Rex Grizell was born in Brighton and educated at grammar school and at Exeter College, Oxford. He had intended to teach languages, but while at Oxford was invited by a national magazine, to which he had contributed short stories, to join their staff as a feature writer. He thus became a journalist, remaining in Fleet Street as a feature writer and executive on newspapers and magazines for thirty years. Ten of those years were spent as Travel Editor of the *London Evening News*, during which time he visited all five continents and about a hundred different countries.

He and his French wife travelled both privately and on business in France for more than twenty years, but since 1983 have lived on a small fruit and cereal farm in the heart of Aquitaine.

Rex Grizell's interests include period furniture and nineteenth-century painting, rough carpentry, photography, and restoring old houses and gardens. He divides his time between writing, travelling, and helping round the farm. He has two sons, one daughter, and two grand-daughters.

**Other Harper Independent
Traveller guidebooks include:**

Southern Italy
Soviet Union
Greek Islands
Mainland Greece
Turkey
Spain
Portugal

The Harper

INDEPENDENT TRAVELLER

SOUTH-WEST FRANCE

REX GRIZELL

Series Editor Robin Dewhurst

PERENNIAL LIBRARY

Harper & Row, Publishers, New York
Grand Rapids, Philadelphia, St. Louis, San Francisco
London, Singapore, Sydney, Tokyo, Toronto

Note

While every effort has been made to ensure that prices, hotel and restaurant recommendations, opening hours and similar factual information in this book are accurate at the time of going to press, the Publishers cannot be held responsible for any changes found by readers using this guide.

This work is published in Great Britain by William Collins Sons & Company Ltd.

THE HARPER INDEPENDENT TRAVELLER: SOUTH-WEST FRANCE. Copyright © 1989 by Rex Grizell. All rights reserved. Printed in the United States of America. No part of this book may be used or reproduced in any manner whatsoever without written permission except in the case of brief quotations embodied in critical articles and reviews. For information address Harper & Row, Publishers, Inc., 10 East 53rd Street, New York, NY 10022.

First PERENNIAL LIBRARY edition published 1990

Series Commissioning Editor: Louise Haines
Maps by Maltings Partnership

Library of Congress Cataloging-in-Publication Data

Grizell, Rex.
    South-west France / Rex Grizell. — 1st Perennial Library ed.
       p.   cm. — (The Harper independent traveller)
    Includes bibliographical references.
    ISBN 0-06-096459-6
    1. France, southwest—Description and travel—Guide-books.
  I. Title. II. Series.
  DC609.3.G74 1990
  914.4′704838—dc20   89-45663

90 91 92 93 FG 10 9 8 7 6 5 4 3 2 1

Contents

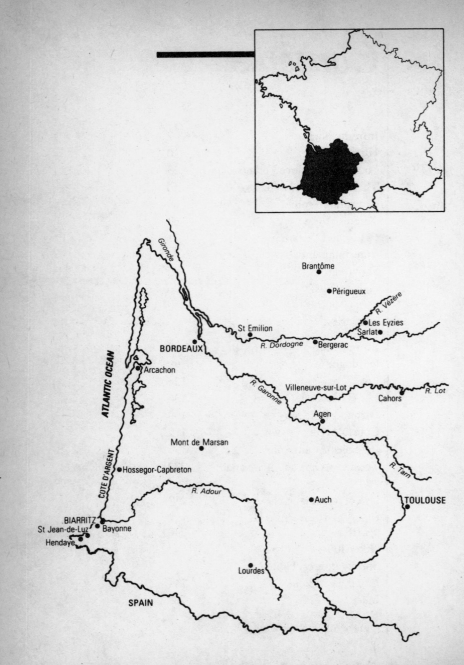

Gironde

Brantôme

● Périgueux

R. Vézère

St Emilion

● Les Eyzies
Sarlat ●

BORDEAUX

R. Dordogne   ● Bergerac

ATLANTIC OCEAN

● Arcachon

R. Garonne

Villeneuve-sur-Lot
●

R. Lot

Cahors ●

Agen
●

● Mont de Marsan

CÔTE D'ARGENT

● Hossegor-Capbreton

R. Adour

● Auch

R. Tarn

TOULOUSE

BIARRITZ
St Jean-de-Luz ● ● Bayonne
Hendaye ●

● Lourdes

SPAIN

Introduction

Before starting this book I had a look at an old home movie of our first holiday in south-west France. There was my six-year-old son leaning on his spade, staring across an endless stretch of empty white sands, wondering how many castles he could build. There was my fat two-year-old daughter, as brown and round as a hazelnut, with a red bucket full of water for the moat, slopping it everywhere. There they were rolling down the great sand dune at Pyla, the highest in Europe – on one side the violet blue of Biscay, on the other the dark green forest reaching to the horizon.

Now, more than twenty years later, the sands are no longer deserted, for the south-west has been 'discovered' and 'developed' to a certain extent. But it is spacious and there is room for all; that forest covers 20,000 sq km, and that beach is up to a kilometre wide and 228 kilometres long.

Yet the sands and the forest form only a part of the south-west. From the wooded hills of Dordogne in the north to the great river valleys in the centre and the majestic Pyrenees in the south, the scenery is as varied as it is beautiful. It is a landscape also of ancient towns and villages, battered castles, Romanesque churches and inexhaustible history.

The countryside basks through long, hot summers and serene autumns, gold and purple on the vine. It is a place for sun-lovers, wine-lovers, gastronomes and gourmets, walkers, riders, cyclists, boat lovers and anglers. It is hard to think of any type of holiday which cannot be enjoyed here.

Areas covered South-west France is not a precise term. In this book it includes the whole of the official administrative region of Aquitaine – that is, the departments of Dordogne, Lot-et-Garonne, Gironde, Landes and Pyrénées-Atlantiques. The towns of Cahors and Toulouse and their surroundings, which belong to the Midi-Pyrénées administrative region, have also been included, Cahors because it is a natural gateway to the south-west and Toulouse because it is a colourful and interesting city, close to the Aquitaine border, which has a vital impact on the life and economy of the south-west.

There are other regional names which you will see and hear in the south-west. Guyenne is said to derive from the rough pronunciation of English soldiers in the Hundred Years War – Aquitaine, Kee-ten, Guyenne. Today it is an area name, without specific limits, of country north of the Garonne and the Lot but south of the Dordogne, and west of Quercy.

Quercy is a former province, named from the oak trees that grow there (Latin: *quercus* = oak), now covered by the departments of Lot and Tarn-et-Garonne.

Gascony, a major part of the south-west with the department of Gers at its heart and its capital at Auch, stretches south from the Lot Valley to the Basque country and the mountains.

Rivers

Although there is something of everything in Aquitaine, as its name suggests it is first and foremost a land of water, sectioned by great rivers, the Dordogne, the Lot and the Garonne. Here they ripple through gorges or narrow valleys, where perched villages and spectacularly sited castles challenge each other across the water; there they run slow and deep where poplars line the banks and fishermen nod in the warm shade. There are innumerable smaller streams, and lakes both large and small.

Crops

Water brings fertility, and south-west France is and always has been a land of farmers and peasants. Outside the bigger towns there is little industry, apart from plants for bottling or canning fruits, vegetables and other local food produce. In summer the valley fields and hillsides are a colourful jigsaw of orchard and vineyard, with the greens and gold of maize, soya, sunflowers, tobacco and wheat. Other important crops are tomatoes, beans, melons, strawberries, apples, pears, plums and peaches.

Variety

I live in the heart of the south-west, and when I try to call it all to mind I see a series of images. In Dordogne I recall the Arcadian valley and the silver sweep of the river, viewed from the heights of Domme or Belcastel. In Lot-et-Garonne it is the washes of pink and white as the orchards come into flower in spring, or the view of the Château of Bonaguil, France's swan-song to feudal times, the last and most romantic of all Aquitaine's ruined fortresses. In Gironde I see the procession of the *Jurade*, the councillors of the wine, in their scarlet and silver robes, passing among the old stones of St Emilion; or the armada of gaily coloured sails on the huge bay of Arcachon.

Further south, in the Landes, the spume-feathered rollers thunder in across the sands, while just inland the distant shores of mirror-still lakes are lost in the heat haze. In Pyrénées-Atlantiques I think of the great bastion of the mountains, snow-capped even in summer, seen from the terrace below Henry IV's castle at Pau, or of a fat trout dozing in the shade of an ancient bridge in some old mountain village. All these are aspects of the south-west, which could be multiplied in a dozen different ways.

This part of France has always seemed to inspire extreme behaviour, the stuff of legends. It is the country of the *Chanson de Roland*, an epic woven on the roads where pilgrims in their thousands made their way towards the Pyrenees and over and on towards their dream, St James of Compostella.

Personalities

It is also the country of larger-than-life characters, like Eleanor of

Aquitaine, who was in her time the richest and most powerful woman in the world; and of her son, Richard the Lionheart, soldier and troubadour, who was an indifferent King of England but a great Duke of Aquitaine. It was the land of Henri III, the rustic Protestant king of out-of-the-way Navarre, who turned Catholic on becoming Henri IV of France, telling his friends back home in Béarn that 'it was through Béarn that France was annexed to Gascony' – a typical piece of Gascon *braggadocio*, a *gasconnade* which was not entirely lacking in truth.

Gascony was also the land of Pothon de Xantrailles and of La Hire, the lieutenants of Joan of Arc, who led the troops which she inspired. It was the home of D'Artagnan, and the cadets de Gascogne, the daring and boastful soldiers, younger sons of poor landowners for whom the only chance of fame and fortune was gained with a sword in their hand, and whose reckless deeds have inspired shelves of novels, plays, films and television series, from *The Three Musketeers* to *Cyrano de Bergerac*.

Peace

Although the history of the south-west was made in blood and marked in stone for more than a thousand years, it is peaceful now. The trumpet blasts of war have long since faded, and the only battle cries heard today are those on the rugby grounds. Nowadays it is a place to enjoy life and leisure. It offers the visitor everything from sandy beaches and sunlit seas to bracing mountain valleys and shady woodland streams, salt-tanged, pine-scented unpolluted air, good food, superb wines, café terraces and château hotels.

Where to choose?

The south-west of France is a large region, bigger than some countries, and somewhere in this region it is possible to find just the right holiday, just the right place for every taste. But where? In this book I am attempting to tell you enough of the qualities and differences of this warm and welcoming land to help you make the choice that will suit you.

History

The Romans

History, as distinct from prehistory, begins with the arrival of the Roman legions in Aquitaine during the century before Christ. The Romans already knew of the local tribes, to whom Greek and Roman writers had referred as early as the fifth century BC, calling them collectively Celts or Gauls. They had a long-established reputation as skilful metal workers in bronze, a craft which had been taught them a thousand years earlier by Phoenician traders, who used to bring them the tin for the alloy from mines in Cornwall. Even as long ago as that, Phoenician ships sailed into the estuary of the Gironde and unloaded their cargoes on the south bank.

It was Publius Crassus, a lieutenant of Julius Caesar, who completed the formal conquest of Aquitaine in 56 BC. During the long Roman peace which followed, towns developed – Burdigala which was to become Bordeaux, Vesunna which became Périgord, Aginnum which became Agen, as well as Saintes and Cahors and many smaller **Roads** places. In the early twenties BC, the Emperor Agrippa had a network of roads constructed in Aquitaine and throughout Gaul, some of which are still followed by the N-roads of France. Every 1,500 metres – a Roman mile – these roads between major towns were marked with 'milestones', showing the distance from the point of departure and to the destination. One of these stones was unearthed in 1969 beside the N137 at St Ciers-sur-Gironde.

Every forty-five kilometres, relay stations were set up where couriers delivering official letters could change horses. Like the Pony Express horsemen in the early American West, these riders became famous for the distances they could cover. Ninety kilometres a day was the norm, but one man became renowned for travelling 300 kilometres in twenty-four hours. As inns for the use of non-official travellers grew up beside the post-stops, it soon became possible to travel from one end of the Roman Empire to the other, sleeping in complete security every night.

Aqueducts The Romans also constructed aqueducts – some as long as seventy-five kilometres – to carry water to the principal towns of the south-west. The one which served Saintes was still in use in the nineteenth century.

Spas   The first spas were established by the Romans. If there was no natural mineral water, they built public baths and filled them with water, which had been filtered to avoid pollution. Even the smallest cities had these baths, which had heated swimming pools, as well as private bathrooms, gymnasium, rest rooms, shops and gardens. The spas at Dax, Bagnères de Bigorre, Cambo, Amélie-les-Bains and Luchon were all first established during the reign of Augustus, and are still popular today.

Wine   It was also during Roman times that wine was first produced in the Bordeaux region. The local farmers became jealous of the profits made by wine producers in the Narbonne area, near the Mediterranean coast, but found that the same vines did not thrive in their own poor soil. So they searched all the Mediterranean countries for a more suitable vine, eventually finding one, on the Greek shores of the Adriatic, which was suited to their stony soil and produced a good, long-lasting wine. Soon they were exporting it from Burdigala to Roman settlements in Britain, and Bordeaux has been a wine port ever since. The pruning-knives used by these earliest cultivators of the vine, identical to those in use today, can be seen in the Aquitaine museum in Bordeaux.

Visigoths   When the Roman Empire in the west came to an end, it was followed in Aquitaine in the fifth century AD by an invasion of the Visigoths, who ruled the area for about a hundred years. Their kings were admirers of Roman culture and allowed things to continue as before. They left nothing of their own, apart from a few place names such as Alaric's Mountain, near Carcassonne, and Alaric's Camp, near Villeneuve-sur-Lot.

The Dark Ages

At about the end of the seventh century Europe entered what is known to historians as the Dark Ages, because the scarcity of documents surviving from that time has left them in the dark as to what was going on. It may sound like a pun but it is the simple truth.

In Aquitaine, names and shadowy figures do emerge from the bloodthirsty turmoil, but who exactly they were, where precisely they ruled, and what they did is conjecture rather than certainty. In general, these chieftains – who were variously known as princes, kings or dukes, a word that at that time still had the sense of the Latin *dux*, or leader – were commonly engaged in slaughtering rivals, including their close relatives, and despoiling their neighbours' property.

Charlemagne   One figure to emerge clearly from the historical murk is Charlemagne, who rose to the top of the heap and created an empire which stretched from the Pyrenees to Poland. In 778 he decided to make Aquitaine a kingdom for his newly born son, and in 781 the boy, Louis, was crowned by the Pope in Rome. A few weeks later the three-year-old child, wearing a helmet and breastplate and seated on a huge horse, took official possession of his vast kingdom.

Louis grew up to be a good soldier, and added a large part of north-east Spain to his kingdom, but when Charlemagne died in 814, the empire which he had built crumbled in the hands of lesser men. In 877, the French king, Louis the Stammerer, put an end to the independent kingdom of Aquitaine, and its dukes and counts became his vassals. At least, that was the theory. In fact, within ten years the Dukes of Aquitaine were refusing to accept the authority of the new king of France, Charles the Simple.

The Dukes of Aquitaine

One of these dukes was William the Pious, whose lands covered a vast part of France, including Burgundy, Berry and Auvergne, in addition to Aquitaine. In his will, made in 910, he left his favourite hunting estate at Cluny, in Burgundy, to a group of Benedictine monks, who founded there a monastic community, which became the most influential in the Christian world of the Middle Ages.

One William followed another as Duke of Aquitaine, each extending the duchy so that when William VIII died in 1086, after a reign of fifty years, Aquitaine covered more than a quarter of what is France today.

William X

While William IX was a brave soldier, a first-rate poet and an indefatigable womaniser, the tenth William was a ruffian of the first magnitude. An exceptionally strong and vigorous man, he was said to have eaten as much meat at one meal as eight normally healthy young men. He also loved fighting, to the extent that when there were no genuine battles to be fought, he set his vassals against each other so that he could enjoy the excitement. His sexual appetites were as unbridled as his gluttony. According to one early chronicler, his fondness for murder and incest made him a second Herod, and like Herod he carried off his brother's wife, keeping her by him for three years. He had two daughters, of whom he spoiled the elder, allowing her to be present at whatever roguery was going on in court. Her name was Alienor or, in English, Eleanor.

At thirty-eight, after a life of excesses, William X became conscience-stricken and set off for St James of Compostella to make his peace with God. No one knows for sure what became of him. One report says that he died a few miles from his destination, another that he disguised himself as a Spanish peasant and made off into the mountains to live as a hermit, praying and catching crayfish. Whatever the truth, he was not heard of again.

Eleanor of Aquitaine

Before he left he had made his daughters wards of the French king, Louis the Fat, and had made a will naming Eleanor as his heiress. Louis was pleased to accept the responsibility, relishing the opportunity it gave him to unite the great duchy of Aquitaine with the French crown by marrying his son and heir, another Louis, to Eleanor. The marriage took place in Bordeaux five months before the disappearance of William X.

It would be difficult to imagine a couple less suited to each other. Louis was a bloodless, physically feeble and intellectually ineffective young man, totally unfit for the responsibilities of kingship or marriage, while Eleanor had inherited some of the strength and wildness of her father, allied to the lightness and fire of the Midi. Her attitude to men resembled that of her grandfather, William IX, to women – there were not enough of them about. She held her Courts of Love and flirted with the troubadours, while Louis said his prayers and read the lives of saints. Eleanor enjoyed luxury, excitement and the conviviality and red wine of her own Aquitaine, all of which were carefully avoided at the court of Louis the Pious. His idea of a good time was to dress up in the black habit of a monk and sit down to a bowl of boiled oats and water. Eleanor thought him something worse than a bore.

She did accompany him on a Crusade to the Holy Land, an expedition which she regarded as an oriental jaunt. As a Crusade it was a complete disaster. Louis and his barons abandoned their soldiers and left them to their own devices, while Eleanor went on to visit her uncle Raymond, Count of Poitiers, in nearby Antioch. Considered the handsomest man of his day, he gave Eleanor a good time, receiving her with rather more than the normal avuncular fondness.

Back in France, as Louis became more and more pious, Eleanor became ever more bored. All the same, what followed was surprising, even for those unpredictable times.

The Plantagenets

In 1151, Geoffrey Plantagenet, Count of Anjou, paid a visit to the court of King Louis and Queen Eleanor, taking with him his wife, Matilda, who was a great-granddaughter of William the Conqueror, and their nineteen-year-old son, Henry.

In their efforts to secure the royal succession, Louis and Eleanor had produced two children, but both were daughters. The elder, Marie, was five. While paying homage to his king, Geoffrey of Anjou hoped to arrange for the betrothal of his son to Marie, who, if Louis had no son, would become Queen of France. Because Henry, through his mother, was heir to the throne of England, he would thus in due course reign over both England and France.

It was a good idea, but the thirty-year-old Queen Eleanor, still beautiful and aching for excitement, soon had a better one. Looking at the strong, handsome, young prince, she decided to marry him herself, and sought a divorce, claiming that her blood relationship with Louis was too close. This was nonsense; the great-grandfather of the grandfather of Louis had married the sister of the great-grandfather of the grandfather of Eleanor, but that was all. However, the royal couple did not get on and Louis, knowing nothing of her passion for Henry, readily agreed to the divorce. He also agreed to return her dowry, the whole of Aquitaine, on condition that she let him keep their children. Eleanor consented.

Henry II

Eight weeks later, on 18 May 1152, Eleanor and Henry were married at the Church of St Pierre in Poitiers. Henry was as different from Louis as it was possible for a man to be. He was of average size, but strong and unceasingly active, with great powers of endurance. He would hunt from dawn to dusk and then keep his companions up half the night carousing. He never sat down, except for meals, and hated the confinement of church services, during which he talked and drew cartoons.

Within two years of his marriage Henry became Henry II of England. He was already Duke of Normandy and Count of Anjou, so he and Eleanor now reigned over the whole of south-western and central France from the Channel coast to the Pyrenees, as well as over England.

Henry's great energy was not confined just to fighting and horse-riding; he also satisfied a succession of mistresses. Like most wives with a much younger husband, Eleanor was jealous, but managed to keep him close enough to bear him five sons and three daughters in fourteen years. They governed as a team, standing in for each other in London or Bordeaux as circumstances dictated. Eleanor was herself a person of great stamina: whether about to have a child or just having had one, she was always ready to travel anywhere in the cause of government.

Richard the Lionheart

Her favourite son was Richard the Lionheart, who was not only a brave soldier but a singer and musician of talent. She gave him the job of governing Aquitaine, which he did with firmness and ability. Many castles associated with him are still in existence today, some rebuilt, like that at Beynac in Dordogne. Others, like that at Penne d'Agenais from which he controlled the Valley of the Lot, were reduced to a heap of stones by later rulers.

Eleanor was eventually imprisoned by Henry, remaining captive for sixteen years until he died, but by then their energetic government had laid the foundations of prosperity for Aquitaine. In those days, because the language of government and influential people was still French, the merchants of Bordeaux were as much at home in London, as the London businessmen were in Bordeaux.

Eleanor outlived both her husband, who died in 1189, and her son, King Richard, who died of wounds received in battle in 1199. The indomitable old lady continued to rule actively over her domains, making extensive tours even at the age of eighty. She died aged eighty-two in the year 1204, at the Abbey of Fontevrault, having lived enough in every sense for a score of ordinary people.

The Hundred Years War

The solid foundations laid by Henry II and Eleanor ensured the prosperity of Aquitaine throughout the thirteenth and early four-teenth centuries, during which time the revenues of the duchy exceeded those of the kingdom of England. However, the kings of France, notably Philip V and then his brother Charles IV, were envi-ous of the wealth of Aquitaine and determined to make it part of their kingdom.

About 16 kilometres from where I am writing there is a small village called St Sardos. I doubt whether any of its 200 inhabitants – with the possible exception of the village priest – know it was an incident here that sparked off the Hundred Years War between England and France.

The beginnings

When Charles IV came to the French throne in 1322, King Edward II of England, as Duke of Aquitaine, should have paid him homage, but was too busy with war and revolt in Britain to do so. When the French king complained, Edward replied that he would come to France when he could, and added, in passing, that he did not appreci-ate the construction of a French *bastide*, St Sardos, in territory which had been English since 1303. Charles IV countered that he was defending the priory at St Sardos, a dependence of the Abbey of Sarlat which was French.

The first attack

When a number of Anglo-Gascon barons responded on behalf of Edward II with a punitive expedition against St Sardos in 1323, sack-ing the priory, the French king retaliated by sending an army into Aquitaine the following year, under the command of his uncle. Almost all the Plantagenet territories in the south-west were taken, but only a year later Charles IV offered to return them on condition that Edward

Temporary truce

II should declare that his son, the future Edward III, would, as Duke of Aquitaine, be a vassal of the French king. The reason for Charles's action was that, being childless, he was the last of the Capetien kings and would be succeeded by a remote cousin, Philippe de Valois. On the other hand, because Edward II's wife, Isabella of France, was a Capetien, her son Edward would have a stronger claim to the French throne than Philippe de Valois. The return of the conquered territories was therefore a bribe, intended to prevent an English claim to the throne of France.

Edward II agreed, but two years later he was imprisoned, and later assassinated, on the orders of Roger Mortimer, Isabella's lover. A year later Charles IV died, and the new antagonists were Edward III of England and Philippe VI of France.

New antagonists

The two kings met and exchanged promises which meant nothing, the French continuing their attacks on Aquitaine, and Edward III refusing to pay homage to Philippe VI. Only a few months after their meeting, Philippe VI confiscated Aquitaine, and in retaliation Edward III declared himself King of France, being immediately recognised as such by the majority of the nobles of Aquitaine. In 1345 an English army under Henry of Lancaster landed at Bayonne, reconquering the territory which had been occupied by the French. The following year,

Battle of Crécy

after an English victory at Crécy, life returned to normal in Aquitaine.

Although a state of war existed between England and France for a hundred years, the fighting was intermittent, with long intervals between major battles. Meanwhile, the close association between Bordeaux and London continued; the citizens of one were citizens of the other, to the extent that one Bordelais even became Lord Mayor of London.

English fortunes in the war varied according to the energy and interest of successive monarchs. Edward III pursued the war with vigour. In the autumn of 1355 he appointed as Lieutenant General of

The Black Prince

Aquitaine his son, the Black Prince, who had first distinguished himself as a youth of sixteen on the battlefield of Crécy. The young prince took the job seriously.

In September 1356, at the Battle of Poitiers, a small English army led by the Black Prince completely routed a much larger French force led by King Jean II, who had succeeded his father, Philippe VI. In the course of the battle the French king was captured, then taken to England and held to ransom.

By the Treaty of Brétigny in October 1360, the French king obtained his freedom, Edward III renounced his claim to the French throne, and practically the whole of the Aquitaine of the Plantagenets two hundred years earlier was restored to England.

In 1362, Edward III made Aquitaine a principality instead of a duchy, the Black Prince becoming Prince of Aquitaine until his death in 1376, a year before that of his father.

Edward III was succeeded by his grandson, Richard of Bordeaux, who became Richard II of England. His attitude was more conciliatory than that of his father and grandfather, and he hoped to establish peace between England and France. In the years following the death

Loss of Aquitaine

of the Black Prince most of Aquitaine, apart from Bordeaux, was recaptured by the French. Far from retaliating, Richard made a truce with the French king, Charles VI, agreeing to evacuate certain French towns and paying homage to Charles for Aquitaine.

His actions were strongly opposed by John of Gaunt, Duke of Lancaster, and Richard made things worse in England by appropriating the estates of his cousin, Henry of Lancaster, an action of which Parliament also disapproved. Richard was imprisoned in Pomfret Castle where, according to *Holinshed's Chronicles*, he was murdered by Sir Piers Exton and a group of knights, to be followed on the throne by Henry of Lancaster, as Henry IV.

Although neither Henry IV, nor his successor Henry V, ever visited Aquitaine or set foot in Bordeaux, Henry V was anxious to show that the House of Lancaster could be just as successful in battle against the French as the Plantagenets had been more than fifty years earlier at Crécy and Poitiers. In 1415 he defeated the French at Agincourt, but having proved his point he showed little interest in Aquitaine apart from collecting his taxes. He died, still a young man, in 1422.

Battle of Agincourt

He was succeeded by Henry VI, a king who was never in command of the situation at home or abroad. Meanwhile, Henry V's brother, John, Duke of Bedford, continued the war in France with some success for a few years, but when Joan of Arc appeared on the scene, and with her lieutenants succeeded in raising the siege of Orleans in 1429, the English fortunes began to decline. Joan was burned at the stake as a witch, but this savage action served only to strengthen French resolve.

Joan of Arc

In Aquitaine the situation deteriorated steadily, so that in 1452 two of the Bordeaux nobles went secretly to London to ask Henry VI to send an army to expel the French from Aquitaine. The king sent John Talbot, Earl of Shrewsbury, with an army of 6,000 men. At first Talbot had considerable success, but at the Battle of Castillon in July 1453, he was killed and his army routed. It was to be the last battle of the Hundred Years War, marking the end of the three hundred years of opposition, which had started with the marriage of Eleanor of Aquitaine and Henry Plantagenet, and had been fuelled by the rivalry between the Plantagenets and the Capets, the Plantagenets and the Valois, and finally between Lancaster and Valois. It was over.

Battle of Castillon

In Aquitaine they have never forgotten, and in the small town where it all finished, now called Castillon la Bataille, the final battle is refought every year in a magnificently staged spectacle for tourists.

The D'Albret family

One of the many distinguished French officers killed at the Battle of Agincourt was Charles le Connetable, who was a member of the D'Albret family, one of the oldest of Gascony. They were a family who, by determination, aggression and astute marriages, were to exert a great influence on the history of France for the next two hundred years. At the death in 1522 of Alain le Grand, Sire D'Albret, Viscount

Tartas, the family domains extended over much of Gascony, Limousin, Brittany and Normandy. In 1484 he had seen his son, Jean II D'Albret, become King of Navarre through the marriage he had himself arranged with Catherine de Foix, heiress to Béarn and the kingdom of Navarre. In 1499 his daughter, Charlotte D'Albret, married Cesar Borgia, son of Pope Alexander VI.

In 1527 his grandson, Henri D'Albret, King of Navarre – who had fought at the side of the French King François I at the Battle of Pavia in Italy – married Marguerite D'Angoulême, the sister of François. It was from this time that the D'Albrets began to have more than a purely military interest in the political affairs of France.

Marguerite D'Angoulême

Marguerite D'Angoulême was an attractive and also a learned and witty woman whose literary works, particularly the *Heptameron*, are still read today. She was interested in a wide range of subjects, and welcomed to her château at Nérac writers and philosophers as well as religious thinkers, many of whom were influenced by the Protestant doctrines of Martin Luther. Her secretary, the poet Clement Marot, became valet and official court poet to her brother, the king. Although Marot remained a Catholic his tolerance towards the Protestant cause led to his being imprisoned, and in 1534 he returned from the court to Nérac, at a time when the great teacher of Protestant thought, Jean Calvin, was also spending several weeks at the Château of Nérac.

Although Nérac was from 1530 onwards a most important centre for the dissemination of Protestant beliefs, neither Marguerite nor her husband ever renounced their Catholic faith. But their daughter, Jeanne D'Albret, became a dedicated Protestant. She married Antoine de Bourbon, a Catholic member of a family which already included some leading Protestants, in 1548.

When Marguerite D'Angoulême died in 1549, Henri moved to his castle at Pau, leaving the château in Nérac for his daughter, Jeanne, and her husband to live in. When she became pregnant, though, he asked her to come to Pau to have the child, and there, on 13 December 1553, she gave birth to a son who was to become Henri III of Navarre, and later Henri IV of France.

As Queen of Navarre, Jeanne D'Albret was fanatical in her promotion of Protestantism and her suppression of Catholicism in her domain. The new faith was taken up by many influential figures in royal, political and military circles, including the Prince de Condé, the Vicomte de Turenne, and Admiral de Coligny.

The Religious Wars

The struggle between Protestants and Catholics became more and more a military conflict. During the 1550s La Rochelle, Saintes,

Marmande, St Foy la Grande and Bergerac all fell to the Protestants, with Catholic churches damaged, their treasures stolen and Catholics killed.

Catherine de Médici

In 1563, Catherine de Médici, Regent of France during the minority of her sons, appointed an experienced Catholic general, Blaise de Monluc, Commissar Extraordinary of Aquitaine, with instructions to crush Protestantism.

The campaign was ferocious, cruel and bloody, with atrocities committed on both sides. The Catholics of Cahors massacred the town's Protestants; the Protestants in Agen set fire to a Catholic monastery; in Condom, Protestants were killed and thrown in the river. Many towns of the south-west were attacked, pillaged, burned or reduced to ruins, first by one side then the other.

Catherine de Médici was a devout Catholic, but being more tolerant as a person than she was as a ruler, she had hoped for reconciliation between the two sides. Her Regency ended when her son, Charles IX, came of age, but the new king was of weak character, ill and easily influenced.

Catherine, who had tried to influence the course of events with her 'flying squad' of beautiful and aristocratic girls, whose job was to seduce leading Protestants and 'convert' them, followed the same line of thought in proposing the marriage of her daughter, Marguerite de Valois, to the Protestant Henri of Navarre. The marriage took place at Notre Dame de Paris on 18 August 1572. Six days later Charles IX authorised the St Bartholomew's Day massacre, in which four thousand Protestants were slain.

Henri III

Charles IX was tubercular and died in 1574 at the age of twenty-two. He was succeeded by his brother, Henri III, a man who combined an unusual number of unpleasant qualities, being cunning, treacherous and degenerate. He used lotions to improve his complexion and make-up to enhance it, wore white gloves in bed to preserve the softness of his hands, and was an enthusiastic transvestite. While having no religious faith himself, he felt that the *status quo* should be maintained, and so gave the Catholic leaders a free hand against Protestantism, although he was more interested in the petty gossip of his favourites than in politics. He had married but was childless, so the Valois line came to an end when he was assassinated in 1589.

Henri IV

The heir to the throne was Henri, King of Navarre, a direct descendant of Louis IX, but the Catholics opposed him, preferring a republic to a Protestant king. Henri, who was a realist first and a Christian second, is said to have shrugged his shoulders saying 'Paris is worth a Mass', and destroyed their opposition by becoming a Catholic.

In 1598 he brought the religious wars to an end by signing the Edict of Nantes, which allowed the Protestants considerable freedom of worship. In 1607 he united his own kingdom of Navarre with that of

France. During his reign his popularity and his just authority enabled the balance between the religious factions to be maintained, but in 1610 he was assassinated. His son, Louis, was only nine years old, and the queen, Marie de Médici, his second wife, was a vain and silly woman unable to govern effectively.

Louis XIII

The religious strife soon broke out again, and when he came of age Louis XIII, who had been brought up a Catholic, sometimes took part in the fighting. By 1620 several of the Protestant towns of the south-west, including Nérac, St Emilion and Bergerac had been recaptured by the Catholics.

In 1635, the unrest was increased when the whole town of Bordeaux rose in revolt against the heavy taxation to which it was subjected. Several tax collectors were lynched by the mob, and it was only when the Bordeaux Parliament decided to suspend collection of the taxes that peace was restored.

The Fronde

In the middle of the seventeenth century Bordeaux played an important part in the civil strife known as the Fronde, the revolt of the Paris Parliament against the government of Cardinal Mazarin. One of the most dramatic incidents of this rebellion occurred when a full-scale battle was fought in the Rue St Catherine, the main street of Bordeaux, which is now a pedestrian shopping street. The struggle between the citizens of Bordeaux and the royal troops left more than four hundred dead in the street.

Once these differences had been settled, however, Bordeaux and the south-west prospered throughout the seventeenth and eighteenth centuries.

The French Revolution

The citizens of Bordeaux supported the Revolution when it began in 1789. The Bordeaux political party, the Girondins, were in the majority in Parliament but, as has always been traditional in Bordeaux, they wanted a strong measure of independence to enable them to run their own affairs. Robespierre disapproved of this, suspecting them of wanting federation, and had the leading members of the Girondins arrested and put on trial. However, they put up such a strong defence that Robespierre stopped the trial and summarily executed twenty-one of them.

Bordeaux, which was the leading port of France, suffered badly in Napoleonic times from being blockaded by the English navy, and it was not until the Restoration that the economy began to improve again.

The nineteenth century

In 1853 Paris was linked to Bordeaux by a railway, which was soon extended further in the south-west. Easier communications naturally gave the economy a boost, as well as bringing the first tourists to the south-west.

The wife of Napoleon III, the Empress Eugénie, was fond of Biarritz, where she had several times stayed as a girl. Her husband also liked it, so much that he had the enormous Villa Eugénie built there. Many years later it became the Hôtel du Palais. Biarritz became fashionable, remaining so throughout the nineteenth century and well into the twentieth.

In the late 1850s the building of a deep-water jetty and a railway connection with Bordeaux led to the development of a second important resort in the south-west, Arcachon. At about the same time the railway was extended to Dax, which had been known as a spa since Roman times. The town took the opportunity to renew many of its thermal establishments, and has enjoyed a steady popularity ever since.

Drainage and forestation

The second half of the nineteenth century also saw completion of the tremendous task of stabilising the huge coastal sand dunes of the Landes, and the planting of a vast forest of pines in the desert scrubland, which had been created by centuries of windblown, drifting sand. Underneath this drifted sand there was a layer of impermeable rock, which prevented water from draining away, resulting in much unhealthy swampland. This problem was solved at the same time, by breaking through the hard rock in key places to establish a system of drainage. When the forest of pines and cork oaks matured, the Landes changed from being the poorest to one of the richest departments of France.

Economy

The prosperity of the south-west was further increased by a considerable expansion of the Bordeaux wine trade towards the end of the nineteenth century.

In the Franco-Prussian War of 1870, during the First World War, and again at the start of the Second World War, the French government moved from Paris to Bordeaux.

In recent years, the history of the south-west has been one of social change. Agriculture was the main occupation of the people for hundreds of years, but with the advent of mechanised farming the numbers employed have steadily declined, and there has been a drift from the land. Yet overall production in farming has increased and agriculture remains a major factor in the economy of the south-west.

Before the Second World War there was little industry in the south-west, but since the 1950s there has been a steady expansion. Bordeaux has become an important centre of the space industry, including missile construction and allied electronic industries. There are also important chemical and medical products factories in the south-west, as well as plants making paper and cellulose products from wood from the Landes forest.

South-west France Today

When, in Roman times, the first literate men came to south-west France and wrote about it, they described it as a country of idleness and luxury, a place where life was happy and easy – what later writers meant when they wrote of a 'land of Cockaigne'.

Fertility and variety

It is still, after two thousand years, a place whose inhabitants can count themselves fortunate, a region rich with the fertility and variety which made the Romans love it. What idleness there is today is enforced, for the south-west has not escaped the scourge of increasing unemployment and there is little luxury in the modern sense of the word, although there is comfort of all kinds, for both the body and the spirit. Indeed, a recent survey in a German magazine described south-west France as the region that offered the highest all-round amenities for modern living in the whole of Europe.

The westerly winds bring in pure air from the vast spaces of the Atlantic, and the climate is kind and sunny, with enough rain to ensure that crops thrive. In the fertile valleys of its rivers, particularly the Garonne and the Lot, there is nothing, apart from tropical and sub-tropical fruits, that will not and does not grow. The housewife in south-west France can buy three-quarters of all the fruit and vegetables she wants, absolutely fresh, grown within a few kilometres of where she shops.

The rivers are full of fish, including such gourmet's delights as trout, salmon, shad, pike-perch and even lampreys and the occasional sturgeon. The numerous farms produce countless chickens, ducks, geese and turkeys; there are sheep on the hillsides and cattle in the meadows, with innumerable cheeses being made from their milk. The mountain slopes, the woods and forests are full of game birds, deer, hares and even wild boar, while the vineyards produce the world's finest wines and the superb Armagnac brandy.

The landscape

This rich countryside is also beautiful. Its rolling hills and secret valleys, its oak and chestnut woods and great pine forests, the orchards drifted in blossom or heavy with fruit, the hilltop castles and the panoramic views all combine to please the eye and soothe the mind.

In summer, families take their children to the sandy beaches of the Atlantic coast, where many of them have a second home or holiday

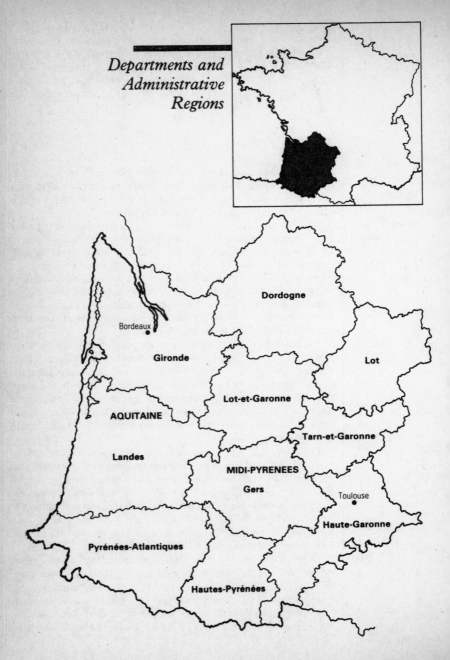

Dordogne

Bordeaux

Gironde

Lot

Lot-et-Garonne

AQUITAINE

Tarn-et-Garonne

Landes

MIDI-PYRENEES

Gers

Toulouse

Haute-Garonne

Pyrénées-Atlantiques

Hautes-Pyrénées

chalet within an easy drive of any part of Aquitaine. In winter, they can go to the ski resorts of the Pyrenees, a short morning's drive from the furthest corner of the south-west. For a change they can go to the Mediterranean or across the mountains into Spain, both an easy drive from much of Aquitaine. They can sail in all seasons on some of the largest lakes in France, or on the 150 sq km of the bay of Arcachon. They can walk or ride in the wild foothills of the Pyrenees to the south, or of the Massif Central to the east.

The people of the south-west who share all this diversity live side by side in two separate and very different societies. The modern society of the towns is numerically much the largest, but it is the smaller yet all-pervasive, traditional society of agricultural life outside the towns with which most independent travellers are likely to have closer contact.

Change

Visitors to whom the forests, beaches, and rambling countryside of Aquitaine are new are likely to be surprised by its spaciousness and apparent emptiness in many parts. This is not a false impression, for the average population is only 24 per sq km, towns included, and is as low as 10 in some areas.

Recent changes

But those who remember the region from twenty or thirty years ago find it very much changed, the most obvious aspect of this change being the visual one. Only twenty years ago the coastal strip, for example, was so utterly deserted that the empty strands and silent forests were the subject of a television documentary. Today there are made-up roads where there were footpaths, summer chalets where there was only the breeze on the sand dunes, television aerials among the trees, camping sites and caravan parks where there was wilderness.

But do not be misled. These new aspects, noticeable to those who knew the region before they appeared, make very little difference to the overall spaciousness. The sandy beach is more than 228 kilometres long and a kilometre wide at low tide, without a stone on it, and it is still backed by 20,000 sq km of pine forest.

Development in towns

True, the towns have changed. When I first visited southern France as a student about thirty years ago, I was struck, as were many travellers in those days, by the number of towns and villages which looked as if they had been unchanged for hundreds of years, and without a new house or a fresh coat of paint anywhere.

Today every village and town has new residential development on all sides, whether in small building estates or in houses scattered through the near countryside. The new houses are usually single-

25

storeyed with red-tiled roofs, buff-coloured walls, brown-painted shutters, a covered terrace and a neat garden. It gives a very different look to the towns from that of the grey stone, often gardenless, town houses of the past.

Spacious countryside

But the fact remains that you can still drive for kilometres through the great forest of the Landes without seeing a house, and there are many country roads in Dordogne, Gers, Gironde, and even fertile Lot-et-Garonne, where you can stop on an empty stretch and have to search the hillsides to spot a house half hidden by trees. It is still a spacious, peaceful countryside, often with nothing to be seen in the way of modernity – not a factory chimney, not a car on the road, no railway, rarely a tractor in sight despite the many ploughed fields, and away from Bordeaux or Toulouse a sky usually empty of planes.

The drift to the towns

In south-west France, as in other rural areas throughout Europe over the past hundred years, there has been a steady drift from the land, which has been accentuated in recent years. There are now many farms for sale, and many farmhouses have been bought and modernised for use as permanent or holiday homes by successful business and professional people in the larger towns.

The drift from the villages to the towns and from the towns to the cities, first Bordeaux and Toulouse and then further afield to Paris, Marseilles and Lyons, was sufficiently significant to bring about a steady fall in population, so that by 1946 there were fewer people in Aquitaine than there had been in 1872. In recent years there has been an increase of about 1 per cent per year, and today the population of Aquitaine is about 2.75 million, more than one-third centred in the single city of Bordeaux and its agglomeration. This represents one-twentieth of the population of France, scattered through about one-twelfth of the total area.

Cosmopolitan society

During the past fifty years it has steadily become a more cosmopolitan society and now about 5 per cent of the population is of foreign extraction. There has been immigration from Spain for many years, with a surge at the time of the Spanish Civil War. In the 1930s many Italians left Mussolini's Italy and, liking the climate, settled in south-west France. Today the children of those immigrants form a hard core of skilled artisans in building and allied trades. In the 1950s, and following Algerian independence, many North Africans with French citizenship settled in the south-west (Algeria was a part of Metropolitan France for more than a hundred years). There are enough English residents in northern Aquitaine, particularly Dordogne, for there to be English shops and even an English newspaper. This influx has occurred in the past twenty years and is still going on. Another 5 per cent of the inhabitants are French people who have retired to the south-west from other parts of France, particularly from the Paris area. The local people recognise them as French, but still regard them as foreigners.

Politics

France, which has a population of between 55 and 56 million, is divided into ninety-five departments, including the island of Corsica, which make up twenty-two regions. The departments are divided into cantons, and the cantons into communes. It is a democracy with a freely elected government, headed by a President who holds office for seven years, though at the time of writing there is a move to reduce the term to five years to coincide with the normal life of a government.

Suffrage

There are two kinds of suffrage in France: universal direct suffrage, by which the people as a whole elect the President, the members of Parliament, the regional councillors, the general (departmental) councillors and the municipal councillors. Those elected in this way then become a privileged group of electors who themselves elect the members of the Senate, the upper house equivalent to the House of Lords. This is known as indirect universal suffrage.

Government

Though only three-quarters the size of Texas, France is a large country by European standards, more than twice the size of Great Britain, and much of the work of government is decentralised. The affairs of the regions are directed by the regional councillors, those of the departments by general councillors – one of whom is elected from each canton – and those of the communes by municipal councillors. There is thus a freely elected network of authority from the *Maire* and the councillors in the communes, right up through the departments and the regions to the central government and the President.

There has been a succession of republics in France; in times of crisis the constitution has been changed and a new republic formed. The present, the Fifth Republic, was created in 1958 by General de Gaulle, following the failure of the Fourth Republic and the demission of its government during the Algerian War, at a time when France itself was in economic difficulty.

The Fifth Republic

The Fifth Republic differs from all the previous ones, the changes in its constitution having been put forward by General de Gaulle to enable him, he said, to govern effectively. They were agreed by a referendum of the people, who showed themselves more than two-thirds in favour.

This new constitution gives a great deal more power to the President himself, at the same time reducing the power of Parliament. It lies somewhere between a dictatorship and a true parliamentary government, rather closer to the latter than the former. One of the most important differences is that under the Fifth Republic there is no Council of State. In all previous republics the Council of State, which was a kind of successor to the old monarchical council, was requested by the President to form a cabinet, which had to be confirmed in office by a vote of the members of Parliament. The President of the Council of State and all the government ministers were obliged to be members of Parliament.

Under the Fifth Republic the President names the Prime Minister himself, and the Prime Minister proposes his ministers to the President, who may accept or refuse them. The Prime Minister and the ministers do not have to be members of Parliament, but in practice they almost always are. There were thinking Frenchmen who considered de Gaulle a dictator, and in theory the constitution of the Fifth Republic would allow the President himself to form the entire government and to control it. In theory there need be no member of Parliament in it, although it is certain that such a situation would be tolerated by neither Parliament nor the people as a whole. However, with the rise in popularity of the National Front and its Fascist leader, Jean Marie Le Pen, the possibility gives food for serious thought.

So this hybrid form of government has moved some way from complete parliamentary democracy, though Parliament retains some power and the people have a free vote in elections at every level. However it may be classified, the Fifth Republic has already lasted thirty years and, so far, has seemed to work well. Its governments have been stable, remaining in power for several years with only occasional ministerial changes, and it seems to be popular with the people, although there remains a nucleus of influential businessmen and academics, both right and left of centre, inclined to resist any further moves away from true democratic government.

The political parties

There are two parties of the left – the Communists, who have lost favour steadily in recent years and who now have between 5 and 10 per cent of the vote, and the Socialists, the largest single party, with about 35 per cent of the vote. The right is divided between the RPR (*Rassemblement Pour La République*), the UDF (*Union Démocratique Française*), which is nearer the centre, and the extreme right National Front, who now have between 10 and 15 per cent of the vote nationally and considerably more in the Marseilles region.

Parliament

Parliament sits for about five and a half months of the year. If television coverage of important debates is to be believed, it consists largely of rows upon rows of apparently comfortable, though empty, seats – indoors, of course, but otherwise resembling Wembley Stadium as it might be for a mid-week friendly with a touring Patagonian football team or Madison Square Garden for a display of Armenian folk dancing.

Regionalism

The most significant aspect of French political life is its regionalism. Regardless of which party is in power, or who its dominant personalities are, the outlook of the average man in the southwest remains almost entirely regional. I have heard local farmers, and even teachers, say, 'France begins south of the Loire'. Their attitude is similar to that which exists in the United States where, for example, the people of Florida will have heard of the state of Oregon, but may well want nothing to do with it. No doubt the same feeling exists between Kazakhstan and Armenia, and between regions in any large country. In south-west France the central government often seems remote, and would seem more so were it not for the ritual appearances on television of its key members. The 'national' newspapers of Paris have a very small sale in the provinces, where every region has its own paper devoted almost exclusively to local matters.

Identity cards

The French bureaucratic system is highly developed. It can be enormously long-winded and pernickety, but for those who conform it can also be rather easy-going. The French find it difficult to believe that the British are not required to carry any identification, for in France your 'papers' are of paramount importance. Anyone stopped, for example, for a motoring offence is at once asked for the documents relating to the car, a driving licence, *and* a personal identity card. For foreigners a driving licence and a passport (it can save bother always to carry it in France) are sufficient, but whatever else he can show, a Frenchman who cannot produce his identity card is at once suspect to the police and will be closely questioned. The French are brought up always to have their identity cards with them and to expect to have to produce them. If they cannot, there may well be a serious reason.

Livret de Famille

In addition to identity cards, every family is expected to have a family booklet, the *Livret de Famille*, which is given to every couple at the time of their marriage and to every unmarried mother. It contains spaces in which to record the birth and names of each child and any deaths which occur in the family, as well as any other events such as divorce, remarriage, adoption and so forth, and it is obligatory to present it at the *Mairie* on each such occasion to be duly stamped and officially signed. Its possession facilitates the solution of any subsequent problems relating to identity, such as nationality, inheritance, or the loss of an identity card. Without it you can be swept back and forth on the endless tides of bureacracy.

Efficiency

All systems are most fairly judged by results and by this rule the French system is sound and well thought out. The towns are clean and well lit, the rubbish is collected and disposed of efficiently, the postal service is reliable, the trains are clean and run on time, the telephone system works well, no aspect of the superb road network is neglected, and the hospitals are modern, efficient and comfortable.

The Mayor

For the average inhabitant bureaucracy begins and ends with the Mayor (*Monsieur le Maire*). He it is who registers the births and deaths of the citizens of his commune; he can marry a couple, if at least one of them lives in the commune, and if they live together outside marriage he can provide a certificate of concubinage, which allows them certain tax and other advantages. If crops are damaged by hail, if there is a domestic or hunting accident, or a quarrel between neighbours, and in countless other events of daily life, the Mayor is the man on the spot to establish the facts.

29

On the face of it he does all this for limited expenses, fixed at a national level according to the numbers of inhabitants in his commune. In practice he is likely to be no more disinterested than the councillors in any average small town, whose businesses, in some mysterious way, thrive so well. It is also a fact that the route to the top in French politics very often begins in a *Mairie*. Every major political figure, almost without exception, is also the Mayor of a large town and carries the major part of its vote with him into Parliament.

Imitations of de Gaulle

The modern generation of French politicians still seems to be in a hypnotic trance imposed upon them by the memory of Charles de Gaulle. Even those who are anti-Gaullist have often adopted his mannerisms, his deliberate and exaggerated cadences of speech, even actual phrases. This tendency produced a vaguely musical-comedy atmosphere during the presidential and legislative election campaigns in 1988, as one candidate after another gave in physical, if not always political, terms his own impersonation of de Gaulle – even those who, like François Mitterrand, were more than a foot shorter. It was as if they had all been listening to recordings of de Gaulle's speeches and telling themselves, 'It worked for him, perhaps it will work for me'. But for the most part they are smaller men in every way.

Demonstrations

French politics often tend to become physical, with frequent banner-waving marches and demonstrations. Two areas which arouse particularly intense emotions are education and agriculture.

Education

National education is in a state of flux, and is said by many parents to be in decline. In the past French education was effective, producing a population with a high average level of culture, but little individuality. It was so standardised and formal in the intellectual sense that the majority of French people tend to waltz through arguments in an identical one, two, three fashion. Discipline in French schools was previously rather strict, but this has been somewhat relaxed of late, causing over-reaction among pupils, with widespread smoking and, to a lesser extent, drug problems among the young.

Memories of 1968

The events of 1968 – when a student revolt against proposed university reforms was quickly joined by the trade unions in violent protest against the rising cost of living, leading to clashes with the police and three deaths – are still fresh in the minds of politicians and public alike. It is not uncommon to hear writers, singers and professionals of the media saying, 'I was there in '68, on the streets . . .' or words to that effect. Most of the students who fought the police in May 1968 are now themselves parents, but public and political memory is still hypersensitive. When last year the government again proposed changes to make university education – which at least in theory is now open to everyone – more selective and more closely related to genuine ability, there was immediate opposition from students and an immediate withdrawal by the government. The minister for education was replaced.

**Agricultural
protests**

Political activity is a term which the farming community of the south-west has tended in recent years to take literally. This was especially the case during the run-up to Spain's entry into the EEC. Farmers in the south-west found their markets shrinking because Spanish produce was lower-priced, owing to cheaper labour in Spain, and it was reaching the markets a week or two earlier because of the warmer climate. Every year there were demonstrations in which hundreds of tonnes of tomatoes were dumped in front of town halls, so that motorists were soon driving through a sea of tomato purée. On other occasions a glut of apples or peaches would be disposed of in the same way, while sometimes hundreds of tractors would arrive in a town centre and drive slowly round and round, causing total traffic chaos before their owners parked them anywhere and retired to local bars to discuss the agricultural situation. At one time imports of Spanish wine resulted in the burning of hypermarkets which sold it.

There were numerous occasions on which Spanish lorries loaded with fruit and vegetables were delayed at the frontier by long-winded formalities, or had their cargoes emptied over the road, either by infuriated farmers or by French lorry drivers, who were in their turn delayed by Spanish formalities.

The situation has become somewhat less tense since the Spanish entry into the EEC, the French government having succeeded for the time being in persuading farmers that it is not a one-sided agreement and that France also benefits from it.

**Towards
united
Europe**

So what is the future of this curious Fifth Republic with its powerful President, its separation of the executive from the legislative power so that ministers do not sit in Parliament and do not even have to be members of it? French politicians of all parties consider the unification of Europe in 1992 with deadly earnestness, tinged with a slight but positive sense of panic, and all of them are busy selling the future Europe to the electorate as a Europe which will be led by France.

But they may well find the reality more difficult to put into practice than it seems on paper and in animated discussion. In the first place the French character, for all its many qualities, *is* chauvinistic. Frequently convinced that their way is the best (as it is in some areas), they are slow and reluctant to change. To the impartial observer, and there are some in France, it often seems that the industries of other European countries are quicker off the mark. South-west France, for example, is already flooded with Spanish and Italian consumer goods, and all kinds of small household items.

Secondly, French politicians suffer from a disease common to politicians everywhere – that of believing that talking at length about a problem is the same thing as solving it – but they have the sickness more seriously than most. President Mitterrand's soothing bedside manner contains no remedies for anything at all.

Finally, the French economy is in a serious condition, largely because they have paid themselves too much for too long, not only in their social security services, which are heavily in debt, but also to workers in key industries which now find it very hard to compete in world export markets. The Socialists are pleased with themselves now, but if they run true to the form of previous such governments in France there will be bills to pay by 1992, and France may not be able to cut quite the figure she would wish in the new Europe. If this should be the case, the Socialists are likely to be blamed for it.

Religion

France has never been a totally Roman Catholic country in the sense that Spain and Italy are Catholic, for it has always had important religious minorities. The history of the Church in France has been bloody and bitter, nowhere more so than in the south and south-west, where **Albigensian** religious strife began with Pope Innocent III's Albigensian Crusade **Crusade** against the Cathares, supporters of the Albigensian heresy. In 1209 the army of the Pope's Crusaders took the town of Béziers and killed the whole population, regardless of religion. 'God will know his own,' said their leader.

In the following year Simon de Montfort captured the town of Bram, took one hundred of the inhabitants, put their eyes out, cut off their lips and noses and sent them to the next town, led by a one-eyed man, to terrify its defenders. The killing and burning at the stake went on over the whole region between the Rhône and the Pyrenees and south of the River Lot, and was followed by a hundred years of Inquisition. Nevertheless, there are still some Cathares in the Carcassonne area.

Wars of The long wars between Catholics and Protestants more than **Religion** 300 years later were no less bloody, and affected every town in Aquitaine and Auvergne. Now, nearly 400 years later, there is still a strong Protestant minority in the south-west and throughout France. The Prime Minister at the time of writing, Monsieur Michel Rocard, is a Protestant.

Because these persecutions took place with the approval of existing governments and monarchs, a traditional association grew up in France between politics and the Church. The Revolution was as anti-church as it was anti-nobility and anti-privilege.

Decline In modern times, Gaullism was strongly Catholic. But since the Second World War the importance of religion has steadily weakened in France, a decline so marked in some areas, especially near the Mediterranean coast, that the term 'dechristianisation' is often used. In the 1950s, in France as a whole, 30 per cent of all Catholics attended Mass regularly. By the 1970s this figure had fallen to 7 per cent attending, not regularly but once or twice a month. The figures have fallen further since, but perhaps rather less in the south-west than in some other regions. Another significant fact is that between 1964 and 1975 (later figures are not available) the number of Catholic priests being ordained fell by 70 per cent.

Alternative activities

Among the reasons put forward for the falling off of religious worship are the steady increase in alternative weekend occupations, especially the development of leisure and sporting activities which has been very marked in France, the increasing ownership of cars and other private transport enabling family visits to be made, and the increased importance of scientific and technical instruction.

Modern attitudes

Catholicism has suffered more than Protestantism, because the liberation of women, the use of the Pill and more relaxed attitudes towards contraception and abortion have all brought modern couples into direct conflict with the parish priest, whose interference in their lives is tolerated less and less. Modern wives do not want to be told when and under what conditions they should sleep with their husbands. This change of attitude is illustrated by the decline in the birthrate in the south of France, where the mathematical rate is between 1.45 and 1.85 for each woman of childbearing age.

Not only have church attendances fallen off, but there are fewer religious marriages and baptisms. Today most of the devout are old, although among younger people the Church still has what it calls festive or occasional Christians – those who attend church only for family celebrations such as marriages and baptisms. Most young people in France, even those who describe themselves as Catholic, have a derisory attitude towards confession.

Religion and politics

Modern research has shown the persistence of the link between religion and politics, especially in the south of France. Although socialism is widespread, it is strongest in those areas where the Protestant minority is also strong. Communism is strongest in those areas where dechristianisation is most advanced, and is no doubt a contributory factor. But as the Church becomes weaker, this link between politics and religion, forged so long ago, also steadily rusts away. For many of the young it is broken already.

Still a presence

Nonetheless, religion is still a presence. In the south-west you will find votive candles burning in almost any church you enter, and in farming areas village churches are still crowded for marriages. Farmers are also not above asking the priest to pray for rain; they may do it jokingly, but they do it.

There is a Gascon story of a village priest who was unrivalled in diverting storms from his parishioners' crops. One day, when a storm threatened to ruin the harvest, some of the congregation called at the church to ask him to work his miracle. He was absent, so they asked the bell-ringer, who, greatly honoured, seized the statue of the Virgin Mary and began to intone, *'Exsurge Domine . . .'.*

At this moment the curé returned, asking, 'What on earth are you up to?'

'It's obvious, Monsieur le Curé, I'm chasing the storm away.'

'Idiot! Do you expect to turn aside a storm with a statue of the Holy Virgin? Don't you know it's not woman's work? Fetch me the statue of Jesus.'

I'm not sure what that story says about religion, but it says something about Gascons. There are plenty of villages in Gascony where it would be laughed at – but not too loudly.

Social security

France is a highly developed welfare state whose social security benefits are generous by the standards of many other countries. Its health service, though at present under stress, offers a very wide range of medical benefits at low cost, including many medicines. Even visits to masseurs, physiotherapists and spells in spas to take the waters are paid for, provided they have been authorised by a doctor. Some treatments are reimbursable at 100 per cent and others at 70 per cent, while private medical insurance is available to cover the balance of 30 per cent.

There are unemployment benefits and generous family allowances according to the number of children, a system which encourages large families among the poor and unemployed, who are sometimes able to live almost entirely from these benefits.

Unemployment

There has been high unemployment in France in recent years, with no apparent change for the better. Unemployment figures are slightly above the national average in south-west France, where there are 22 per cent fewer people engaged in industry than there were at the turn of the century, although the decline has been slight during the past twenty-five years. In agriculture, the number of workers has declined from 51 per cent in 1901 to 13 per cent today, but in general business, the retail trade, consumer services, the media and so on there has been a steady increase throughout the twentieth century.

Crippling costs

The high cost of social security is gradually bringing the internal economy to its knees, with the deficit increasing every year. The system at this level is virtually self-destructive. Small employers, for example, are closing down by the thousand because they cannot afford the social security charges they are obliged to pay for each employee. Some of their men are able to find other work, but many swell the ranks of those collecting unemployment benefit, ultimately increasing the charges on the remaining employers, so that yet more of them give up. One government after another scratches around, desperately trying to find a solution that will not cost them votes.

34

Beggars

Visitors may be surprised at the number of beggars in the towns of the south-west. Most of them sit around the most frequented shopping areas or market places and often have a dog as a companion, while some haunt car parks and try to catch people as they enter or leave their cars. Many of them are clearly alcoholics, but sometimes schoolchildren will ask for money, saying they have no change for the telephone.

Cash will do nicely

The difficulties due to unemployment, inflation and rising cost of living have produced a widespread black economy. If you have some repairs or maintenance work done on your house, the man who does it will give you a normal bill, including VAT at 18.6 per cent if he has had to buy materials to do the work. If he has supplied nothing but his labour, particularly if it was not a long job or if he has chosen to do a longer job over a number of weekends, he will be happier to settle for cash.

Occasionally a van will arrive with a load of kitchen chairs, or other products which can be made in a workshop by artisans. They will be offered at the normal price, but will be sold below that and without VAT if you pay cash. Such sales do not appear in the books.

Clearly, any small entrepreneur has to provide enough facts and figures and evidence of purchases and sales to show that he is conducting a genuine business, but people like plumbers, carpenters and many others tend to mix up their jobs, doing a day here, half a day there, half a morning somewhere else. He knows how long everything should take and what he is up to, but no one else does. It all depends on how long he is prepared to work, whether he will work outside normal hours and at weekends, and on how much he declares that he has earned. So long as he keeps within reason, the authorities cannot establish that he has done more than he says.

This preference for cash is rather more common than having two jobs, although there are plenty of factory workers on early or late shifts who do another job before or after their normal work. A machine operator in a factory may well be a part-time gardener, while a garage attendant may repair lawn mowers privately. There are many retired craftsmen who carry on working privately, discreetly and in an irregular fashion – and always for cash.

The two societies

There are only two large cities in the south-west – Bordeaux and Toulouse – each, with its suburbs, having a population in excess of 600,000. Other towns rarely exceed 40,000, a more usual figure being between 10,000 and 20,000.

The life of those people who live and work in the cities and towns does not differ greatly from those who live in towns anywhere else, although some aspects of the daily pattern of life will be unfamiliar to first-time visitors from abroad.

The working day

As in the United States, everything generally begins earlier in the day in France than in Britain, for example. With few exceptions the working day starts at 8 a.m., shops, offices, even banks included. No workman in France would dream of taking any kind of break from the time he starts until he stops for lunch. On the other hand, except when alone – and sometimes even then – they talk all the time.

Lunch time

In our local town, which has a population of about 35,000, a siren is sounded every day at 12 noon, including Sunday. This is the signal, particularly for men working in the fields or tradesmen working in houses in the near countryside, and for everybody in town, that it is time for lunch. In some parts of France the sanctity of the two-hour lunch break is being eroded but not yet in the south-west. In many towns everything stops at midday. All shops close, except food shops, which stay open until half past twelve so that people can buy something for lunch on the way home. The only exception in our town is one large hypermarket, with a popular self-service restaurant, which remains open in case people who lunch there may want to buy something.

Almost everybody goes home to lunch, by car, and returns to work at 2 p.m. Most food shops do not open again until about 4 p.m., remaining open until about 7.30 p.m. Offices usually close at 6 p.m.

Life in the countryside of the south-west, however, is very different from that in the towns.

Down on the farm

Not long ago a national magazine in France conducted a survey in which readers were asked what income they would require before they considered themselves rich. The answers varied from a hundred thousand francs to a million francs a year, the lowest figure being the average response of the peasant farmers, the *agriculteurs*. But all is relative.

Many of the farmers live in the family house, built and paid for generations ago, and thus have no rent or mortgage liability. Because they have often married into another farming family, there may well be a second house. I live on a property which lies between a prosperous commercial fruit farm and a more traditional farm. The fruit farmer has his own large house, in which he was born and brought up his children, and there is another house for his son and his family. The farm is now worked by the family co-operative, a *Groupe Agricole Economique Coopérative*, GAEC for short. The family as a whole has recently had a small house built in the Pyrenees, which the younger members use for skiing holidays, while the older members take summer breaks there.

On the other side is a farmer of a different kind – a subsistence rather than a commercial farmer. He lives with his wife, daughter and his mother in the old family house. They also own the mother's farm, with an equally large house on the other side of the village, but that house remains empty, although they farm the land around it.

Both these families are representative of thousands of farmers in the south-west. So when they say one hundred thousand francs, some farmers may be thinking in terms of spending money rather than survival money.

Mechanisation

Not many years ago a farmer in the south-west could live well on 12 hectares of fertile land, but costs have increased at a rate which has not been matched by income. Until about twenty years ago the land was worked with teams of horses or oxen, a pair of which could work economically for several years, during which time they provided natural fertiliser, before being sold to the butcher for approximately what they had cost. Today the land is worked by tractors, which have a long life but do not last for ever, and when the time comes for replacement, the farmer often cannot afford it.

Contract harvesting

Sophisticated harvesting machinery is out of reach of all but the biggest farmers in the south-west, so that harvesting cereal crops is now a specialised job in itself. Companies buy machines costing possibly hundreds of thousands of francs and contract with farmers to harvest their crops. As all the maize ripens at about the same time, all the wheat in its time, all the sunflowers in their time, harvesting can be completed before crops spoil only by working day and night. In my first year here I was surprised to wake at midnight to the sound of machines harvesting wheat by the light of headlamps.

The high cost of farming machinery, as well as artificial fertilisers and sprays, means that most farmers have to borrow at high rates of interest and are heavily in debt. Though they have low household bills and enjoy favourable social security and insurance costs, they find it very hard to meet production costs.

Subsistence farming

My neighbour and his wife work to live off their farm. They have turkeys, guinea fowl, geese, ducks, pigeons, chickens and their eggs. He has a few cows and their calves, and so milk; he grows all his own vegetables and fruit; he makes enough wine for his own use and to have a regular clientele who buy at three francs a litre; he sells potatoes to a few neighbours, and he makes enough prunes from his plums to sell to people who call, as well as making prune and walnut liqueurs. He also has his own water supply.

He rarely buys clothes, since he works every day (as does his wife) in work clothes that are replaced only when they begin to fall apart. His *bleu de travail*, the blue overalls still worn by all workmen in the south-west, are so grimed that the blue has long since disappeared. His household expenses are confined to a few things which he cannot produce himself – sugar, coffee, rice, pasta and books and clothes for his schoolgirl daughter. He does not even buy bread. Instead he gives an agreed proportion of his wheat harvest to the baker, who delivers his bread – a system of barter which is not unusual in the south-west.

The general result of the changes and difficulties in agriculture in recent years is that land prices have fallen sharply, and there are many farms for sale. They do not sell readily.

Love and marriage

There seems, to the British or American mind, to be something different about the French idea of marriage. Although numerous marriages fail throughout the Western world, they frequently begin with an atmosphere of mutual commitment. In France, however, there is from the start a certain reservation on both sides.

The marriage contract

This is most obviously expressed in the marriage contract, which establishes at once the strong material element in French marriage. It can be a contract either creating common ownership of property or separating the property of the wife from that of her husband.

There is also a certain reserve at official level, a hint that at best it is a temporary arrangement. When Claudine Dupont marries Pierre Dubois, she becomes Madame Dupont as far as neighbours, tradesmen and business colleagues are concerned, but to the state she is Claudine Dupont first, wife Dubois second, and remains Claudine Dupont *épouse* Dubois as long as she is married to him. If Monsieur Dubois dies first, she becomes Claudine Dupont, widow Dubois. The same applies in reverse to Pierre Dubois, *époux* Dupont.

Perhaps the lack of commitment from the outset is the reason for the high rate of divorce in France. In the Paris area one marriage in two ends in divorce, in the south-west the figure is one in three.

Concubinage

There are also many homes in France in which people live together officially without the formality of marriage. This situation is known as *concubinage*, and raises no eyebrows whatever. Illegitimacy rates are similar, perhaps lower at 22 per cent, than those in Britain or the States.

The wedding

Marriages may be civil but are also, in the country, frequently performed in church, and in the south-west are great festive occasions.

Saturday afternoons, always busy, are further enlivened by long processions of decorated cars touring round and round the town, all horns blasting. Houses where the daughter has just been married can often be recognised, especially in the country, from the custom of placing bushes decorated with white ribbons at the entrance.

As you drive through Aquitaine you will notice that many farms have a small plantation of poplar trees. It was, and still is to some extent, the custom to celebrate the birth of a daughter by planting such a wood. Poplar takes little more than twenty years to reach maturity, so the plantation is ready to be cut down and sold to pay for the festivities when the daughter marries.

Extra-marital activity

Whether there is more extra-marital sexual activity in south-west France than there is in Britain or America is anybody's guess. It certainly seems so, but this is no doubt due to some extent to the overt attitude to such things. Our local weekly give-away paper contains several pages of fascinating reading under the heading *Rencontres* - meetings. About half of them are advertisements inserted by genuine matrimonial agencies (which abound), trying to match up ageing widows and widowers, divorced people and unmarried mothers. Others are privately inserted, a proportion presumably coming from serious young people trying to find a partner. This section also features many announcements of a more Rabelaisian flavour.

'Man in his forties, divorced, free to spoil any woman who is truly feminine and insatiable.'

'Young woman, sexy, dissolute, exhibitionist seeks erotic meetings with lustful men or women, forty-five to sixty. Write with your sexual dreams and out-of-the-ordinary fantasies. Discretion. Reply guaranteed.'

'Young married couple, fun-loving, seek young women for pleasant evenings and intimate games.'

And so on. There are also many display advertisements from prostitutes, some of which have the amusing sub-heading 'Erotically yours – every day except Sunday'.

Psychic services

These same give-away newspapers contain other advertisements offering a range of rather more unusual services. In the many years I lived in Sussex I do not think I ever saw anything like the following in the local paper:

'The Brothers André and Vincent, disciples of the Abbot Julio, for the lifting of spells, exorcism, protection against the evil eye, love reborn, blessing of houses and businesses etc. Will work from photographs, or travel anywhere in France.' Expenses paid, of course.

Someone called Renato offers to sort out sexual misunderstanding between couples, treat handicapped children and counter harmful waves both psychic and earthly.

And there are many women claiming to be mediums, clairvoyants, and to read your palm or tell your fortune in the tarot cards. By appointment only. Some of them, for a suitable fee, are prepared to do rather more than hold hands.

In rural France the people tend to show a degree of credulity far in excess of that which one would expect to find in Britain or America. One of these self-declared healers succeeded in persuading a considerable number of his clients that, in addition to charming away their warts, his magic powers enabled him to double any money they chose to leave in his open suitcase for a week. It worked so well as he moved from place to place that he left his getaway rather late, and his early clients having complained, he was arrested as he was about to leave France with a suitcase full of banknotes.

Family life

Despite these extra- and intra-marital aberrations, family life in France is still of great importance, especially in the rural areas. In the countryside the family has traditionally been a work force as well as a blood relationship. Even the farmer's wife, in addition to running the household, cooking for the family and other workers on the farm and looking after the farmyard with its chickens, ducks and pigeons, is expected to help with the harvest, pick fruit, or drive a tractor when necessary.

Family council

Matters of importance may still be decided by family council. In times of emergency any member of the family can call a *conseil de famille*, the majority decision of which has legal force. The matter raised usually concerns inheritance, or important sales or purchases.

Senior citizens

In the country it is usual for the family to take care of its older members. The peasants who survive their sixties often live to the late eighties or into their nineties. The *mémé* and the *pépé*, the grandmother and grandfather, continue to do whatever they can around the farm as long as they are able. The *mémé* prepares the vegetables for meals and the fruit for jam-making, plucks the chickens and may do some mending if her sight is good enough. The *pépé*, although officially retired and enjoying his pension and the social benefits of the *troisième age* (senior citizens), may still do work around the farm according to his physical strength, and will long continue to look after the family vineyard and potter in the vegetable garden.

There are comfortable homes for old people in France but it is not usual, certainly in the countryside, for families to put away their old parents in such homes. This attitude is traditional rather than peasant reluctance to spend money when it can be avoided, for it seems right to them that people should die where they have lived and worked. When the mother of my neighbour, the fruit farmer, died at ninety-two, she died in the house to which she came as a bride of twenty, and in the room where she had given birth to her children.

Head of the family

French families are traditionally headed by the oldest member, man or woman, without whose approval important decisions are not normally taken. When a farmer says, 'Well, I might sell you that piece of land, but not just yet', it could mean that he does not intend to sell, or that he would like to but that his mother or father will not permit it. Many a farmer in his sixties has a parent in the eighties who still keeps a tight hold on the family purse strings, those with strong personalities dominating every aspect of family life as long as they have their wits about them. One young farmer told me that his grandfather had refused to allow them to spend money on installing a bathroom and an indoor toilet. 'I have lived all my life without either, and I'm eighty,' he said. 'You don't need them. It's a waste of money.'

Visiting relations

Relatives who live within reasonable distance of each other often exchange visits, usually on Sundays, and eat in each other's houses. It is the usual custom when visiting friends or family to take with you not a bunch of flowers or a bottle of wine but, in tune with the French love of food, a cake from the *pâtissier*. On Sunday mornings in every town and village the *pâtisseries* are crowded and a succession of customers can be seen leaving with beribboned and carefully wrapped boxes of delicious *gâteaux*. They are eaten after the family Sunday lunch, and in summer it is a common sight in the south-west, where virtually every house has a terrace, to see large family groups still sitting out at the lunch table late in the afternoon.

Those who do not eat in each other's houses often form a family group, small children included, and book a large table in a restaurant for Sunday lunch. For this reason it is advisable for visitors travelling in the summer high season to book in advance at restaurants.

Death

The people of the south-west are very respectful towards their dead. During the Second World War the Resistance was strong in this area, and the old soldiers' associations, the comrades of the Resistance, the *gendarmes* and so on still turn out in force with medals, flags and music on every date associated with the war, such occasions being treated with great respect by the general population.

On the whole people seem to remember their dead in a more obvious manner than in many other countries, visiting and decorating the graves more frequently. Very many families visit the cemeteries on All Saints' Day, a date which also often produces the highest number of fatalities in road accidents.

Feeding the family

The French spend a lot of their income on food, and with all the temptation put before them they would surely have to be superhuman not to do so. Hypermarkets with parking for hundreds of cars are to be found on the outskirts of even small French towns. In them you can buy all the necessities of everyday life.

Hyper-markets

For example, our local hypermarket, and there are four others around the town, sells more than sixty kinds of cheese, including Dutch and Italian – but no English. There are more than twenty kinds of bread to go with it, and well over a hundred different wines.

There is a clothes section which sells everything from slippers to straw hats, as well as a gardening department where you can buy everything from a lawn mower to pre-packed plants and the fertilisers and weed-killers to go with them; then there is a do-it-yourself section with all the tools, car furniture, sanitary fittings and so on necessary for car upkeep and house maintenance; plus another large area for consumer goods ranging from microwave ovens to televisions, another for glassware, china and kitchen utensils, and a sports department with everything from table tennis tables to guns and fishing equipment. In short it is not easy to think of something you cannot buy under this one roof. Bowler hats and cricket bats come to mind, but not much else.

Traditional markets

You might think with all this so easily available that there would be no place for the traditional market, but you would be wrong. There is a market every day in the larger towns, twice a week in the smaller towns and once a week in the large villages.

They are all fascinating, and although they are mainly markets for food and clothing, they often have surprises. I remember walking through the Friday market in a local small town and hearing the *muezzin* calling the faithful to prayer. Looking around, intrigued, I found a stall selling a variety of household articles including mantel clocks which, instead of chiming the hour, reproduced at appropriate times the Muslim call to prayer. As there is a small Muslim population in the south-west, following the exodus from North Africa, I have no doubt that the enterprising stallholder found a buyer.

The traditional markets thrive throughout Aquitaine. The farmers use them not merely to sell their produce and to restock with baby chicks, ducks, geese and so forth, but also as a meeting place. These are the only occasions apart from the few official meetings each year, usually to protest about something, when they get together and exchange information about prices, new ideas they have heard of or tried, and also to gossip about family and friends. They are what markets have been for thousands of years, since men first began to live together in communities. When you walk through them, you are sharing in one of the timeless activities of society. Everywhere you will find knots of three or four men and women, discussing the price of something they themselves grow, or the health of a friend or relative (almost invariably not what it was), or the marriage recently past or forthcoming (and none too soon) of someone they all know, or the recent birth of a girl, or better, a boy.

Ecological markets

In addition to these general markets, there are regular ecological markets selling untreated fruit and vegetables and, in the small villages, Sunday morning markets for home-made produce. This is where you can buy farmhouse cheeses, jams, local honey, featherlight tarts and sponges, and such famous regional dishes as *confit* of duck and goose (joints roasted, salted and bottled in their own fat).

Mushroom markets

Then there are specialised markets, like that which takes place in autumn in Monpazier, the *bastide* village which calls itself 'the capital of mushrooms'. This is the great market for the *cèpes de Bordeaux* – a mushroom which figures in many regional recipes – and for about fifteen other varieties of mushrooms commonly eaten in the south-west, including truffles. Restaurateurs come from as far afield as Paris to get their supplies fresh at Monpazier, where *cèpes* and truffles can reach very high prices.

Contract buying

A common practice for keeping down the food bills, used by many housewives who live in town but near the country, is to contract with a farmer in advance to buy his lambs, calves or turkeys at maturity. At lambing time, for example, the farmer makes a list of names of people who want a lamb, and at the right time the animal is slaughtered and delivered to the housewife for her deep freeze. The farmer knows where he is from the start and the housewife gets prime quality meat at well under half the price, nearer a third, of what it would cost from the butcher.

Homes and houses

Périgord farmhouses

The more traditional domestic architecture of the south-west includes some very attractive styles. If you rent a holiday home in Dordogne, you may find yourself staying in one of the lovely old Périgord farmhouses which are such a wonderful blend of strength, practicality and romantic charm. They have certain things in common, such as an outside staircase leading to the living accommodation on the first floor, and at least one tower, usually rectangular but sometimes round. In the old days the rooms at ground level were used for livestock and the storage of fodder, both of which helped to insulate the living accommodation in winter. In some working farms, this is still the case.

The design is so popular that it is used today for modern houses in

Aquitaine, still with the outside staircase and balcony, but the ground floor is now occupied by a large workshop for the man of the house and a large laundry and drying room for the wife, as well as a spacious deep freeze, storage space for wood, a garage, and often a bedroom.

Landais houses

Another attractive style, just as original, but quite different, is that of the typical houses of the Landes forest. They usually have one spacious living room, often with an open, circular fireplace in the middle, and an adjacent kitchen which is sometimes built around the well, for there are many artesian wells in the Landes. There will probably be one or two main bedrooms on the ground floor, and although the houses are essentially single-storey, some of them have an additional sleeping area under the roof.

These Landais farmhouses, known locally as *bordas*, are often of beam and plaster construction, with the beams exposed. The roofs are widespread with a gentle pitch, the windward side often sloping closer to the ground to afford protection against the spring and autumn gales which harass the forest from the Bay of Biscay.

The smallest houses in the forest were known as *maisons des brassées*, the *brassée* or *brassier* being the poor peasant who had nothing but his hands and the strength of his arms with which to work.

Fireplaces

The open-air terrace, used for meals throughout the long summer, is one of the symbols of home in the south-west. The other, representing winter comfort, is a huge fireplace. There are woods and forests on all sides and the winters in some areas have spells which are cold enough to call for fires in the house. In the farmhouses of the past these great fireplaces were not only the sole source of warmth but the cooking area as well, and there are still many such houses where the kitchen chimney place has a turning spit and a trammel, the adjustable chain and hook on which to hang the stew pot. The people keep them and use them, even though there may be a microwave oven as well.

The imposing fireplace is also an important selling feature of new houses, with a certain snob value. Several companies produce glossy catalogues offering a splendid variety of stone and/or brick fireplaces, sometimes topped with an old oak beam, and including storage places for logs. They are often named after a classic period of architecture or a region of France where that particular style is traditional. The designs and level of workmanship are of a kind not found in Britain except in important town houses and country mansions. Instead of the turning spit and trammel, new houses have equally imposing fireplaces, but with back boiler and hot air distribution systems which augment or replace central heating.

Large houses

The average Frenchman in the south-west, especially if he lives outside the towns, usually has a considerably larger house than his counterpart in, say, Britain. There are more large though unpretentious houses and fewer cottages than is general in Britain. Among the

44

houses built by prosperous farmers in the past there is a great variety of styles, each seeming to have been determined to outdo his nearest neighbour in matters of towers, turrets and gables, and none of them feeling any need to consult an architect. For example, my house, which is a traditional regional farmhouse, featured pillars and porches wherever a former eccentric owner had felt he could add them to the original simple building.

There is no main drainage in the countryside of France, and because of the large distances between towns, villages and even houses, there is never likely to be. Many fine old houses have only recently had bathrooms installed.

Mortgages

Not long ago the system of buying houses on mortgage was almost unheard of in France, but it has developed over the past few years and is now quite common. Money is normally advanced either directly by a bank, or by a merchant bank specialising in credit for purchases, or by the builder backed by such a bank.

Municipal housing

Aquitaine has few council estates, but most towns, and even large villages have municipal housing on the outskirts in the form of large and often hideously ugly blocks of flats. These *habitations loyers moyens* (low rent homes) are always called HLM for short.

Flats

Blocks of private flats do exist in the towns but, perhaps because of the great amount of space, the majority of people who can afford to buy live in their own detached house. New semi-detached or terraced property is unusual. A five-roomed house, usually in the form of a long, low bungalow with kitchen, bathroom, garage and terrace, costs about 300,000 francs.

Gardens

With the spread of house ownership other changes have come about. In the past the French were not, in general, a nation of gardeners, but in the last few years one of the boom areas of the economy in the south-west, where the climate is ideal for them, has been the development of nurseries and garden centres. Every year new ones open, and the competition is fierce. This has been paralleled by the great surge in DIY centres, *bricolage*, as the French call do-it-yourself, now being the national pastime. They believe it saves them money, and as the average Frenchman is very good with his hands, it probably does.

Many of the new houses scattered in apparently odd places in the deep country are there because farmers have the right to build, without the usual planning permission, an additional house on their own land for the use of a member of their family. This is an inducement for a son, when he marries, to stay on the farm.

Staying put

The British resident in France, coming from a small country in which most people move about frequently, is surprised to find that in France a great many people are very much tied to their own locality, their own *pays*. The farmers in particular move about very little; for one thing they are too busy, working every day of the year if they live on a subsistence farm. The farmer's wife next door to us has been once to the sea – at Arcachon, only two hours' drive from home – in the twenty years of her married life. Her daughter went to school in the local village and, until she was sent to a more senior school 26 kilometres away in Agen, at the age of sixteen, she had never been to a town.

Artisans and delivery men from the nearest town often have to be given detailed instructions on how to reach our hamlet, which is only 11 kilometres outside the town.

In the course of conversation with older people I have often been surprised to find that, apart from one or two key towns in their own department which they may have visited for shopping or medical reasons, they know hardly any town or village not connected with their own work or family needs.

Cars

One of the reasons for this apparent insularity is that the people in south-west France do not motor for pleasure, and would not dream of going for a weekend drive. It would seem to them a ridiculous waste of time and money. When they get in their cars, it is for business, shopping or to visit relatives nearby, although once or twice a year they may take the children on a skiing or summer holiday, or may visit relatives in some more distant part of France. On such journeys they invariably take the shortest main-road route, so that France, which has far and away the finest and most diverse road system in Europe, regularly suffers from 30-kilometre traffic jams at certain points on key holiday departure and return dates.

This is a boon for visiting motorists who, if they avoid main-road routes, can often drive for hours and see few other cars, even in the height of summer. For those who enjoy motoring this is one of the great pleasures of south-west France.

Very few people in the south-west are too poor to run a car. Those who live away from towns are obliged to do so, for distances are considerable and, apart from school buses, public transport is almost non-existent. Often there is no more than a once-daily return service between towns, and a service once or twice a week from villages to towns for market days. There are bus stops to be seen on country roads, but in five years of driving in this region I have only twice seen a moving bus on the road.

However, cars are expensive to run, and many are both unlicensed and uninsured. A recent estimate suggested that there were 300,000 uninsured motor cycles alone on the roads in France.

Artisans

Life in south-west France is enriched by the existence of a large artisan class, not a 'working' class, but a body of men who are genuine craftsmen rather than the kind who will make you a fancy wrought iron gate, or burn designs on leather, or offer oddly designed hand-made furniture at exorbitant prices.

Masons

In England and the States they have bricklayers, but in France they have masons. A French mason, many of whom in this part of France are of Italian, Spanish or Portuguese extraction, will build you a house in brick, or dressed stone, or stone as it comes from the quarry. They will build anything from a bridge over a stream to a family mausoleum, and I am quite sure that, given the time, our village mason could build a cathedral unaided.

Blacksmiths

Every centre of population still has its *forgeron*, a blacksmith who can do anything the farmer may require, from making new parts for ancient agricultural machines, special tools such as the long-handled iron gouge used to lift asparagus – not required in sufficient numbers to interest commercial manufacturers – or the strong secateurs used for pruning fruit trees and old-fashioned bread guillotines, to the irons and fire dogs used in the great chimneys. He can also shoe a horse for the pony club and make wrought iron gates.

Furniture

Artisans also have an important place in furniture making. There are basically three kinds of furniture available in France. The mass-produced article is usually rather expensive and often rather nasty. Above this there is a range of well-made furniture in a variety of attractive woods, including wild cherry and pear. Some is skilfully aged and some is made from monumental old furniture which has already served for generations.

Then there is a good deal of fine furniture which, though not entirely made by hand has a lot of hand work in it, and can be made to order. When I remarked to a man in a good furniture shop, 'That table is what I want but it is a bit too large', he did not shrug and walk away but told me to supply the exact dimensions and he would have it made at the same price. So I now have a solid oak table made by hand in a workshop in the Pyrenees, and at no greater cost than the one I saw.

The man who made it does not sign his work with a mouse or a bear; it's just his job and whether he makes something for a shop or an individual, it is all the same to him as long as he makes a good table. I am sure that the one he made for me, which takes two strong men to lift it, elegant though it is, will still be in use somewhere in a couple of hundred years or more, short of destruction by fire.

Local craftsmen

Talking of age, it is interesting that when a corner of my 200-year-old barn was brought down in a violent storm, I had no difficulty in finding three men who were prepared to rebuild it with solid oak beams and rafters exactly as it had been done when it was new. None of them lived more than eight kilometres away.

Income

Though they do not bring them fortunes, some of the trades practised by artisans bring a very comfortable income. Many mothers are satisfied to see their daughters marry, for example, a chef, a pastrycook or a *charcutier*. The *pâtissier*, the man – and it almost always is a man – who makes all those delicious *gâteaux* and French pastries, is often one of the more prosperous men of the village.

There can be few trades which bring a bigger return for individual labour than that of the *charcutier*, a kind of glorified pork butcher. He begins with a pig, and by the time he has finished turning every single part of it – from the trotters to the ears – into some much appreciated delicacy, he must have multiplied its value scores of times. In the south-west the *charcutier* also practises his art on geese, chickens, quail and rabbits, transforming each of them into all kinds of prepared dishes.

Art

Nowadays painters are not classed as artisans, though many of the greatest painters and sculptors of classical periods thought of themselves as ordinary craftsmen, similar to masons and carpenters. But in France, certainly in Aquitaine, painting is a less rarefied occupation than elsewhere, and art in all its forms is a familiar presence. In London or New York, one has the impression that pictures are generally collected by well-to-do people. Here, though, at any one time there will be dozens of posters in shop windows advertising two or three different exhibitions of the work of contemporary artists, usually regional but sometimes from any part of France or Spain.

Every small town in southern France has its own shop and art gallery, as well as its own group of professional artists. It is a trade felt to be open to all, and many of the best French artists still come from artisan families. A man, now retired, who sometimes helps me with the garden, spent his life as a *cantonnier*. This is the man who, in small villages, was responsible for the condition and upkeep of the local roads –

a job now replaced by gangs and mechanised equipment from the municipal works department. His son is a well respected local painter in oils.

Respect for painting

Painting thrives in France because of the almost universal respect for this art form. Any man who does well in life buys paintings – the businessman and shop-owner, the professional man, accountant, lawyer and doctor. It may be considered an outward sign of his increasing prosperity, but more often it is just an aspect of French life. It is rarely done with any pretence at knowledge of painting, or with thought to investment, for it is the not-yet-known working artists who sell pictures. People buy what takes their fancy; they may listen to what a local gallery owner tells them if it suits their taste, and they may ask the artist to paint a particular subject for them. It is not too much to say that small town society often feels an obligation to support working artists.

Nothing is underpriced in France, and it would be misleading to suggest to the tourist that he can buy good paintings cheaply. He may later find that he has done so, but even a small picture by an unknown though competent artist is likely to cost two or three thousand francs. On the other hand, there are so many practising artists that among them there are without doubt some who will be counted geniuses in the future.

The impact of tourism

Though it has brought some changes, tourism has not had the dramatic effect on everyday life in Aquitaine that it had, for example, on the grindingly poor farmers and fishermen of the Spanish Costa del Sol, who for centuries struggled for existence against the sun-withered near-desert and barren seas of that coast before the advent of tourism. There, the quick thinkers turned from farming and fishing to bars, restaurants and hotels, moving from poverty to riches in a generation.

Old resorts

In Aquitaine, Arcachon, Biarritz and St Jean-de-Luz are old resorts, already fashionable a hundred years ago. Dax has long been one of the most popular spas in France, and the Pyrenees have for many years attracted travellers.

New trends

But in the past twenty years, slowly at first, the volume of tourism to south-west France has increased considerably, doing much to balance the decline in agriculture and shipping and the loss of work due to technological development. Changes due to tourism are most noticeable in the coastal and mountain areas and in the Périgord Noir, around Sarlat.

South-west France is still comparatively little-known to British and American holiday-makers, who are outnumbered by the Dutch, the

The beaches

Belgians and the Germans, although by far the largest number of visitors are from the Paris area and northern France.

When, twenty years ago, we used to take our family holidays in the Arcachon area, we had only to drive a few kilometres out of the town to the south, and then take a footpath through the forest for a few hundred metres to find ourselves alone, as far as we could see, on the largest beach in Europe. On the days when we saw another sun umbrella a few hundred metres away, it was worth a comment. Those same beaches are frequented today by thousands of people. In the high season some sections are like Brighton beach on a Bank Holiday. Yet the beach is so vast that it is still possible to find plenty of space, if you do not mind a walk from your point of access and do not mind bathing where there is no lifeguard supervision.

Summer homes

Places like Mimizan – an unknown village when Winston Churchill spent part of a painting holiday there before the Second World War – and Biscarosse, once nothing more than a few houses around an old church, now have hundreds of summer homes, built in the Landais style, scattered in the forest all around them.

Camp sites

Throughout the whole length of the coastal strip there are a number of large and well-equipped camp sites. For those who enjoy camping holidays there can be few better sites than these, situated in the shade and shelter of the forest with sun-scorched ocean beaches on one side and spacious lakes with smaller sandy beaches on the other.

Winter tourism

There has also been a marked though less important development of winter tourism, with new ski resorts being built on both the French and Spanish slopes of the Pyrenees. At present these are used chiefly by the population of the south-west, who can drive to them for a day's skiing at any time during the season, and by visitors from other parts of France who come for longer skiing holidays.

Some habits and customs

Shaking hands

The average Frenchman in this part of the country probably shakes hands as often every day as most Britons do in a year. It is usual to shake hands with everyone you meet, new acquaintances or old, every time you meet them and every time you say good-bye. A workman or a farmer may hold out his hand to you with the fist closed, because his hands are dirty, and it is usual then to take him by the wrist or forearm as a substitute for a handshake.

Greetings

The small politenesses of life are observed with considerable formality in the south-west. When somebody enters a shop and says, *'Bonjour, messsieurs, 'dames'*, it is not because he knows the customers already there. It is simply a common courtesy widely observed in shops, restaurants, post offices, banks, doctors' waiting rooms and similar places where strangers meet. It is also usual to say, *'Au revoir, messieurs, 'dames'*, on leaving.

When separating before meal times, the French in this area always wish each other *'Bon appetit'*, the first to say it usually being answered with *'De même'*, the same to you.

It is normal for men and women to address each other as *monsieur* or *madame* when opening, and from time to time during conversation. Exceptions are members of the same family, or old friends, who may be addressed by a Christian name. I have noticed that the *monsieur* and *madame* tend to get louder and more pointed when there is a difference of opinion in the air. If you want service in a shop, or to ask a question of someone in the street, perhaps a *gendarme*, you are likely to gain attention more easily if you begin with a clear but polite *'S'il vous plaît, monsieur'*.

Tu and vous
As far as the use of *tu* and *vous* is concerned, it is simpler not to try to understand the nuances, and to use *tu* to children and animals and *vous* to everyone else. *Tu* is used between old schoolfriends and genuine friends, but it is also used by those aspiring to an intimacy which does not, and probably never will exist. On television and in show business it is frequently used by interviewers hoping to suggest a closer degree of acquaintance than has ever existed between himself and the famous subject who is being interviewed.

Money
The French attitude to money is basically the same as that of most other races: they like it. But in France the feeling is greatly intensified.

Dress
The formality of manners is not accompanied by formality of dress. It is rare in the south-west to see a man formally dressed in a suit and wearing a collar and tie, unless he is a politician posing for an election poster, or wishes to be mistaken for a television news reader, or is perhaps on his way to a wedding or a funeral. Informality is the rule, even in the evenings, and in restaurants men will often hang their jackets on the back of the chair.

Nudity
Informality is continued on the beaches where, although there are specific naturist areas, it is not unusual everywhere to see young couples and whole families from grandparents to tiny tots in the nude. If they are not nude, most young women with a reasonable figure go topless on the Atlantic beaches.

Chic
The reputation which French women have for being chic is often justified, but it costs money and so applies in general to those women who work themselves or whose husbands have good jobs. On the farms of the south-west there are still many older women whose daily dress is peasant black with perhaps a flowered apron and a wide-brimmed straw hat against the sun. French women, like American women, tend to wear more perfume and a lot more jewellery than is usual among British women, a trend which is encouraged by the way in which the *speakerines* who announce television programmes are presented, with expensive clothes, elaborate hair styles and wearing

jewellery which sometimes seems to have been borrowed from a Christmas tree.

Regional characteristics

Almost all the south-west is part of the Midi of France, the south, where people are much more Latin in temperament than they are in the north. A good part of Aquitaine consists of the old province of Gascony, and the Gascons are famous throughout France for their swagger, boastfulness and joviality. They make and break friendships easily, and make and break promises equally easily. A 'Gascon promise' is proverbial in France as a measure for something of little or no worth, not to be taken seriously.

Punctuality   As far as personal appointments are concerned, punctuality is not a strong point with people of the south-west. On the other hand, shops open on time and when the workmen start, they start on time, although they do share with builders and plumbers of other nations the inability to arrive on the day promised.

Hospitality   The Gascon is genial, and hospitality is a matter of honour with him. An elderly relative of mine who set off to walk to the nearest village became tired and took what he thought was a short cut back only to find himself in a farmyard faced by a bewildered farmer. Neither spoke each other's language but they enjoyed a good-natured though incoherent conversation over a glass of the farmer's home-made sparkling wine, and the host eventually made clear to his guest how to find the road back.

Specialities   Almost every town in the south-west claims to be the capital of something, from artichokes to asthma, which usually means that they produce a lot of something or specialise in curing a particular malady. It may be coincidence that it is a small Gascon town, Moncrabeau, which is the capital of liars. Every year a grand fair and Liars' Championship is held there, the teller of the best lie being ceremoniously crowned King of Liars for a year. It is fair to say that not all the contestants are Gascons, for the event attracts competitors from all over France.

Law and order

Responsibility for the maintenance of law and order in France is divided between the police, who are civil servants, and the *gendarmerie*, who are attached to the army. The police operate in the towns and the *gendarmes* in the villages and the countryside.

Car parking

The people in south-west France do not care much for rules and regulations, a characteristic that the motorist from abroad is bound to notice when it comes to parking his car. All towns have authorised parking-places, some with meters, some free, but if you walk along a row of meters with parked cars, you will see that only one in four will have had any money put in it. This is about the average rate in country towns. In other places 'No Parking' yellow lines marked on the kerbs will often be completely hidden by parked cars. Hospital and fire station exits are spared, but not much else. Most French drivers will make an attempt to find a proper parking place, but if he has no quick success the average motorist gives up and parks where it suits him. There are traffic wardens, but never enough to cope with even a quarter of the offenders, although things are stricter in the *préfectures*, presumably because they control the departmental budgets.

Speeding

Both police and *gendarmes* are indulgent towards tourists who commit minor motoring offences, although speeding is an exception, and on-the-spot fines are levied. For some time now the police have been out to raise money for modernising the force, and are therefore a good deal more vigilant than was the case a year or two ago.

Theft

The tourist in south-west France is not likely to be mugged, or to have his pocket picked. It could happen, but only in the cities and rarely – much less often than in London or New York. On the other hand it is wiser not to leave expensive cameras, radios or other valuables in a parked car overnight, or to leave them for long unattended on a beach.

Law-breaking

Mushrooms offer a good example of the regional attitude to regulations. A few years ago there was little restriction on the gathering of mushrooms, and searching their favourite woods for *cèpes* or other mushrooms for supper was a popular way for townspeople in Dordogne, Lot-et-Garonne, and other departments to spend a Sunday afternoon. But since prices have soared, there are 'Mushroom picking forbidden' notices everywhere.

The local paper recently reported an amusing case. Some mushroom pickers, defying the notices, were making their way back to their car with full baskets when they were stopped by two men with guns. Had they not seen the notices forbidding the picking of mushrooms? No, where was that? There is one behind you. This is my land and you are making off with a valuable crop. I could prosecute you.

After discussion, the 'farmers' agreed not to prosecute, but insisted that the trespassers leave the mushrooms with them. The mushroom pickers drove off and the 'farmers', making their way back to their own car, had gone only a few steps when the real farmer emerged from the undergrowth. 'Not a bad dodge,' he said. 'Bad luck for you, but I am the owner of this land and I can prove it, which you cannot. My mushrooms, if you don't mind.'

53

Despite the average Frenchman's readiness to disregard regulations of all kinds, I would nonetheless describe France as a law-abiding country as far as important issues are concerned.

Private property

In the country some of the liberty in the *Liberté, Fraternité, Egalité* comes into play. Few French farmers object to people crossing their land to fish in a river or to picnic under a convenient tree, provided crops are respected. I have never seen the equivalent of a 'Trespassers will be prosecuted' notice in this part of France. The 'Private property' notices which one does see almost invariably refer to residential properties rather than working farms.

Low life

There is a drug presence rather than a drug problem in Aquitaine. Prostitution is not uncommon; even small towns still have their *madames* and their 'houses'. There are also occasional reports, in the local press, of bars and restaurants in remote parts of the forest and the countryside where the owners have been charged with keeping two or three girls on the premises. These arrangements have usually been made by gangsters in Bordeaux or Toulouse as a diversification, which they hope will escape the attention of the law. They usually come to light as a result of a *règlement de comptes*, a favourite phrase of the French police, which means a settling of accounts between rival gangs.

Sport

In modern France success in sport is regarded politically as an important source of national prestige. In the south-west all sport is taken seriously and rugby union is almost a religion.

Sports facilities

Towns and villages are remarkably well equipped with facilities for a wide range of sporting activities, even small towns being likely to have an indoor sports stadium with an Olympic swimming pool, halls for basketball and other indoor games, as well as rooms for such sports as boxing, judo and karate. There is also likely to be an outdoor stadium with running tracks and football pitches, and usually there is a separate lawn tennis club with approximately one court for every two thousand of the town's population. Even villages are likely to have a tennis club with at least two courts and floodlighting.

Rugby

The national sports of France are cycling and football, but although they are popular in the south-west, their importance is far outweighed by devotion to the game of rugby football. Every town and village from the Mediterranean to the Dordogne has its rugby fifteen, and many of them play the thirteen-a-side game as well. The only town in the south-west where soccer is more important than rugby is Bordeaux, whose local side, the Girondins, is one of the great French teams.

Media coverage
The importance of sport in the south-west is reflected in the local papers, *Sud Ouest* and *La Dépêche du Midi*, whose every issue contains at least five pages devoted to sport – more than twice the coverage given to national and international news – plus a separate eight-page supplement on Mondays.

Tennis
The French have always produced some good tennis players, particularly in the days of the great Suzanne Lenglen, Henri Cochet, René Lacoste and Jean Borotra, but it is only in recent years that the game has been organised on a national basis, with all club members being registered and their level of play assessed, rather as golfers are handicapped. The result is that France now has a number of rising young tennis players at international level.

Golf
Rather belatedly, the French have recently become enthusiastic about golf, and are now organising it in the same methodical manner. There have always been some fashionable golf courses, although they were few compared with those of the USA, Britain and some other countries, but in the past few years fifty new courses have been or are being laid out, and even villages are beginning to have their own nine-hole, or if there is not sufficient space, six-hole courses. Good French golfers at international level are as scarce as Olympic pole-vaulters in Britain, but the new effort and a system designed to encourage the young and find new talent will no doubt change this situation during the next few years. The French are extremely competitive by nature, and once they take up a sport on this scale it becomes a matter of national pride to do it well. On television it often seems that the national interest is the only thing that matters, and it is not unusual for reports to tell how the French competitor performed – even if he or she came only fourth or fifth – without telling you who won.

Cycling
Cycling is a spectator sport in France throughout the summer. Visiting motorists can find themselves held up unexpectedly in some out-of-the-way town or village which happens to be on the route of a regional cycling event. If you happen unwittingly to cross the route of the *Tour de France*, you are likely to have no alternative but to park the car wherever you can and join the local inhabitants, who stand for hours, rain or shine, waiting to see the cavalcade of the nation's greatest sporting event sweep through their village.

So sport in modern France is taken very seriously, and nowhere more so than in the south-west, where rugby and its great players are treated with the reverence formerly accorded to princes.

The Weather and When to Go

The climate of south-west France is in general very pleasant and livable. The winters are mild; spring is an erratic continuation of winter, becoming slowly warmer; the summers are long and hot, like those remembered from childhood; and autumn is calm, sunny and fruitful.

Winter In winter frost is rare, particularly along the coastal strip, where the gardens are yellow with mimosa in January and February. For snow you have to go to the mountains, although every thirty years or so there is a hard winter. In 1956 frost killed some vines and in 1985 almost every mimosa in France died. That year even pine trees were killed by the cold, and you could have danced a small elephant on the snow-covered ice of the swimming pool. But that was in 1985, and in the normal course of events such a winter should not occur again until about 2020.

Spring Spring is predominantly rainy, although I have known sunny Februarys, and Aprils when the sun shone every day and the water was warm enough for bathing. In the Biarritz area, spring can be very pleasant, although in most of Aquitaine the weather is in and out until the end of May, when summer arrives seemingly overnight. One day you need a pullover and a couple of days later you can sunbathe in comfort. Suddenly it is warm, and then hot. Temperatures reach the **Summer** nineties in July and August every summer, and sometimes in June and September as well. The hottest area is inland between the Lot and Toulouse, while the most temperate is the Atlantic seaboard. The Pyrenees, like other European mountain ranges, are cloudier and more stormy than the lower country.

Summer heat can be broken by storms which are tropical in violence and during which a great amount of rain falls. On the other hand, there are summers in which no more than a distant rumble of thunder is heard, and no storm arrives. An official drought has been declared in three of the past four summers. Between these extremes, summer rain normally falls in heavy showers, often quickly followed by bright sunshine.

There are many still days in summer, and windy is not an adjective one would use of the climate of Aquitaine. The wind comes mostly from the south-west, but not always, hot weather often being brought by a south wind from North Africa. In spring and autumn a fitful east wind called the *vent d'autan* brings bright sunny weather for a few days, followed by rain, while winter's cold spells are often accompanied by a north-west wind.

One of the nicest things about the climate of the region is that whenever the sun comes out, even in December and January, its warmth can be felt. At any time of the year, many days which begin by looking grey and cloudy turn out to be sunny, because the sun has burned off the cloud by mid-morning.

In spring and autumn the nights can be fresh, so that you may be glad of a pullover, although you would be unlikely to want one in the main summer months, except while visiting caves or high in the mountains.

Snow

There are now a number of ski resorts in the Pyrenees. Those who want to be certain of snow might be advised to leave their holiday until after Christmas, for although there is sometimes snow earlier, it can be late. In the winter of 1987–88, there was virtually no snow on the ski-runs anywhere in the Pyrenees during the Christmas holiday season, but this was rather unusual.

When to go

High season

The French almost all take their own holidays between mid-July and the end of August, with the peak in the first two weeks of August. The south-west is very popular with people from the Paris region and the north of France, as well as with the Dutch and the Germans, who take their holidays in exactly the same period. The result is that the coastal resorts become crowded during this time, many coming alive only towards the end of July and going to sleep again at the end of the school holidays.

In inland areas there is much less of a problem. Tourism is not yet considered sufficiently important for local people to stop thinking of August as their own holiday period, and as in Paris, a good many shops are closed at some time during the summer high season. In our village both the bakers close on the same dates. Some hotels and restaurants with a high proportion of business customers also take their own holidays sometime during the summer, so this is something which should be checked.

September

September can be a very pleasant time for a holiday in the south-west, especially in the bigger resorts such as St Jean-de-Luz, Biarritz, Hossegor and Arcachon. The French, Dutch and German tourists have returned home, but there is still a certain amount of life in the hotels and restaurants – and it is ten times easier to find a parking

Self-catering

place for your car. The weather can be very pleasant and the sea is at its warmest.

Self-catering holidays inland are enjoyable at any time from June to October, and are particularly interesting as summer moves into autumn, for there is activity all around you as one crop after another is harvested, and the time for the picking of the grapes and the making of the wine arrives.

Travelling Around

The great majority of the residents of south-west France use their own transport to travel around – car, mobylette and, for short distances, bicycles. They do this because it is the most practical way. Bus services are few and far between, and most of the small railway lines have been closed, only the larger towns being linked by rail – and not all of them. There are a few air services, but in terms of air travel the distances are so short that, when you take into account getting to and from the airport, they have no real advantage over fast trains.

In most places outside the larger resorts, tourists will find that a car is essential, if only for shopping, and those who do not bring their own car should consider car hire.

By road

The south-west has an excellent road system. From the A62, the *Autoroute des Deux Mers* which links the Atlantic and the Mediterranean coasts, down to the smallest local byway the roads are well maintained, and all main roads have useful road markings. There is an extensive network of alternative routes which allow enjoyable exploration by car, especially as French motorists almost invariably keep to direct main-road routes, leaving the side roads free of all but minor local traffic. Most of them serve only villages and outlying farms, but they offer splendid views, countless picnic spots, and the occasional old church, forgotten castle or sleepy hamlet which once had its place in the cut and thrust of history, like St Sardos (see p. 15) which now lies on a little side road to nowhere in particular.

Signposting   In addition to being well maintained, the roads are mostly well signposted, although the system is not consistent. Some point slightly or frankly down the road to the destination they name, while others, admittedly easier to read, lie at right angles to the correct road, which is behind the sign, not to the left where it seems to point. It is important to be sure you have understood what is meant when finding your way out of a large town, for a wrong turning can take you into a maze of one-way streets, involving quite a loss of time and much frustration. French drivers behind foreign-registered cars are reasonably considerate, which they are not always with each other.

Minor roads

On minor roads, remember that it is farming country and there may well be a slowly moving tractor, or a lorry loaded with crates of fruit or fertiliser, just round the bend. It often seems to me that the only car you ever meet on these byways comes round a blind corner on the wrong side of the road, so place yourself carefully on bends, in case one of the more haphazard drivers is coming your way.

Police

Although the police are, on the whole, indulgent towards tourists, they are unlikely to overlook speeding offences. If you do happen to be stopped by the French police, courteous apologies will ease the situation and you will probably be sent on your way with just a warning. Bluster and argument are likely to have a less satisfactory outcome. If they take you to a van and start to make a typewritten report, be careful what you say, for they will include anything you say which they feel strengthens their case. It's best to agree with them, saying as little as possible while expressing surprise and regret.

The police have also become stricter about parking offences in the past year or two, but are rather more lenient towards tourists. If you park in the wrong place in a small town, you are more likely to find a warning note than a 100-franc fine. But if you are going to break the parking regulations, do it discreetly – don't block the police station exit.

Garages and petrol stations

If you find your car needs attention, do not hesitate to take it to a local garage. Workmanship is first-class and labour rates are low.

Petrol has no fixed price, the only invariable rule being that it is more expensive on *autoroutes* than anywhere else. If you are driving off the beaten track on Sundays, even in summer, it is wise to make sure you have enough in the tank, for many petrol stations are closed on Sundays, and in country districts finding an open one is a matter of luck.

Car hire

It costs from about 200 francs per day (VAT included), plus about 3 francs per kilometre, to hire a small car from a reputable company, although if you want a Mercedes, it will cost more like 700 francs plus 7 francs per kilometre. Rates for longer periods are proportionately cheaper.

Another alternative to taking your own car is the fly-drive holiday in which you pick up a car at your destination in France. These holidays are offered by a number of tour operators.

Cars (and bicycles) can be hired at most mainline railway stations.

By bus

Except for the two large towns, Bordeaux and Toulouse, where buses bring people in to work from the suburbs and home again in the evening, bus services are very limited in the south-west.

60

Some towns, whose railway services have been discontinued, have short-radius bus services to other towns in their locality, of the two or three per day variety, and villages may have one or two per week to the town for market days. Long-distance services are so infrequent as to make day return journeys impractical and organising a bus tour a real headache. Tourists are therefore best advised to forget about them. If you really want to travel somewhere by bus, and are of a patient disposition, go to the bus depot in the nearest town and try to sort something out. There are no cheap-rate or touring tickets on buses.

By train

French trains have the deserved reputation of being fast, clean and punctual. The south-west is served by two main lines. The first is Paris–Bordeaux–Toulouse–Marseilles–Nice, which serves eleven towns between Bordeaux and Toulouse, including Agen, with a connection at Toulouse for Carcassonne. Arcachon, Dax, Bayonne, Biarritz, St Jean-de-Luz and Hendaye are among other places served by train from Bordeaux, and there are trains from Bayonne to Pau and Lourdes.

The second main line is Paris–Agen via Limoges, which serves northern Aquitaine via Thiviers, Périgueux, Le Buisson (for the upper Dordogne Valley), Monsempron-Libos and Agen.

There are several cheap-rate systems for train travel, for students and young people under twenty-five, and for people over sixty. Available to foreigners as well as French nationals, they offer 50 per cent reduction on some services, and 20 per cent on others. Full details can be obtained at any mainline SNCF station, or from the SNCF Office at 179 Piccadilly, London W1V DAL. These cheap rates are useful mainly for journeys to and from the south-west, for with the cost of the pass included they would represent little saving within the area on short journeys.

By air

Both Bordeaux (Merignac) and Toulouse (Blagnac) are international airports with frequent flights from London, Amsterdam, Brussels, Frankfurt, Geneva, Madrid and Milan. The internal French air service, Air Inter, is a cheap and quick way to travel to and from Aquitaine from other parts of France, but although Bordeaux and Toulouse are linked by Air Inter, train or road travel is really more practical than air within the south-west.

By taxi

Taxi services are available in most places, even villages. The present tariff is a basic hire charge of 8.50 francs plus 2.40 francs per kilometre. In practice this is 4.80 francs a kilometre almost everywhere, because you have to pay the taxi's return journey, there being virtually no hailing of taxis. Rates are increased to 3.45 francs (6.90 francs) per kilometre from 8 p.m. to 7 a.m. and on Sundays. No extra charge is made for additional passengers, and taxi drivers do not expect to be tipped. Waiting time works out at about 1 franc per minute on the meter.

All-day excursions by taxi, for example to Lourdes from the north or to Les Eyzies from the south, are a matter for negotiation.

Where to Stay

Traditional hotels

An old, romantic song has the refrain, 'There's a small hotel, by a wishing well . . .'. It is evocative, calling to mind the kind of hotel familiar to all those who know France. True, it is not often by a wishing well, but it might be beside a lake, a stream or a canal, or it might have a view over wooded valleys and hills, snowcapped mountains, or just the village square where the old men play *boules*. There is probably some creeper on the walls, or window boxes overflowing with geraniums, and a flowery terrace with tables shaded by gaily coloured parasols. The dining room is on the sombre side, with a beamed ceiling, faded wallpaper, old brass and copper and a grandfather clock that stopped long ago. The bedrooms have roomy double beds with thick mattresses, riotously flowered wallpaper found only in French farmhouses and hotel bedrooms, and wooden shutters to the windows.

It is a family affair. Papa looks after the bar, or he may be the chef, while Maman keeps an eye on everything else and looks after the accounts. Ideally there are two pretty daughters, who serve with a smile at mealtimes, and a son-in-law, who runs the restaurant or may be making himself a reputation as a chef.

There are still many hotels like this throughout south-west France. Indeed, ten years ago you would have found very few others, apart from the bigger, city hotels, but now the hotel scene in France has altered. Chains of modern hotels proliferate all over France, among them Sofitel, Novotel, Ibis, Climat, Mercure, Campanile and others. They are functional hotels, whose design has been strongly influenced by accountants dictating the number of rooms (and so their size) which must be put on a particular site in order for it to be profitable at the required rate. Not surprisingly, such hotels have no more character or interest than the office blocks built to similar specifications.

Modern chains

The tight-budget versions of these hotels often approach disaster. There may be an *en suite* bathroom, but one in which only dwarfs would be comfortable. People of average size can get into the bath, sitting up with knees bent, but six-footers take a look and give up, only to find that the shower is at shoulder level. When I see a bathroom like this, I always remember one in a hotel in Corsica where I stayed about twenty years ago. The bath was so high that the mahogany bath stool had two steps on one side to help you climb into the bath safely, and once in, it was so large that even half-full it was dangerous to non-swimmers. It would have given any modern accountant a heart attack just to look at all the wasted space, but I preferred it to the cramped tourist boxes of today.

To be fair, the better hotels of the modern type do have rooms which are quite large enough, the beds are invariably comfortable, and the *en suite* bathroom is satisfactory, though rarely spacious.

Uniformity

The fact that when you have seen one of these hotels, you have seen them all, can be an advantage, for once you have established a relationship with a particular chain, you know exactly what to expect. And because people know what to expect, the modern hotels receive a lot of bookings from holiday motorists who have not planned ahead and, at the end of a long day's drive, do not want the bother of looking for something which may be marvellous or may be a dud, and prefer to settle for what they know.

They are strictly functional hotels, and are often efficiently, if impersonally, run. In the old traditional family hotel, you are somewhere and you are somebody. You may even, after a day or two, be addressed by name. In the modern chain hotel you are in the same limbo, wherever it may be, regarded more as a cheque or credit card number to be computer processed. Many people do not mind this at all, but those tourists travelling by road who really prefer a hotel with some character and charm may find it worthwhile to book ahead, and to make the route and the overnight stops additional pleasures rather than unavoidable boredom.

Choosing a hotel

There are as yet practically no hotels in south-west France which rely on package-tour business. The vast majority never see any at all, and outside the prehistory areas of Dordogne and the major seaside resorts, there are many that never see a coach party. The south-west is still the realm of the independent traveller, where the hoteliers are geared to pleasing them, whether they are business guests or tourists. So you are unlikely to find yourself stumbling about among piles of other people's luggage in French country hotels. The only thing that disturbs their general calm is the occasional wedding reception or business lunch.

Star ratings

When it comes to choosing a hotel in France, modern or traditional, you should not pay too much attention to official classifications, except in the most general way. It is reasonable to expect a four-star hotel to be better, as well as a lot more expensive, than a one-star hotel. On the other hand it does not necessarily follow that a two-star hotel is better than a one-star, or a three-star better than a two-star. Official classification is based on the physical nature of the hotel and its amenities, and has nothing to do with the atmosphere or the efficiency of the way it is managed. Star rating is concerned with things like the number of bedrooms and their size, whether or not there are telephones in the bedrooms, the size of the reception area, what percentage of rooms have private bathrooms, availability of lifts in relation to the number of floors and so on. Even in one-star hotels more than thirty requirements are listed, more in higher grades. Some of the distinctions are of little interest to the average tourist, though they may matter to businessmen. No hotel, for example, can have two stars or more unless it has a telephone in every bedroom.

When you want to stay just one night, it is important to realise that the best rooms in a one-star hotel will be better than some of the rooms in a two-star, and so on up the scale. The official classification does not help you with this, nor does it give points for management, so that a well-run two-star hotel may be quite a bit better than an indifferently run three-star. This is where guides which specialise in hotels and restaurants and which do take such things into account can be useful.

Even in the modern, functional hotel a lot still depends on the manager. Some hotels are impeccably run, while in others you will see messy breakfast trays left outside bedroom doors for hours. Some are clean and some have months of fluff under the beds.

What to look for

Is it possible to know much about a hotel before you commit yourself to it? You can, at least, get an inkling. The style, character and standards of a hotel are always focused in the reception area. In a large hotel, the doorman, lift boys, receptionists, furnishing, decor, tidiness, the state of the carpets and ashtrays, missing light bulbs, a dozen different things combine to produce an effect. If there is any sloppiness or indifference there, you can be sure it will be repeated throughout the hotel.

In smaller hotels, similar things apply on a smaller scale, and the warmth and courtesy of the welcome count for much. All these points seem obvious, yet every day thousands of people walk into hotels, book a room at reception and take the key, without even looking around.

In France, indeed in most places except perhaps eastern bloc countries, you have the right to see the room and are expected to do so – and to refuse if it does not suit you. It is part of the French way of life that everyone is expected to look after his own interests. So if you do not look at the room, it may be assumed that you are indifferent, and you are more likely to be given one next to a lift or a public bathroom, or above the back entrance where the rubbish is collected noisily at five in the morning, or facing an all-night garage across the street. The other side of the corridor may have rooms overlooking a peaceful garden. It's up to you to ask for one.

Double or twin beds

In the typical French family hotel and in older, large hotels in south-west France, a double room still very often means a double bed, so that if you prefer twin beds it is important to specify this at the time

65

of booking. In most modern chains there are rather more twin-bedded rooms, and where there are double beds there is often a convertible sofa for an additional bed. If you are stuck with twin beds and would have preferred a double, you will not be in trouble if you push them together and cross-mattress them, although sometimes, but not often, they are fixed to a wall headboard.

In most of the chain hotels you are expected to cope with your own luggage, but if you are helped a sensible tip is often a good investment.

Prices

Repeat business is important to all hotels, especially those outside large cities. For this reason, in resorts or country towns where there are several hotels, you can expect prices to be competitive for comparable accommodation. Rather than attempting to give actual prices, which vary from room to room within the same hotel, and from year to year or sometimes from season to season, this guide simply gives an indication of what to expect in the hotels named. The words 'average' or 'moderate', qualified with 'above' or 'below' and with an occasional 'cheap' or 'expensive', have been used. In the kind of family hotel which has been described, in the country or a village, average means from 140 to 300 francs (for the best double rooms), above average means from 250 to 500 francs, and below average means from 100 to 200 francs. If the hotel is in a seaside resort, you may have to add 50 to 100 francs for each of these categories. The average price of a double room with bath in a middle-range hotel in a city such as Bordeaux or Toulouse would be about 300 francs. Country house hotels, château hotels, *Relais de Campagne* and so on charge from 600 to 1,000 francs a night. Some may be a little cheaper and a few more expensive.

These are guideline prices for 1989–90. Until two years ago, hotel prices in France were controlled by the government, who authorised a small percentage increase each year. Now this control has been dropped, hotels may charge what they like, with competition the only control. Hotels are supposed to display all their room prices in reception where they can be easily seen. Most of them do, although some have a curious idea of what easily means.

Chain hotels

Hotels in modern chains such as Novotel, Ibis, and those linked to marketing chains such as Mapotel and Inter Hotel, can normally be relied upon to be satisfactory, efficiently run and price-competitive with comparable independent hotels. Novotel charge 300 to 380 francs for a room large enough for three, and there is no extra charge for up to two children in the parents' room. The Climat group charge from 200 to 260 francs, with a supplement of up to 30 francs for a third person. Ibis Hotels are similar in style to Novotel, but rooms, bathrooms, public areas and restaurant menus are more restricted. Their rates are similar to Climat. All these chains will make reservations from one hotel to another within their group, free of charge.

Logis de France

The Logis de France group is a marketing organisation specialising in small country hotels, mainly in villages or small towns. Membership of the organisation has often enabled proprietors to borrow money at low rates of interest to upgrade their hotels, particularly in providing better bathrooms. In return for marketing services, including listing in the annual guide, Logis de France members pay a subscription and are expected to maintain certain standards. These include offering a warm welcome to guests, providing comfort in line with official standards (most of them are one- or two-star establishments), offering menus which feature regional dishes and some specialities from the chef, and giving value for money at prices which include service.

Logis de France and Auberges de France (inns with too few rooms to qualify for star rating) are normally required to be in a tranquil situation, although this is not a certainty. The annual handbook, which can be obtained from the French Government Tourist Office, 178 Piccadilly, London W1V DAL, contains examples of Logis on a main road and on the edge of large towns, but giving the population of their commune, perhaps only a few hundred, while the town of which it is a suburb may have fifty thousand. So check when you reserve, and do not simply assume that it will be in the middle of peaceful nowhere.

The most important thing when travelling is to be able to find a room. The 'Where to stay' suggestions in this guide therefore include, wherever practical, a hotel with a fair number of rooms, on the grounds that it is more likely to have one available. Other criteria which have been taken into account include the existence of a good restaurant in or near the hotel, pleasant grounds, swimming pools, shady terraces and interesting views, all of which can add enjoyment even to a brief stay.

Overbooking

There was a time not so many years ago when it was safe to start looking for that night's hotel early the same evening. This is no longer the case in the June–September period in France. The problem is aggravated in high summer because some French motorists, uncertain of how far they will get in the day, have taken to making reservations for the same night in two or three different hotels spaced out along their route. Hoteliers have realised this and overbook to cover themselves for those who do not turn up – an inexact science which sometimes leads to difficulties all round.

Booking ahead

The best procedure is still to book in advance yourself – even if it is done only at lunch time for the same evening, although a day ahead is better – telling them that you intend to have dinner and, most important, arriving in good time. French hoteliers normally ask when you expect to arrive and, if you are much later than the time you have given, may well have disposed of the room.

On Saturdays and Sundays you stand a good chance of getting a room, even in high season, if you book ahead to one of the modern chain hotels situated, as many of them are, in the *zones industrielles* on the edge of the larger towns. This is because they are primarily businessmen's hotels, used less at weekends. Private hotels which cater for businessmen may close their restaurants on Sunday night, especially outside the high season.

Car parking at hotels

It is unwise to leave your car parked in the street near your hotel if it obviously contains anything of value or importance to you. This is particularly true in the Channel ports of France and in the larger towns, where so many cars are broken into that the police merely shrug and tell you they have other things to do.

If the hotel has private parking it is therefore sensible to use it, even if there is a small charge. If not, take valuables with you and leave the car in the best-lighted spot you can find.

Breakfast

Many hotels overcharge for breakfast, and especially for continental breakfast served in your room, which is likely to be overpriced anyway and will have expensive room service on top. It is also true of the enticing help-yourself buffet breakfast which is *de rigueur* in the modern chain hotels. They have everything from ham and cheese for the German tourists to cornflakes and boiled eggs for the British, with a great deal besides. If you like a hearty breakfast, this is the place to tuck in, but do not expect to pay less than 30 francs a head.

If you want to economise, do not breakfast in the hotel, but stop instead for coffee and croissants at the first likely-looking café.

Apartment hotels

Some of the coastal resorts have apartment hotels, although these are not general in south-west France. They are blocks of holiday flats with one, two or three bedrooms, bathroom and kitchenette, as well as some of the amenities of large hotels, such as swimming pool and tennis court. You can buy your own food and prepare some of your meals, so they may work out cheaper over a period, and you are not tied to meal times as you might be *en pension* in a hotel.

Rented accommodation

One of the most enjoyable ways of spending a holiday in France is to rent a country cottage or a seaside villa.

Gîtes

Country cottages are known as *gîtes ruraux* (strictly speaking *gîte* by itself means a lodging of any kind). A number of British tour operators specialise in providing holidays in these country cottages in France, and there are several advantages in booking through such an operator. The holiday price includes the Channel crossing, and documentation gives advice on routes and driving times, as well as recommending overnight hotels vetted by the tour operator. Most important of all, because this is now a highly competitive business the operators are able to set their own standards and expect *gîte* owners to meet them according to contract. Regular inspections are carried out to see that they do, and unsatisfactory *gîtes* are dropped.

Most of the *gîtes ruraux* are owned by French farmers. It has always been difficult to separate a French peasant farmer from his money. Although they understand that they must pay for seed and fertiliser if they are to have a good crop, they seem incapable of making the same association for tourism, and show themselves reluctant to spend anything on improving existing properties, except in the most basic fashion.

Well aware of this attitude, the French government some years ago took the initiative by offering advantageous loans for making improvements to potential holiday homes in the French countryside. *Gîtes de France* is an association of such properties, and has a British section which publishes an annual handbook listing hundreds which can be booked from Britain. The handbook can be obtained from the French Government Tourist Office in London (see p. 70 for address). Owners who have taken advantage of the loan scheme have to undertake to let their property through *Gîtes de France* for a number of years, so there is always a large number of such *gîtes*. It goes without saying that the earlier you book, the wider the choice.

Last-minute bookings

Some people prefer not to organise holidays too much in advance. There are some countries where this attitude might be ill advised, such as Yugoslavia and Bulgaria, but France is one country where it can work, and if you are the happy-go-lucky sort, you can take the car across the Channel and leave finding accommodation until you reach the other side. The local Tourist Office or *Syndicat d'Initiative* usually have a list of *gîtes* in their area, and may well have a system of classification indicating the level of comfort. But it is very much a question of pot luck and, in the high season you will be getting the leavings, if any. Either side of the season is much safer.

Tour operators

The best *gîtes* in most areas are taken by British tour operators. This is because they can offer the owners a longer letting season than they would get with French holiday-makers. The pioneers in this field, and the one the others are still trying to catch up with, were *Vacances Franco-Britanniques*, of St Margaret's Terrace, Cheltenham, Gloucestershire, who have more than four hundred individually approved *gîtes* throughout France, about forty of them in the south-west.

Villas or flats in seaside resorts in the south-west are offered by tour operators who specialise in this, but may also offer country cottage holidays. Villas can also be rented directly in the major resorts of the south-west by dealing directly with local estate agents. You would be lucky to find one in the July/August high season, but either side of it there will almost certainly be a choice to offer you. In this case, of course, all you pay is the rent of the villa, regardless of the number in your party, instead of buying a holiday each.

Camping

Outside the high season you can drive on to any French caravan or camp site which is open (some close pretty promptly when school holidays end) and pick your own position from the many that will be available. But if you plan a camping holiday in France in July or August, it is best arranged through one of the numerous British companies who offer such holidays, many of them specialising in particular areas. Try to deal with one that has some years of experience. Camp sites in France vary from the most primitive and overcrowded to four-star luxury, and should be chosen carefully, never booked blind. As *Vacances Franco-Britanniques* were the pioneers fifteen years ago of *gîtes* holidays, the pioneer camping company is Canvas Holidays, of Bull Plain, Hertford, Hertfordshire, who have a choice of sites in the south-west.

Lists of all tour operators offering holidays in France, including all forms of self-catering, country cottages, seaside villas, mountain chalets, camping and caravanning can be obtained from the French Government Tourist Office, 178 Piccadilly, London W1V DAL.

Eating and Drinking

The French passion for food is deep, patient, totally serious and eternally watchful.

We cook with bottled gas, and a man comes out from town when necessary to change the cylinders, a job which normally takes him no more than five minutes. The connection is on the wall of an outbuilding at the back of a flower bed.

Last time he came here, he stopped suddenly, apparently transfixed, his arms still round the cylinder. They are heavy, and I thought he had slipped a disc.

'Ah, you have snails,' he said in a reverent tone. 'Do you mind if I look around?' We left him to it.

He returned happily more than half an hour later, saying that the job was done, and he had found sixteen snails. Together with those he had found the day before he now had nearly forty, a veritable feast.

'These are the Petit Gris, the Bordeaux Petit Gris, the finest tenderest snails you can get, far superior to your Burgundy snail.'

'Are you going to have them for lunch?' I asked in polite interest.

'Not this week,' he said. 'Snails take the flavour of whatever they have been eating. It might have been a plant with a bitter leaf. You have to feed them on something good for a week, so that they take on a fine flavour. I keep mine in a dish of vermicelli; some people feed them on barley. It's a matter of personal taste. It took me a few years to find out, but I can tell you nothing beats vermicelli. In a week's time they will be delicious, oh, delicious.'

The patience, the seriousness, the alertness are all summed up in that simple story. On a higher plane, for me, since I do not care for snails, there was the time when four of us stopped (three of us thought by chance) at a small fishing inn on the banks of the Dordogne, not far from the village of La Roque-Gageac. It was not much of a day, a bit out of season, we were the only clients and the landlord was afraid that there was not much choice, but if we left things to him he hoped we would be satisfied.

We sat down in one of those old-fashioned French country dining rooms where the owners have never heard of interior decoration, and would not pay any attention if they had. What was good enough for their parents was good enough for them; and the parents were still there, in elaborately framed 1930s photographs on the wall.

With a bottle of wine to encourage us, we waited and hoped and wondered. The meal began on a quiet note with a huge tureen of vegetable soup so good that we all took two helpings in case it represented the high point of the meal. It did not. The next course brought a touch of confidence and authority which promised well. Nothing is more variable than omelettes, and these were wonderfully light, stuffed with chopped truffles, near perfection.

A pause followed during which we began to feel rather contented, murmured approval to each other, and through the window watched a boy pottering about in a red canoe on one of the loveliest rivers in Europe. Next came grilled trout with a subtly flavoured creamy sauce. By now we realised that a country feast was being orchestrated for us, and that the friend who had said, 'I know a little place', and whose job was promoting holidays to Dordogne, had telephoned in advance.

After a decent interval, a dish of *confit d'oie* was brought in, succulently crisp, and served in the classic way with sliced potatoes, which cook and absorb the fat as the *confit* is reheated. There was no hurry and between courses the landlord brought in more bottles of an unlabelled, deep purple wine, which seemed to go well with everything. I began to be careful as I was driving, but the others were still eating and drinking like Roman soldiers.

Now came the main course, lamb's tongue and capers, a masterpiece that melted in the mouth. What remained was a challenge to be accepted. The landlord insisted that we try his wife's home-made goat's cheese, and then her strawberry *gâteau*, consisting almost entirely of fresh strawberries and whipped cream.

Own produce

I admit this was a special meal but I tell the tale because it does illustrate several interesting points. I have always remembered the landlord telling us afterwards that everything we had eaten, with the exception of the truffles which came from a wood a few miles away and the trout which had been fished from the river outside his door, came from his own land and his own livestock, and the wine from his own vineyard. No doubt because of the time we had taken, the sensible portions, and the cook's lightness of touch, the feast did not lie heavily on the stomach, and we went on our way, three hours after our arrival, happy and at ease with the world.

Not all restaurateurs use their own produce to this extent, but fresh raw materials are a key factor in the cuisine of the south-west. The good restaurateur goes to market regularly, of course, but in the south-west he almost always has relatives or friends from whom he obtains freshly caught fish, or duck, chickens and eggs from the farm, or game from the woods. The other characteristic of the best cuisine of the south-west is that the chefs treat all these rich raw materials with remarkable lightness.

Inexpensive

It is also surprising how cheap eating out in the south-west can be, for there is certainly no need to spend a lot of money to eat very well indeed. A good three-course meal with wine included can be bought for 65 francs per head in dozens of places, and even some of the best restaurants have menus at 90 francs on weekdays. It is usual, though not universal, practice for restaurants to drop their cheapest menu on Sundays.

In general, restaurants can be categorised as resort hotel restaurants, other hotel restaurants, restaurants which also have rooms, and restaurants pure – but not necessarily simple. There are differences between them.

Resort hotels

Resort hotels often confine their restaurants to residents, in which case they have captive consumers, who eat rather more cheaply and often less well than those in restaurants who must attract repeat business daily. When a resort hotel restaurant is open to the public, the chef may, in some cases, have become used to aiming less high than he would have to in a more competitive restaurant.

Restaurant hotels

Some hotels, usually not in resorts, are better known for their restaurants than they are for their hotel side. Then it is the quality of the restaurant which attracts clients to the hotel, rather than the hotel clients alone filling the restaurant. These hotels include some of the best places to eat.

There are restaurants, often good or very good, which also offer rooms. Although the rooms may be comfortable, the establishment frequently lacks some of the amenities of a straightforward hotel, perhaps no proper reception area, too few bathrooms or no public lounges, and so does not claim to be one.

Restaurants

Restaurants which are restaurants and nothing else can be divided into two classes. The majority aim to offer sound cuisine to regular customers, passing tourists and businessmen, but have no pretensions towards *haute cuisine*, although they may offer very good regional cuisine. The minority, where ambitious chefs seek or have already made a reputation, are picked out with rosettes, stars, chefs' hats or other symbols in popular restaurant guides. Among these practitioners of *haute cuisine* are those who are satisfied with their ranking and others who are constantly trying, for various reasons, to add another star. It is in these restaurants that you eat best of all. In cooking, as in mountain climbing, when you reach the top there is nowhere to go but down. In these restaurants you can choose a menu and eat marvellously well at a very reasonable price for what you get, or you can let yourself go and spend a lot for a meal including rarities, chefs' specialities, and superb wines. It is still likely to be less expensive than a meal of similar pretensions and rather less performance in some of the world's capital cities.

Relais Routiers

To come down to earth, there is a separate category of restaurants which should by no means be left unconsidered – the *Relais Routiers*.

73

They are meant for and mostly used by lorry drivers (*routiers*), who like all other Frenchmen in the south-west stop for lunch at 12 noon sharp. They do have menus but the great attraction is the *plat du jour*, and any lorry driver knows what will be on offer each day of the week on his regular routes. He arrives a few minutes either side of noon to make sure he gets it, for if you are late there is likely to be none left. Other things, yes, and they will not be expensive, but the one the chef has really worked on will be finished.

'Gastronomic' menus

Many restaurants in south-west France, and in all other regions, offer what they call a 'gastronomic' menu. The vast majority of such menus are nothing of the kind and it is unwise to take one in a restaurant not already known to you. The essence of true gastronomy is quality allied to simplicity with a touch of originality, ideally a meal of light courses built around one superb main dish, accompanied by a good wine. Some would say a superb wine with a couple of good courses built round it.

'Gastronomic' as opposed to 'touristic' menus have nothing to do with this concept. They concern quantity rather than quality and simply have five or six courses instead of three. No miracle happens in the kitchen because the chef is preparing a *magret à la crème de poireaux* for a 'gastronomic' menu. He does it as he always does it. The only astonishing thing in the usual 'gastronomic' menu is the size of the bill. You do get a lot more, and you pay accordingly, which is fair enough if you are rich and hungry. But in truth the term 'gastronomic' is a matter of the restaurant and the chef. In a good restaurant the simplest menu will be 'gastronomic' because of the way a good, conscientious chef works. This, combined with the existence of large numbers of discriminating clients – all spiritual cousins of my gas man and, like him, always on the *qui vive* for something good – is the reason why it is still possible to eat well in so many places in France.

Arrive early

The remarks about arriving early at *Relais Routiers* apply a little less strictly to all restaurants in south-west France. The earlier you arrive, the better the table and the wider the choice of food. By half past one, you just might still be lucky, but in some places where the chef is an outside worker he may already be on his motor-bike.

Choosing a restaurant

When you arrive in an unfamiliar town without the name of or a recommendation to any particular restaurant, choosing where to eat can be a problem. The only ultimate way to judge a restaurant is by what you get on your plate and what you pay for it, but, as with hotels, there are pointers to what you may find. A *Relais Routiers* which has only a couple of lorries outside it at a quarter past twelve is best avoided. By contrast, any restaurant with a good number of cars parked near it is likely to be good value, especially if many of them have the registration figures of the department you are in, which indicates that the locals think well of it.

When you can see two or three restaurants from where you are standing there is not as a rule much difference in price as they are clearly in competition with each other. One is bound to be influenced by the obvious, such as spotless tablecloths and shining glasses, but sometimes the restaurant itself is out of sight behind a bar or reception *Menus* area. I always look closely at the menu, which by law has to be displayed outside, not so much to see what it lists, though this is sometimes an indication of whether they are trying or not, but to see how it is written and presented. I am put off by menus where the ink is so faded that it has evidently not been changed for months. It may mean no more than that they keep to what they know and do it quite well, but it can also suggest a certain indifference and lack of enterprise.

Limited menus in themselves should not be off-putting, especially when clearly presented. As a rule they merely indicate prudent budgeting, and are much to be preferred to those which seem to list every known variety of meat, fish and fowl. No chef does everything well, and a long menu simply means large refrigerators, rather than plenty of fresh raw materials. Such menus are usually not a good sign in the south-west, and if you have no choice of restaurant but one with a long menu, it is better to take the *plat du jour*, or something popular and not too expensive.

Do's and If you want to get good value for money in a French restaurant, **Don'ts** there are some don'ts and a do which help considerably. Don't forget that coffee is always an extra and can easily add 20 francs to a bill for two people. Don't forget, if you are eating *à la carte*, that you are not obliged to take more than one course, and that you will save a lot by missing out a starter or dessert, or both. Desserts are often overpriced. If you are going to drink wine with a meal, do remember that it is better to take the reasonably priced house wine than to pay three times or more (I have seen six times) the retail price for an ordinary wine. Restaurants which have good local trade would never get it without a reliable house wine.

Variations It is always worth asking for a variation in France, unlike some countries where it is virtually impossible to get any dish except as it is described in the menu. I remember being told by a waiter in a Hilton Hotel in the United States that there was 'not a chance, bud' of getting a jacket potato with butter instead of sour cream and chives.

If you would rather not have your sole with the sauce proposed, ask for it plain grilled, or if the menu says *foie de veau lyonnaise* (calves' liver with onions) and you would rather not have onions, ask for it *nature*. This is the normal term for something without sauce or dressing. All good restaurants will be happy to make minor adjustments to suit the client. Incidentally, those people who like liver, kidneys, sweetbreads, brains and so on, will find them first-class in the south-west.

One between Flexibility extends to other arrangements. French couples often *two* share one menu between them, and there is no reason why you should

75

not do the same. Just order it and ask for two covers. Or, if one person wants to eat *à la carte* and another a three-course menu, there is no reason why the person who takes the menu should not give a starter or a dessert to the other, so that you both have two courses.

If you order roast or grilled meat of any kind, you will be asked how you like it done. The accepted grades are: *bleu* – lightly cooked on the outside, almost raw inside; *saignant* – rare or bloody; *à point* – medium; *bien cuit* – well done. All meat in France will be undercooked, unless you specify otherwise. Pork, lamb (and mutton, more generally available than in Britain or the United States), and all poultry are excellent. Beef is less good than the rest, but veal is usually good in restaurants.

Useful terms

Here is a short vocabulary of some of the more unusual terms you may see on regional menus.

Offal

Andouillettes – sausages made with finely chopped pigs' chitterlings and stomach. Served hot. *Andouille*, a larger version, is served cold.

Cervelles – brains (usually *cervelles d'agneau* – lambs' brains).

Ris d'agneau – lambs' sweetbreads. *Ris* means sweetbreads, and should not be confused with *riz* – rice.

Rognons – kidneys (*à la Bordelaise* – with red wine sauce).

Foie gras – the liver of force-fed geese or ducks, cooked and served without sauce. *Foie gras rosé* is very lightly cooked.

Gésiers – gizzards, cut into pieces, cooked and often served warm with salad, or as a snack with aperitifs.

Poultry and game

Civet – stew, usually of *lapin* (rabbit) or *lièvre* (hare) or *marcassin* (young wild boar). Always prepared with red wine and some blood in the sauce, as with jugged hare. Rabbit stew with white wine is called *gibelotte*.

Confit – joints of goose, duck, chicken or pork, cooked in their own fat and then bottled and preserved in it; reheated before serving and should be crisp on the outside but not dry.

Caille – quail.

Cassoulet – a speciality of Toulouse, a stew of goose, kidney beans, mutton, sausages, tomatoes among other things.

Ham

Jambon – ham. *Jambon blanc* or *jambon de Paris* is similar to York ham. The famous *jambon de Bayonne* is ham salted for six weeks and then rinsed and air dried for up to six months. The pigs should come from Béarn, the Basque country or the Armagnac region, and the salt from Saliés de Béarn. If the ham is genuine, the label bears the words *Marque deposée, jambon de Bayonne, etiquette syndicale*. Only about one-eighth of all the ham sold as *jambon de Bayonne* actually bears this label.

Jambon de pays or *jambon de campagne* is salt-cured ham similar to *jambon de Bayonne* but with less finesse about it. It varies from good to something reminiscent of dried penguin.

Mushrooms

Champignons – mushrooms. Those commonly found on menus are *cèpes de Bordeaux* (the best of several kinds of edible boletus, for those who know about fungi), which add a lot to the price of a dish and considerably less to the flavour.

Truffles   *Truffes* – truffles. Any dish including truffles will be expensive; if it costs less than 200 francs you may see some black specks but you are not likely to get more than a hint of flavour.

Fish   There is a large selection in the fishmongers but only a few are found on restaurant menus:

Ecrevisses – crayfish. This small freshwater relative of the lobster, found in rivers throughout Aquitaine, is tasty but needs a lot of patience.

Huitres – oysters. Always in season and fresh in the south-west.

Quenelles de brochet – pike (*brochet*) in small round fish cakes.

Sandre – zander, or pike-perch, one of the better freshwater fish.

Alose – shad. Another river fish common in the Gironde and the Adour, it has a good flavour but is as bony as herring. Sometimes offered in fillets.

Lamproies – lampreys. Cooked in their own blood and Bordeaux wine, they are highly thought of by some. Short season in early summer.

Lotte – monkfish. Gets around a lot on the cheaper menus.

Truite – trout. There are a good many trout rivers in Dordogne and Pyrénées-Atlantiques. Some riverside restaurants have a *vivier* where they keep live trout and fish them out as required. *Truite au bleu* is not, like meat, nearly raw. It should be prepared from freshly caught trout, killed, cleaned and rolled in vinegar, which turns them blue. They are then cooked in a *court-bouillon* made with water, white wine and herbs.

Rouget – red mullet. Good when not too small.

Bar – sea bass. Usually very good.

Cabillaud – fresh cod. Plenty in the shops but not often seen in restaurants.

Dorade – sea bream. The *royale* and *rosé* (red sea bream) are appreciably better than the grey.

Cheese   Apart from a few local goats' cheeses, Aquitaine is not a cheese producing area until you reach the Pyrenees, where there are excellent cheeses made from cow's milk (black rind) and ewe's milk (orange rind). They are found in shops and restaurants throughout the south-west together with the dozens of different mass-produced French cheeses. If you do not like your cream cheeses, like Camembert and Brie, too runny, ask for them *pas trop fait.*

Desserts   *Tourtière* – a tart of wafer-thin Armagnac-flavoured pastry filled with prunes or apples (when it is sometimes called *croustade*).

Coulis – a purée of fresh fruit (or tomato), often raspberries or strawberries, usually served with its own fruit or ice cream to enhance the flavour.

Noix – walnut. There are many varieties of walnut cakes and tarts in Périgord. Not so usual further south.

Wines of the south-west

Apart from the wines of a particular region such as Médoc, Graves, St Emilion and châteaux wines, you will see labels with *Bordeaux Appellation Contrôlée* (or AOC, for short) and also *Bordeaux Supérieur* (AOC). *Bordeaux Supérieur* is not necessarily superior, the only obligatory difference being that it must have 10.5 degrees of alcohol, against the 10 degrees of ordinary Bordeaux. If strength was all that counted in red wines, then most St Emilions, which have up to 11.5 degrees of alcohol, would be more expensive than the finest vintages of the great châteaux of Médoc, which have only 10 degrees of alcohol. So some Bordeaux AOC may be superior to some *Bordeaux Supérieur* AOC.

Sweet white wines, such as Sauternes, Barsac and Monbazillac, with a norm of 13 degrees of alcohol, are appreciably stronger than red wines. Other wines common in the south-west include:

Bergerac – Among the everyday wines of France, Bergerac reds are good, the best of them being Pécharmant, which has its own AOC. Dry white Bergeracs from the Sauvignon grape can be pleasant.

Buzet – Well made and strongly marketed reds from Lot-et-Garonne.

Cahors – Strong, dark, long-lasting wine. Can be good but too much can easily produce a 'head' or a hangover. In the old days the peasants used to test it, not by tasting but by spilling a few drops on a clean part of their shirt – not always easy to find. If the stain was not dark enough, they assumed the wine was watered and went to another producer.

Madiran – A full-bodied red wine from the Armagnac area. It is required by law to spend three years in cask, and improves with some bottle age as well.

Tursan – Local wine of the southern part of Landes department. The dry white goes well with oysters; the red is acceptable.

Jurançon – A strange, unusual wine which looks like an Amontillado sherry in the glass, light golden brown in colour, sometimes described as *pelure d'oignons* (onion skin). It is sometimes slightly sweet, and has a very spicy, flowery flavour. It is produced in the foothills of the Pyrenees, near Pau, from three varieties of grape unknown and unused anywhere else. It was the favourite wine of Henri IV, who was born in Pau. Slightly chilled it makes a good aperitif on a warm day.

Armagnac

If you ask a Gascon, he will tell you with total confidence that Armagnac is the best brandy in the world, and he is often right. A few of the best Cognacs are better than some Armagnacs, and the best Armagnacs are better than almost all Cognacs.

Although brandy has been made in Gascony from time immemorial, it is only from early this century that it has been named Armagnac. Until 1905 it was sold to distributors in Cognac, who sold it as Cognac.

Differences between Cognac and Armagnac

However, it is not quite the same thing; there are several differences. Cognac comes from grapes grown on chalky soil, Armagnac from those grown on sandy soil. Cognac is double-distilled in a pot still, and leaves the still as a clear spirit 70 per cent alcohol. Armagnac is distilled once only in a sort of double boiler, something between a pot still and a continuous still, and the resulting spirit is about 53 per cent alcohol. This lower strength leaves more flavour and scent in Armagnac than in Cognac. Cognac is aged in white Limousin oak, Armagnac in the black oak of the Gers. The brandy ages more quickly in the black oak than the white. Cognac normally has some added sugar, while Armagnac, which does not, is drier. Because they have aged faster, relatively young Armagnacs are smoother than Cognacs of the same age.

Ordinary Armagnac has just its name and that of the suppliers on its label, and if it costs less than 70 francs a bottle it is probably best used for bottling fruit. From 70 to 100 francs it is probably quite good. At a higher price than that it should have some encouraging words on the label, such as *hors d'âge*. The best Armagnacs often have two labels, a small one on the back saying *Recolte 1955* or some other year. This is when the brandy was made and put in the cask. The larger label will have another more recent date on it somewhere, which is the year when the brandy was bottled.

Ageing

Nothing happens to brandy once it is in the bottle. Unlike wine it does not improve, all its ageing and improving having been done in the cask; it is the length of time that it spends there which is all-important. Eight years is good, twenty years is superb, and if you do not mind paying, most good restaurants in Gascony can find you minor miracles that have spent thirty years or more in the cask.

There is no need to treat brandies, even as old as this, gently. They should be given plenty of air in a large glass, warmed in the hand for some time, and swilled around in the glass before being tasted. One famous chef who was philosophising with me over a forty-year-old Armagnac said: 'Don't be afraid to knock it about a bit. Shake it around. It will be better.'

Unlike Cognac, which is mostly made by large companies, Armagnac is made by few companies and many individual producers in three different areas – Haute Armagnac, Tenarèze and Bas Armagnac. The best Armagnac comes from Bas Armagnac. The worst is mixed with unfermented grape juice and sold as an aperitif called Floc de Gascogne.

Entertainment

Cinema Though still a highly respected and popular art form in France, cinema is slowly dying. However, most towns still have at least one cinema, usually offering a choice of three or four films in different viewing rooms. Most are in French, although some may be in English with French sub-titles. Admission is about 30 to 40 francs.

Theatre Most towns also have a theatre. They are surprisingly active, in the sense of live performances, though one-man shows by popular French singers and comedians are as frequent as plays, which are mostly well-known comedies or farce. There are companies of semi-professional players in some villages, such as the Baladins of Monclar in Lot-et-Garonne, who keep to plays and reach a good standard.

Music There are a good number of music festivals in Aquitaine during the spring and summer, mostly classical but some jazz, and many of them taking place in attractive settings. They are well advertised but it is also worth checking at the local Tourist Office.

Discos There is no shortage of discos and dancing clubs. Most towns have at least two or three, and there are many more in resort areas. They tend to have their own sort of clientele, some being for the very young, some for the young, others preferred by older people, and some for homosexuals, so it is useful to get a local opinion. Some of the clubs for older people are of the *Bal Musette* kind, with accordion music. The average entrance fee to all discos is about 60 francs, which includes a drink.

The discos have bouncers, called *videurs*, to deal with any trouble (those who don't look that tough are all judo experts).

Corridas and Courses Landaises In the southern part of Aquitaine, as you get nearer to Spain, most towns have a bull ring (*arènes*) and there are bullfights at regular intervals in summer.

The bull rings are also used for *Courses Landaises*, which operates on the same principle as bullfighting – to taunt the animal until it attacks and then evade it with skilful and graceful movements. In the *Course Landaise* the animals are specially bred, bad-tempered cows, and evading their attacks includes jumping over them with the feet together, or even doing handsprings on their backs. *Courses Landaises* are less artistic, but more entertaining and exciting to the non-connoisseur of bullfighting. The animals are not killed in the French arenas.

Rugby Rugby is the passion, almost the religion, of the south-west, and anyone who likes the game and is in the region during the long season should see some of the good teams. Agen were champions of France in 1984, 1986 and 1988. The matches are usually fast and ferocious.

Horse racing   There are several courses in the south-west, with flat racing and trotting, which is popular in France.

Firework displays   The French like fireworks and put on some splendid displays during the summer, notably on 14 July and 15 August, when even villages put on their own displays.

Summary of annual events

Music   **Bordeaux** – two-week festival in May.

Château de Bonaguil – concerts in July and August (Lot-et-Garonne).

Duras – Music festival in early August (Lot-et-Garonne).

Côte Basque – Bayonne, Biarritz, St Jean-de-Luz and other towns stage a week-long music festival at the end August, beginning September.

Town fairs and spectacles   **St Jean-de-Luz** – Fête de St Jean on 24 and 25 June, featuring a concert, dance, torchlight procession and bull of fire. Also the celebration of the tunny catch in the first week of July.

Ciboure – Tunny Fair on variable date at the beginning of July.

St Sever – *Son-et-lumière* spectacle in costume from Middle Ages onwards around 13 and 14 July (Landes).

Mont de Marsan – St Madeleine's Fair; one week of festivity mid-July.

Bayonne – Traditional fair in the first week of August, with *Course Landaise*, bullfights, concerts, dances and fireworks.

Arcachon – Fête de la Mer on 15 August, with blessing of boats, fireworks.

Biarritz – Major firework display on 15 August.

Bidart – Basque festivities around 15 August.

Dax – Traditional fair in mid-August, with bullfights, bicycle races and fireworks.

Biarritz – Fête de la Mer on the third Sunday in August.

St Emilion – Proclamation and celebration of grape harvest.

Folklore   **St Sever** (Landes) – 5 and 6 August.

Casseneuil (Lot-et-Garonne) – First week of August.

Sporting events   **Brantôme** (Dordogne) – National showjumping competitions on 15 August.

Nogaro (Gers) – Motor racing during the second weekend in September.

History   **Castillon la Bataille** (Gironde) – Reconstruction of the last battle of the Hundred Years War (13 July 1453). Variable date towards the end of July or beginning of August.

Labastide-Armagnac – Reconstruction of historical incident in period costume, with candlelight dinner in the town square, on the last Saturday in August or first in September.

Shopping

Shopping in Aquitaine is interesting and a challenge. Prices of the same things can vary chaotically on the same day in the same town in different shops. Whether it is a bicycle or a bunch of bananas, it can be as much as 20 per cent cheaper just around the corner. Even in the same market, stalls a few yards apart may charge quite different prices for the same vegetables or fruit. There does not seem to be any explanation beyond the normal French desire to do what you feel like.

Food

For the average holiday-maker in France, many of whom in the south-west will be staying in villas or other self-catering accommodation, the most important thing is shopping for food.

Hyper-markets   The easy answer, especially for those tourists whose French is limited, is to shop in the hypermarkets. All towns have at least one of a chain such as Mammouth, Intermarché, Match, Champion or Leclerc, and some have them all. For the tourist there are several advantages in using them. First, there is easy and ample parking space. Trolleys are provided, for which you must put a ten-franc piece in a slot which frees the first trolley from the others. When you have finished shopping and loaded your car, replace the empty trolley by plugging it into the one in front, press the side of the slot and your ten-franc piece pops up. Keep one handy in the car.

The next advantage is that the price of everything is marked, either on the tin or packet itself, or on the shelf near it. Meat is graded by law and must be marked with its grade – first or second choice beef, for example – and must be marked with the price per kilo for that grade, and the weight and price of that particular cut.

A third advantage is that in addition to most kinds of food (not all hypermarkets have a fish counter), you can buy most other household goods, such as washing-up liquid, shampoos, cosmetics, some medicines not needing a prescription, sweets, clothes, bathing suits, sports equipment and so on. You name it, they have it. You can therefore do all your essential shopping in one place.

Super-markets   One step down from the hypermarkets are the supermarkets. They, too, usually belong to a chain, of which two of the best are Casino and

Codec. They are smaller and do not usually have their own parking area. They sell only food and household basics – in a more restricted range than the hypermarkets, and at slightly higher prices – but are useful when the hypermarket is a long way off, or for the odd item you may have forgotten.

Then you will still find some ordinary French grocers, called *alimentations*, which sell the same range of goods as the supermarkets. *Epiceries* are also grocers' shops, but they sell a slightly more 'up market' range of foods.

Butchers

There are plenty of butchers. Their meat is not pre-packed and priced, as in the hypermarkets, but they must display the official controlled price of the various meats. The maximum price of certain foods, notably meat, bread and milk, is government controlled, and it is not a bad idea for tourists to be seen studying this list.

Bakers

There are also many bakers. Factory-baked bread does exist and is sold in hypermarkets, but it is not popular. Almost all bread is baked by individual bakers, every village having at least one, and even small towns having possibly ten or a dozen. No two bakers' bread is ever the same, so every Frenchman has his favourite baker. They all like it fresh.

A baker of average size will probably have five ovens, which he uses in rotation, baking every hour from five in the morning until ten or eleven. The first and second bakings are for early-morning shop customers; most of the third baking is, in the country, delivered to farms and houses outside the village. At the entrance to many farm drives you will see a cylindrical tin, often rusty, placed horizontally on a post. This is where the baker delivers the long loaves, leaving them sheltered from rain or hungry birds until the farmer has time to collect them. The fourth and fifth bakings are sold in the shop for the rest of the day.

Getting your bread warm and fresh from the baker is one of the minor pleasures of being in France. The typical long French loaf is called a *baguette*, a *flute* when it is thinner, and a *pain* when it is bigger. The crusty *pain de campagne* is slightly more expensive, makes very good toast or fried bread, and lasts several days without going stale, unlike the *baguette* which quickly goes hard. Wholemeal bread is made by them all, and is called *pain complet*.

Poultry

Poultry is of a high standard, and is best bought in the hypermarket. In addition to normal brands they also sell *poulet fermière*, which is supposedly raised on the farm, at a much higher price. It is not worth it. Buy the farmer's wife's eggs, if you are staying in the country, and her fresh vegetables, but not her chickens or pigeons, unless you like them tough as well as tasty.

Fish

Fish is very good and absolutely fresh in Aquitaine. The best fishmonger is usually in or near the town's covered market.

Wine

There are not many wine merchants (retailers) in the south-west;

wine is sold in hypermarkets, supermarkets and *alimentations*. Hypermarkets may have up to a hundred different wines, mostly everyday AOC wines, the majority of which connoisseurs would consider too young for drinking. Anything more than three years old is unusual, except for château-bottled vintage wine which is expensive. Ordinary table wines are usually priced well below half the cost of the same wine in Britain. Whisky and gin are also cheaper, but champagne only slightly less. For those who are genuinely interested in wine, it is always possible to arrange a visit to a co-operative or a château and to buy the wine on the spot. It will not be cheaper, but it is a more interesting way of buying.

Markets   Apart from doing basic food shopping in hypermarkets, tourists should also visit the weekly or bi-weekly market in their local town. They vary slightly in emphasis – fruit and vegetables in Lot-et-Garonne, mushrooms, truffles and poultry in Périgord and so on – but they are all fascinating. You will see vegetables rarely seen at home, as well as a great variety of herbs.

Souvenirs and other purchases

Most people take wine back home with them. Even if you take so much that you have to pay duty on some of it, it will still be a bargain. Prunes, peaches, greengages or other fruit bottled in eau-de-vie or Armagnac are delicious and very characteristic of the south-west.

For the kitchen, French-made cast iron cooking pots enamelled in attractive colours, or copper pans for jam-making, are cheaper in France than when they have been imported somewhere else. Ironmongers and market stalls have a wide selection of useful kitchen tools and gadgets, some not easily found outside France.

Especially in Dordogne and Lot-et-Garonne, there is a good choice of baskets in all shapes and sizes and for all purposes, beautifully made by hand.

In Dordogne, Lot and Pyrénées-Atlantiques, whole sheepskins, or sheepskin coats can be bought, including some charming models for small children. Espadrilles tend to come from the Far East these days, but they were first made in the Basque country, and you can still buy the genuine hand-made article in places like St Jean-Pied-de-Port.

Every town in the south-west has two or three hunting and fishing shops, and it is worth looking at the wide range of equipment, including clothing, on sale both in these shops and the hypermarkets. There are vast numbers of anglers in France so prices have to be competitive.

Antiques are usually expensive in France, but all through the summer there are *foires de brocante* in various towns throughout Aquitaine. *Brocante* is a useful term describing second-hand furniture and household objects not good enough to be described as antiques but somewhat better than junk. They sometimes include items not often seen in Britain or the States, such as kneading troughs (*pétrins*) and small preserve cupboards (*confituriers*).

Most large towns have a flea market (*marché aux puces*). There is a famous one in Toulouse, but almost everything in all of them really is junk.

General Basics

Consulates

- **British Consulate**, 353 Blvd President Wilson, 3073 Bordeaux, tel. (56) 42 34 13. Has a British Library and newspapers.
- **American Consulate**, 26 Cours Maréchal Foch, 33081 Bordeaux. Tel. (56) 52 65 95.

Conversions

- 1 kilo is equal to 2.2lb. A half kilo is 500 grams, and is often called *une livre*, which means a lb and is equal to just over one Imperial lb.
- 1 km is equal to 1.6 miles; 10 km is approximately 6 miles and 50 km about 30 miles.
- If you subtract 2 from a Centigrade temperature, then multiply by 2 and add 30, the answer gives the approximate Fahrenheit temperature.
- Most dress and shoe shops know the British and American equivalents of European sizes.

Documents

Citizens of the UK and Eire must have a valid passport, and it should always be in your possession in France. The police will ask to see it, even if there is no special reason other than that they are making a routine traffic check. They may be satisfied with your driving licence, but do not bank on it. They may also ask to see the car insurance documents.

Visitors from non-EEC countries must have visas to enter France; apply for one in advance from a French consulate in your own country.

Electrical current

The electrical current in France is 220 volts, so transformers are not
required for European appliances. However, plugs have to be changed
to the round-prong French type, and sometimes a two-pin instead of a
three-pin. The correct plugs can be bought singly in any electrical
shop or hypermarket, or you can use an adaptor plug.

Health

No vaccinations are needed.

French medical services are first-class. Even in the country villages
there are excellent general practitioners, combining up-to-date knowledge with a family doctor approach. They are quite prepared to visit
outside surgery hours, but charge slightly more for private visits, and
more on Sundays. Normal surgery consultation is 85 francs, while a
visit costs 120 francs, or 225 francs on Sunday.

If you need medicine on Sundays and the nearest chemist's shop is
closed, it should have a notice in the window giving the address of one
which is open. One in each locality has by law to be open on Sunday
morning.

Hospitals in major French towns are very well equipped and nurs-
ing standards are high.

Sun　　Much of the south-west is as far south as the Italian Riviera, so the
sun can be fierce in high summer. Sunbathing should be started
gently, and sun tan creams should be used for the first week at least.

Stomach
upsets　　Stomach upsets are almost always due to eating and drinking too
much – especially of fatty and unfamiliar foods combined with more
alcohol than usual – and very rarely indeed from an infection from bad
food. The best rule is to try anything you fancy, but in moderation if it
is strange to you.

Water　　In the countryside the water supply often comes from a well, so it
may be better to buy bottled water, except for making tea or coffee and
cooking. In hot weather iced drinks should be taken slowly, and not
when you are overheated. This is particularly important for small
children.

Stings　　All nature seems to thrive in Aquitaine and this includes insects.
Wasps and bees are not interested in people and do not sting unless
agitated by waving hands and arms, so if you stay calm they quickly go
away. Most stings occur when people walk barefoot on grass where
there is low-growing clover, which the bees love. Pain is quickly
reduced by an anti-sting spray.

Mosquitoes are not a problem in most areas. They can be kept away with a small electrical device called a *diffuseur anti-moustique*, which plugs into any convenient socket. Mousticologne, available as a spray or cream, also works well.

British visitors

If you do have to go to a doctor, dentist or hospital, show your E111 form (which you should have obtained from your local office of the Department of Health and Social Security in Britain), and you will be entitled to medical treatment in France on the same basis as French citizens. The doctor will fill it in and then give you a sickness form (*feuille de soins*). At the *pharmacie* they will attach small labels to the forms, showing which medicines have been supplied.

Take the *feuille de soins* and the original prescriptions to the local sickness office (*Caisse Primaire d'Assurance Maladie*) – address in the telephone book. They are always crowded but there is usually one person who deals with tourists, and if you ask for that person you may not have to wait long. You will be entitled eventually to a refund of about three-quarters of what you have spent.

Insurance

You could go to France twenty times and never need insurance, but peace of mind is important on holiday. If you travel with a tour operator, an insurance policy covering most contingencies is likely to have been included in the price of the holiday. If you travel independently, take one of the standard travel policies offered by insurance brokers.

Money and banks

Bank opening hours vary slightly from place to place, but are generally from about 8.30 a.m. to 12.30 p.m. and from 2 p.m. to 5 p.m. All bank employees are entitled to two days uninterrupted leave per week, so some banks are closed on Saturday and Sunday, while other branches close on Sunday and Monday. There are thus always some banks open on Saturdays and Mondays, although the first one you go to may be closed. Eurocheques, travellers' cheques and Visa cards present no problem. Be ready to show your passport.

Banks invariably issue money in notes of 20, 50, 100, 200 or 500 francs. A 100-franc coin was issued this year, but few have been seen as yet. The normal coins are 50 centimes, 1 franc, 2 francs and 5 francs (all silvery), 10 francs (coppery), and 5, 10 and 20 centimes (brassy). Five centimes is often ignored, either way, in giving change, and on the ground.

Motoring

Documents

You should always have a current driving licence and your passport with you, plus a valid insurance certificate. If the car is not your own, you will be asked for a letter of authorisation from the owner.

Speeding

In the past couple of years, the French police have become much stricter about speeding offences. The minimum fine is 1,300 francs. If you are stopped for speeding, you will almost certainly be breathalysed and if you are over the limit, you may be fined up to 5,000 francs, payable in cash on the spot. Be careful, particularly within towns and villages. Most speeding offences occur in apparently deserted villages consisting of a few houses lining either side of a main road.

The normal speed limit in built-up areas is 60 km/h but it may be less. On other roads it is 90 km/h, on dual carriageways 110 km/h unless otherwise marked (the French police expect you to be able to read) and on motorways it is 130 km/h. At this speed you will be overtaken by almost every other car, and you are unlikely to be in trouble if you keep under 145 km/h. All speed limits are reduced by 10 km/h if the roads are wet, but I have not yet met a Frenchman who knows this. A newish regulation is that you must not travel at less than 80 km/h in the outside lane of a motorway in normal daylight conditions.

Age limit

The minimum driving age in France is eighteen.

Seat belts

Seat belts must be worn in the front seats. Children under ten must travel in the back seats.

Lights

Beams must be adjusted for right-hand drive, but yellow tinted headlights are not compulsory.

Opening hours

Museums

There are no fixed opening times for museums, but the majority are closed on Tuesdays and public holidays. Many of those not closed on Tuesdays are closed on Mondays. Sunday opening varies. Most museums close for the two-hour lunch break usual in the south-west, but a few remain open all day in the summer season. Entrance fees for national museums vary from 10 to 25 francs, with lower prices for children, students, and senior citizens, and half price on Sundays.

Cathedrals

Cathedrals and churches are normally closed during the two-hour lunch break. There are no guided visits during services, and services must be respected. There may be a charge to visit certain chapels or the sacristy.

Châteaux

Some châteaux are privately owned, others belong to municipalities or departmental administrations. Opening times for those publicly owned tend to be similar to those for museums, that is, they are often closed on Mondays or Tuesdays, and for lunch. In ruined castles such as Bonaguil they will not come looking for you at lunch time so make sure you are not locked in. Some people I know shouted themselves hoarse for half an hour, before being rescued by villagers with ladders.

Private châteaux, with owners more intent on making money, often do not close during the week, except at lunch time. Some are open all day in the summer season.

Many châteaux both private and public are closed for long periods in winter.

Caves and grottoes

No fixed rules but they are normally open every day from spring to autumn, and closed in winter.

Palm Sunday to All Saints Day are the most common limits of the open season for châteaux, grottoes, and other sights.

Post offices

Larger post offices are open from 8 a.m. to 6 p.m. and do not close for lunch. Smaller branches either close for lunch or stay open and close about 4.30 p.m. In the larger ones work is divided, so make sure you are in the right queue. Most post offices have booths from which you can telephone – you ask for a line at the counter and will be allocated a booth. The call is registered electronically at the counter, where you pay after the call. There are also public call boxes in the street. They are normally aluminium coloured, and are not always vandalised, but there are rarely directories. Some accept coins, and some phone cards, so you will need to be prepared. Phone cards can be obtained from post offices in denominations of 32, 40 and 96 francs. There are complete sets of the directories for the whole of France in all post offices, and the Yellow Pages can be helpful in finding any particular service you want.

Prices in centimes

In hypermarkets and some other shops, the price of each article is marked either on the item itself, or on the shelf, in new francs and centimes. But if you ask an ordinary person in the south-west what anything costs, you may be shocked to be given a figure in thousands. This will be centimes, for virtually everybody in the south-west still counts in centimes. Prices are often printed in newspapers in centimes and lottery prizes are won in centimes.

You simply divide the figure quoted by 100. So 12,000 centimes= 120 new francs.

Public holidays

These are public holidays that are celebrated nationally.
- **1 January**, New Year's Day
- **March/April** (moveable), Easter Monday
- **1 May**, Labour Day
- **8 May**, Victory in Europe Day
- **May** (moveable), Ascension Day
- **May** (moveable), Whit Monday
- **14 July**, Bastille Day
- **15 August**, Assumption Day
- **1 November**, All Saints Day
- **11 November**, Remembrance Day
- **25 December**, Christmas Day

Talking to the French

French manners are a good deal more formal at all levels than British or American. If you want to ask a question of a stranger in France, it is important to begin with *S'il vous plaît, monsieur*, or *madame*, as the case may be.

Merci – means 'thank you', except when you are offered a drink, an extra helping of food or something similar. When used alone, it then means 'No, thank you'. If you mean yes, please, just say, *s'il vous plaît* first and *merci* afterwards. *Merci beaucoup* is common in English phrase books but rarely used in the south-west.

Numbers

One	*un*	Twelve	*douze*
Two	*deux*	Twenty	*vingt*
Three	*trois*	Thirty	*trente*
Four	*quatre*	Forty	*quarante*
Five	*cinq*	Fifty	*cinquante*
Six	*six*	Sixty	*soixante*
Seven	*sept*	Seventy	*soixante-dix*
Eight	*huit*	Eighty	*quatre-vingts*
Nine	*neuf*	Ninety	*quatre-vingt-dix*
Ten	*dix*	Hundred	*cent*
Eleven	*onze*	Thousand	*mille*

Useful phrases

Where is . . . ?	*Où se trouve . . . ?*
When . . . ?	*Quand . . . ?*
How much . . . ?	*Combien . . . ?*
Do you speak English?	*Parlez-vous anglais?*
Is there anyone here who speaks English?	*Est-ce qu'il y a quelqu'un ici qui parle anglais?*
Please write it down	*Notez-le, s'il vous plaît*
I'm lost	*Je me suis perdu*
Can you direct me to . . . ?	*Pouvez-vous m'indiquer la direction de . . . ?*
I'm looking for . . .	*Je cherche . . .*
I'd like . . .	*Je voudrais . . .*
It's enough	*C'est assez*
Do you have anything cheaper?	*Avez-vous quelque chose de moins cher?*
Do you have anything bigger?	*Avez-vous quelque chose de plus grand?*
That's too expensive	*C'est trop cher*
The light does not work	*La lumière ne fonctionne pas*
The toilet does not work	*Les toilettes ne fonctionnent pas*
Can you recommend a good restaurant near here?	*Pouvez-vous me recommander un bon restaurant dans les environs?*
Can I have the bill, please?	*Donnez-moi l'addition, s'il vous plaît* (a signing motion in the air is universally understood)
Where is the main shopping area?	*Où se trouve le centre commercial?*
I want to buy . . .	*Je voudrais acheter . . .*
What time do the shops close?	*À quelle heure ferment les magasins?*

Some useful words

Chemists
Aspirin *de l'aspirine*
Disinfectant *un désinfectant*
Insect repellent *de la crème contre les insectes*
Pill *comprimé*
Sanitary towels *des serviettes hygiéniques*
Sleeping pills *des somniferes*
Stomach pills *des comprimés digestifs*

Garage
Brakes *les freins*
Clutch *l'embrayage*
Engine *moteur*
Exhaust pipe *tuyau d'échappement*

Starter *démarreur*
Steering *la direction*
Tyre pressures *pression des pneus*
There is something wrong with the ignition (or brakes, steering etc.)
   Il y a quelque chose qui ne va pas avec l'allumage

Health
Doctor *médecin*
Headache *mal à la tête*
Ill *malade*
Medicine *médicament*
Pain *douleur, mal*
I need a doctor *J'ai besoin d'un médecin*
It's urgent *C'est urgent*
I have a fever *J'ai de la fièvre*
I have a pain here *J'ai mal ici*

Household
Battery *une pile*
Electrical plug *une fiche*
Light bulb *une ampoule*
Matches *des allumettes*
Washing up liquid *liquide vaisselle*

Shops
Baker *la boulangerie*
Bookshop *librairie* (newspapers are bought here or at a kiosk)
Butcher *la boucherie*
Chemist *la pharmacie*
Delicatessen *la charcuterie*
Fishmonger's *la poissonerie*
General food store *alimentation*
Hairdresser *le coiffeur*
Hypermarket *hypermarché*
Supermarket *supermarché*

Glossary of special terms in the south-west
bastide medieval fortified hilltop village
causse barren upland
chai building where new wines and spirits are stored before bottling
chartreuse single storey country house built around a courtyard
château anything from a large farmhouse (in the wine regions) to a
   large country mansion
château fort castle
côteaux hillsides
dépendances farm outbuildings

fermette small farmhouse or farmworker's cottage
gave mountain stream or river in Pyrenees
grange barn
landes lowlying moorland
pech hilltop
pigeonnier pigeon house, dovecote
prune plum
pruneau prune
séchoir (à tabac) tobacco drying shed

Telephoning home

Telephone numbers outside France are obtained by dialling 19, waiting for a new dialling tone, and then dialling the code of the country concerned, followed by the number in that country.

Here are some country codes and the costs of phoning them:

● **United Kingdom and Northern Ireland**: 44. The average cost per minute is 4.50 francs. Calls to the UK are cheaper between 9.30 p.m. and 8 a.m. on weekdays, between 2 p.m. and 8 a.m. on Saturdays and all day on Sundays.

● **United States**: 1. Alaska (1907) and Hawaii (1808) have their own codes. The average cost per minute to the United States and Canada is 9.37 francs. Calls are cheaper between 8 p.m. and 2 a.m. on weekdays, including Saturdays, and between 10 p.m. and 2 a.m. on Sundays.

● **Australia**: 61. The average cost per minute to Australia is 19.10 francs.

● **New Zealand**: 64. The average cost per minute is 21.90 francs. There are no cheap rates for Australia and New Zealand.

Time difference

It is one hour later in France than in Britain, except for a couple of weeks in autumn and spring as the change-over from and to summer time takes place when the time is the same. France changes earlier than Britain. The time in France is six hours later than eastern Canada and the United States in winter, five hours in summer.

Tipping

Service is included in almost all restaurants at 15 per cent. If it is not, the bill should include the words *Service non compris*. If you ask, you may be told that it is up to you. This means that you can give something extra if you wish, and French people do sometimes leave the small change. If it is a *Service non compris* establishment, leave 15 per cent. Waiters in cafés and bars work hard, and most people leave them something, even for just one beer or a coffee.

Useful addresses and telephone numbers

Most towns have their own *Office de Tourisme* or *Syndicat d'Initiative* (same thing under a different name), and the larger ones usually have someone who understands English. They are a very useful source of information on the history, sights, entertainments and sporting facilities of their region, as well as offering lists of hotels in the area.

In villages the *Mairie* can answer most questions, although some are open only three days a week.

Main tourist offices

● **Dordogne**: Syndicat d'Initiative, 1 Avenue Aquitaine, Périgueux. Tel. (53) 53 10 63.

● **Lot**: Office de Tourisme, Place A-Briand, Cahors. Tel. (65) 35 24 97.

● **Lot-et-Garonne**: Office de Tourisme, 107 Blvd Carnot, Agen. Tel. (53) 47 36 09.

● **Gironde**: Office de Tourisme et Accueil, 12 Cours 30 juillet, Bordeaux. Tel. (56) 44 22 92.

● **Landes**: Office de Tourisme, 22 Rue Victor Hugo, Mont de Marsan. Tel. (58) 75 38 67.

● **Pyrénées-Atlantiques**: Office de Tourisme, Place Royale, Pau. Tel. (59) 32 02 33.

French Government Tourist Office, 178 Piccadilly, London W1B DAL. Useful for all general inquiries for holidays of all kinds in south-west France.

French Government Tourist Office, 610 Fifth Avenue, Suite 222, New York, NY 10020-2452. Again, for general inquiries.

SNCF French Railways, 179 Piccadilly, London W1V OBA. They will answer queries and take bookings for Motorail as well.

Written inquiries

Letters (in English or French) inquiring about holidays and amenities in particular departments of the south-west should be sent to the following departmental committees. They deal with letters and professional inquiries, but not callers.

● **Dordogne**: Office départemental de tourisme de la Dordogne, Loisirs-Accueil Dordogne, 16 Rue Wilson, 24000 Périgueux.

● **Lot-et-Garonne**: Comite départemental de tourisme du Lot-et-Garonne, 4 Rue André Chenier, BP 158, 47500 Agen.

● **Gironde**: Comite départemental de tourisme de la Gironde, Loisirs-Accueil Gironde, 21 Cours de l'Intendance, 33000 Bordeaux.

● **Landes**: Comite départemental de tourisme des Landes, Conseil General – BP 407, 40012 Mont de Marsan.

● **Pyrénées-Atlantiques**: Comite départemental de developpement touristique, Parlement de Navarre, Rue Henri IV, 64000 Pau.

Chain hotels ● Novotel and Ibis. Tel. (60) 77 27 27.

● Climat. Tel. (05) 11 22 11.

Wine Maison du Vin de Bordeaux, 1 Cours 30 juillet, Bordeaux. Tel. (56) 52 82 82. Closed Saturday afternoon and Sunday.

Some other wine producing areas have their own Maison de Vin or equivalent. Ask at the Tourist Office.

Wildlife

There is plenty of wildlife in Aquitaine, including many deer, which do sometimes, as the warning signs suggest, leap across the road in front of your car. There are said to be about a dozen Pyrenean bears left in the mountains, but you would be unlikely to find one, even if you searched for weeks, although one or two are kept in captivity in the mountain villages.

The only poisonous snake I have heard of is the adder, which is localised here and there, and I have never seen a report of anyone being bitten by a snake in the south-west. There are grass snakes, but they are both timid and harmless. There is no rabies in this part of France.

There is really no danger to life and limb from animals in Aquitaine. On the other hand naturalists and ornithologists will find a great deal to interest them whether it is eagles, red squirrels, barn owls, tree martens or great green grasshoppers. Some of the local Tourist Offices publish leaflets on their local fauna and flora.

Gazetteer

Introduction

The area of France featured in this gazetteer is extensive, being as large as some small countries. Covering the whole of the administrative region of Aquitaine, and a small part of the adjacent region of Midi-Pyrénées, it is about 320 km from north to south and about 200 from east to west.

The scenery is varied and often beautiful, with mountains, lakes, ocean beaches, forests, wild gorges, nearly barren plateaux and fertile river valleys. It is a region which unfolds the story of mankind from his origin in the mists of time to the bloody struggles of more recent history. It is also a region of special interests, ancient churches and castles, the world's finest vineyards, grottoes, painted caves and other underground marvels.

While it is clearly not possible to include everything that might be considered of interest in such a diverse region, I have tried to include the key points of beauty and interest. However, the gazetteer is to some extent selective, and the traveller is left the opportunity of making some discoveries of his own.

Geographically, the gazetteer covers the five departments of Aquitaine: Dordogne, Lot-et-Garonne, Gironde, Landes and Pyrénées-Atlantiques. It also includes parts of the adjacent departments of Lot and Gers, which are in the Midi-Pyrénées administrative region, as well as Toulouse, the capital city of Midi-Pyrénées.

Each of the sections, which are arranged in a roughly north to south order, concerns mainly one department, although there are overlaps. The resorts of the Côte D'Argent, some in Gironde and some in Landes, have been included together in one section. The Bordeaux area, with its vineyards, has a section to itself, and Gers, including Armagnac, is joined with its nearest big city, Toulouse.

There are considerable scenic differences within the overall area. The department of Pyrénées-Atlantiques is hilly and mountainous, with a broken coastline of sandy coves as well as big beaches, while Landes and Gironde are predominantly flat and forested, sharing a straight, sandy coastline. Dordogne, Lot-et-Garonne, Lot and Gers offer a mixture of farmland, wooded hills and winding river valleys.

Bordeaux and Toulouse are the only two cities in the whole area, and with populations of just over 600,000 each they are, in modern terms, on the small side.

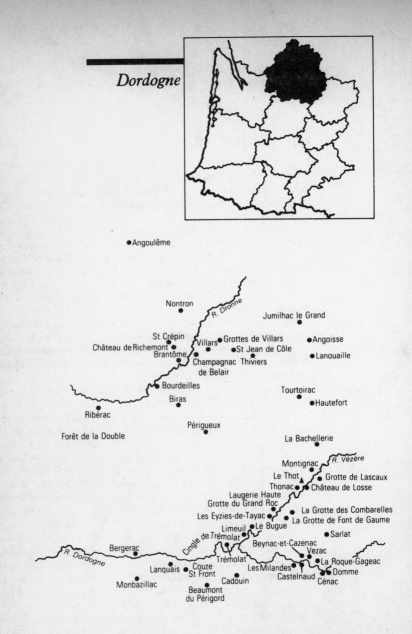

Dordogne

●Angoulême

Nontron

R. Dronne

Jumilhac le Grand ●

St Crépin ● Villars ● ●Grottes de Villars
Château de Richemont ● ●St Jean de Côle
Brantôme● ●Champagnac Thiviers
de Belair

●Angoisse

●Lanouaille

Bourdeilles●

Biras ●

Ribérac ●

Tourtoirac ●

●Hautefort

Périgueux ●

Forêt de la Double

La Bachellerie ●

Montignac ● *R. Vézère*
Le Thot ● ● Grotte de Lascaux
Thonac● ▲ ●Château de Losse
Laugerie Haute ●
Grotte du Grand Roc ●
Les Eyzies-de-Tayac● ● ● La Grotte des Combarelles
● La Grotte de Font de Gaume
Limeuil ● ●Le Bugue
de Trémolat
Bergerac ● *Cingle* Beynac-et-Cazenac ● ●Sarlat
Vezac●
R. Dordogne Trémolat● La Roque-Gageac
Lanquais ● ●Couze Les Milandes● ● ●Domme
St Front Castelnaud● ●Cénac
Monbazillac ● Cadouin ●
Beaumont
du Périgord

Dordogne

Introduction

Some places have a kind of magic about them, a quality that remains mysterious among those that are obvious and creates an attraction which is not wholly definable. This is the case at Delphi and is one of the reasons why the oracles established themselves there. It is also the case with the old province of Périgord, now the department of Dordogne. Perhaps it was this special quality which induced man to choose it for his first home, for although there were other parts of Europe as secure, as full of game for the hunters and with as kindly and livable a climate, men settled here, in the area now called Black Périgord.

In these sheltered valleys mankind developed an intelligence, began to consider how to make life easier for himself, and felt the first stirrings of the notions of comfort, home and society. In short, this is where man began to develop from a savage, hunting animal to a thinking being – *Homo sapiens.*

Whatever the reason, it is a fact that the area still exerts a powerful attraction for many people.

As far as the countryside is concerned the two terms – Périgord, the name of the old province, and Dordogne, the modern department – are synonymous. Except for official purposes, French people, and especially those in the south-west, still tend to refer to the region as Périgord, and think of the Dordogne simply as a river.

Four Périgord regions

It used to be said that there were two Périgords, the White, named from the frequent chalky outcrops on the hillsides, and the Black, named from the dark woods common on the valley slopes. But some years ago, sufficiently long that it is now fully accepted, the communities in the north of the department decided that it would be a good idea for tourist purposes to promote their region as the Green Périgord. So there were three Périgords, and for the past two or three years there have been four, since a tourist official, probably enjoying a good glass of Bergerac, suggested that with so many vineyards in one area, that part should become the Purple Périgord.

There are no precise limits to these four parts of Périgord (nobody ever talks of Black or White Dordogne) but, roughly, Green Périgord occupies the north of the department, White Périgord the centre,

Black Périgord the south-west, and Purple Périgord the south-east. The chief towns of each region are Nontron in the north, Périgueux in the centre, Sarlat in the south-east and Bergerac in the south-west.

Getting there

From the eastern Channel ports the most natural route into this most northerly of the departments of Aquitaine is by the N20 to Limoges, and then the N21 to Périgueux, or for those heading directly for the sites of prehistory, the D704 from Limoges to Sarlat. From the mid-Channel ports the direct route is by the N10 to Angoulême and then the D939 to Périgueux.

Périgueux

The *préfecture* of the department of Dordogne is a modest country town with a population of 37,000, rising to 60,000 with its suburbs. It would be something of an exaggeration to say that it is a worthwhile tourist destination in itself but, because of its central situation, it is a suitable base for excursions.

Roman remains

An old town, founded by the Romans who called it Vesunna, it has a long history of varied fortunes with, until recent times, more downs than ups. Some vestiges of its past can still be seen. The most impressive of the few Roman ruins is the 24 m-high **Tower of Vesunna**. This is all that remains of an important temple built in the second century AD, the golden age of the Roman Empire when, under the wise rule of the Antonine emperors, Antoninus Pious and Marcus Aurelius, all was order and tranquillity. A pleasant garden setting has been made for this tower, and pieces of Roman statuary found during excavations have been arranged around it.

Nearby, archaeologists have uncovered the site of an imposing **Roman villa**, which belonged to a descendant of Pompey, the great rival of Julius Caesar. The remains indicate three huge reception rooms and sixty smaller rooms around what was a colonnaded courtyard, with kitchens, storerooms, central heating, galleries and fountains, which make it easy to imagine the luxurious standard of living that wealthy Romans enjoyed.

Part of the old **Roman wall** of Vesunna can be seen, with a fortified house, the **Château de la Barrière**, built in the Middle Ages on the ruins of the wall.

All that remains of the former **Roman amphitheatre** are the domed gateways and enough of the stones used in its construction to suggest its shape and size as one of the largest in Gaul, with space for more than 20,000 spectators. The oval arena has been made into a public garden with fountains, so that today children paddle where in Roman times gladiators bled to death.

History

As the Roman Empire began to decay, its outlying towns suffered repeated attacks from both land and sea; even the Vikings sailed up the Dordogne and the Isle to sack Vesunna. Slowly the once-noble Roman town was reduced to no more than a ruined village and was virtually abandoned.

It was the coming of Christianity which revived Périgueux. In the sixth century, the miracle-working **St Front** founded a church among the Roman ruins, and when he died a second church to house his tomb was built on an adjacent hill. A town called La Cité developed around his first church, while another town, called Puy St Front, grew up around his tomb, and for hundreds of years there was bitter hostility between the two towns, until they were amalgamated under the name of Périgueux in 1240.

During the **Hundred Years War**, though, the town split into two again, La Cité remaining loyal to the dukes of Aquitaine, who were also kings of England, while Puy St Front supported the King of France.

After the Hundred Years War, Périgueux's recovery was interrupted by a severe epidemic of **leprosy** which began in 1454, but by the end of the fifteenth century the population, which had been reduced by war and disease to 2,000, had climbed again to 10,000. Then in the sixteenth century Périgueux suffered again during the Wars of Religion, being repeatedly attacked by the Protestants. When they captured the town in 1575 many buildings, including the Cathedral of St Front and the Church of St Etienne, were damaged, and the Château de la Barrière was burned.

As it slowly began to recover from these troubles, and with the advent of Renaissance architecture, Périgueux began to take on a new look. Rebuilding their houses, the inhabitants followed an earlier custom, using the stones from the Roman ruins as a quarry, so that stones with Roman markings are to be seen in the walls of Renaissance houses.

The medieval town had been fortified with twenty-eight round towers, one of which, the **Tour Mataguerre**, still stands next to the Place Francheville. It was restored in 1477 by a work force of lepers. The original had been built from Roman stones, as was a bridge over the river.

What to see

Those visitors who enjoy a stroll through the past will find a good deal to interest them in what remains of the old **medieval town**. It forms a rectangle neatly bounded by the River Isle, the other sides being the Boulevard Montaigne, parallel with the river, and the Cours Fénelon and the Cours de Tourny. A clear plan, showing the chief points of interest and a convenient route, can be picked up at the *Syndicat d'Initiative* (see p. 95 for address). Inside this small area, only about 300 m square, there are narrow streets, ancient houses and the vast Cathedral of St Front.

You can see some remarkable medieval houses, including the

twelfth-century building called the **Maison des Dames de la Foi** (because at one time it was a convent) in the Rue des Farges. (*Farges* is an old word for *forgerons* [blacksmiths], and it is interesting that even in pre-Roman times the tribe who founded Périgueux, the Petrocori, were known for their skill as iron-workers.) There are many fine **Renaissance houses**, especially in the **Rue Limogeanne** and facing the River Isle.

Although there has been a church on the site of the **Cathedral of St Front** since the sixth century AD, the present building dates originally from 1173. It was added to, extensively rebuilt and – to put it vulgarly but accurately – generally mucked about in the latter half of the nineteenth century by a pair of architects called Abadie and Boeswillwald.

The result is a large, mosque-like building with seventeen turrets added to the existing five domes, and a 60 m belfry topped by a lantern tower and a conical spire. Abadie, who was also responsible for the Sacré-Coeur in Paris, was no respecter of the past. He got rid of some fine Romanesque sculpture, packing it off to the museum and replacing it with contemporary efforts of dubious merit, and the Gothic chapter house was demolished in favour of a neo-Gothic arrangement. Today the most impressive thing about St Front is its size, and for most visitors, apart from serious students of church architecture, it will probably be enough to see the view of it from the bridge over the Isle. It is said to resemble and to be built on a similar plan to St Mark's in Venice, but where the latter has charm, St Front is just eccentric.

The **Périgord Museum** has an important collection of prehistoric tools and weapons, as well as two skeletons of prehistoric men.

Périgueux today Périgueux has grown considerably since the end of the Second World War. Its chief industries today include the long-established repair yards for railway rolling stock, a clothing industry, cheese production and the printing house for all French stamps, which are acknowledged by philatelists as among the best-designed and best-printed of any.

Where to stay Considering its central position and importance as a *préfecture*, the town has rather limited hotel accommodation.

Hôtel Domino, 21 Place Francheville, 24000 Périgueux, tel. (53) 08 25 80, is comfortable and attractive. It is not in the current Michelin guide, but independent travellers who know France will long ago have discovered that there are numerous good hotels and restaurants which for one reason or another are not in Michelin.

Hôtel Bristol, 37 Rue A-Gadaud, 24000 Périgueux, tel. (53) 08 75 90, is on the small side but modern and comfortable. It does not have a restaurant.

Both these hotels are moderately priced. Slightly cheaper is the largest hotel, the **Ibis**, Blvd G Saumande, 24000 Périgueux, tel. (53) 53 64 58. It has eighty-nine rooms and is one of a large chain of modern and functional hotels with simple but adequate restaurants.

Les Chandelles, Antonne-et-Trigonant, 24420 Savignac-les-Églises, tel. (53) 06 05 10, is situated at Antonne, 10 km outside Périgord on the N21 towards Limoges. It is a charming small hotel in a fifteenth-century house, with only seven bedrooms but a very good restaurant. Prices are reasonable.

Where to eat

The rich and varied cuisine of Périgord is justly famous throughout France. The legendary truffle is still used in many dishes, but as its cost has soared the quantities in which it is used have diminished in proportion, to the extent that the subtle flavour often has to be imagined. The days when you could have an omelette with slices of truffle came to an end about twenty years ago – nowadays you get specks, visible but elusive.

Other stars of this cuisine are *foie gras*, and *confit* – pieces of goose, duck, pork or turkey cooked crisp in their own fat, preserved in it in earthenware pots and served reheated. Périgord is also famous for its strawberries and walnuts, which together with many other delicious locally grown fruits are used in numerous desserts.

Among restaurants where the genuine Périgourdine specialities can be sampled are **La Flambée**, Rue Montaigne, 24000 Périgueux, tel. (53) 53 26 06; **Léon**, 18 Cours de Tourny, tel. (53) 53 41 93; and **L'Oison**, 31 Rue St Front, tel. (53) 09 94 02, a small restaurant which has a Michelin star. It is advisable to reserve a table for either lunch or dinner.

The restaurant of the **Hôtel Domino** (see p. 102) is reasonably priced and has a good reputation.

Red wines of the Bergerac or Cahors vineyards go best with most traditional dishes. Many people like the sweet white wine of Monbazillac with *foie gras*.

Brantôme

From Périgueux, a drive of 30 scenic km north along the D939 brings you to the charming little island town of Brantôme, enclosed between two arms of the River Dronne. Brantôme is not a place redolent with history but, with its five bridges, its old abbey under the cliff, its huge belfry reflected in the river, the old Virginia creeper-covered houses, the weeping willows and a public garden by the riverside, it is a pleasant place to stroll around.

What to see

Despite the fact that the same architect, Abadie, who elbowed his way through the restoration of the Cathedral of St Front, also put his heavy hands on the abbey church, the group of buildings in the **abbey complex** is not unattractive, dignified by the **800-year-old belfry**, which he left untouched, and graced by two **Renaissance pavilions**.

Pierre de Bourdeille

Brantôme's chief renown comes from its association with Pierre de Bourdeille, who can be described as an early gossip writer and whose pseudonym was Brantôme. He was a younger son of François de Bourdeille, high steward of Périgord, and was, within a few years, a contemporary of Shakespeare. He longed for a life of fame, riches and adventure but his older brother, André, inherited the family castle and married a rich and beautiful woman, while Pierre sought his fortune in campaigns in Italy, Morocco and Malta, and as a courtier to the three sickly sons of Catherine de Médici, who were in brief succession disastrous kings of France. He went with Mary Stuart to Scotland, hunted with Henry VIII of England and was a lively companion of the great wherever he went. He knew everybody, famous and infamous – and exactly how well they knew each other.

Though he had never taken holy orders, the king made him honorary abbot of Brantôme, and it was his diplomatic skill which saved it from destruction by the Protestants during the religious wars. In 1589, when he was forty-nine, he fell from a horse and was crippled, was bedridden for four years and had to rest for the remainder of his long life, dying at seventy-six. After the accident, he retired to Brantôme to write his *Lives of Great Men* (*Vies des Grands Capitains*) and his *Lives of Amorous Ladies* (*Dames Galantes*). He was an excellent though cynical raconteur, and as a historian was more interested in human foibles than the strict facts.

Though he did not, in his lifetime, achieve the fame that he would have liked, he did well enough to build himself the **Château of Richemont**, 7 km from Brantôme by the D939 and near the village of St Crépin. He passed the last years of his life here and is buried in the chapel. The castle is open to the public during the high season of July and August, except on Fridays. It is not a building of great interest and only the most committed châteauholics will get much out of it.

Where to stay

Brantôme is not a place which underestimates its own attractions. It has two good and expensive hotels, each of which has a good and expensive restaurant with a Michelin star.

Expensive

Le Moulin de L'Abbaye, Route de Bourdeilles, 24310 Brantôme, tel. (53) 05 80 22, is nicely situated on the banks of the Dronne, with twelve rooms, varying from expensive to very expensive.

Grand Hôtel Chabrol, 58 Rue Gambetta, 24310 Brantôme, tel. (53) 05 70 15, has twenty rooms and is only fairly expensive. If you think that trout is an insipid fish, as some people say, try the Charbonnel brothers' version of trout stewed in red wine (*Civet de Truite au Pécharmant*). It is a small masterpiece, although as Pécharmant is the best of the reds from the Bergerac region, it may give some wine-lovers a twinge to see it used in cooking.

At Champagnac de Belair, only 6 km from Brantôme via the D78 and D83, you can move even further upmarket to the **Moulin du Roc**, 24530 Champagnac de Belair, tel. (53) 54 80 36, which has pleasant grounds, expensive and comfortable rooms, and a two star Michelin restaurant. Try Madame Gardillou's *Poulet Sauté au Vin Blanc de Bergerac.*

Moderate

If, on the other hand, you are waiting for tomorrow and the banks to open before making up the kitty, the **Auberge du Soir**, 24310 Brantôme, tel. (53) 05 82 93, has a simple restaurant and a few rooms at very reasonable prices.

Le Brantôme, Biras, 24310 Brantôme, tel. (53) 46 33 51, 8 km from Brantôme via the D939 (ask for directions when you book), has sixty rooms and is perhaps best described as an average tourist hotel with average prices.

Environs of Périgueux

Bourdeilles

From Brantôme the D78 follows the winding course of the Dronne south-west towards the village of Bourdeilles. At Valeuil, turn right on to the D106 without crossing the river and continue to follow the same bank. This route gives you a fine view of Bourdeilles as you approach it. The château, on a bluff above the river, and the old mill immediately below it beside the Dronne make a picturesque ensemble. The château is really in two parts – the medieval fortress where Brantôme (Pierre de Bourdeille) was born in 1540, and the unfinished Renaissance palace which was built by his sister-in-law, Jacquette de Montbron.

What to see

The **fortress** dates from the thirteenth century and although much damaged during the Hundred Years War it has been well restored. The complex is dominated by a 34 m-high keep with a spiral staircase, by which those sound in wind and limb can reach a terrace at the top with views over the valley.

According to Brantôme, the attractive **Renaissance palace** was designed by Jacquette de Montbron herself. It contains some fine rooms including a magnificent **Golden Salon**, completed in the seventeenth century by an artist called Ambroise Le Noble, but said to have been prepared originally to receive Catherine de Médici, a friend of the family. She never came.

The palace was restored and beautifully furnished by Monsieur and Madame Santiard-Bulteau, who lived there in the 1960s and sponsored the restoration in conjunction with the *préfecture* and the Office of Historical Monuments. The work was barely completed when they both died and were buried in a small fifteenth-century oratory near the entrance.

The château is open to the public – morning and afternoon every day during the high season, and for the rest of the year every day except on Tuesdays. Unlike Richemont it is very well worth a visit, both for its lovely setting and the splendid furnishings.

Hôtel Les Griffons, Bourdeilles, 24310 Brantôme, tel. (53) 03 75 61. Situated beside the thirteenth-century bridge and at the riverside, this is a restored sixteenth-century house converted to a really comfortable hotel, providing an agreeable place for lunch or a stopover. Prices of rooms and restaurant are a little above average but fair.

Ribérac   From Bourdeilles (there is no 's' on the family name; it was added to that of the village by a civil servant who could not spell), it is a pleasant drive through the Valley of the Dronne to Ribérac. Both sides of the river are attractive, and by following the D78 as far as Lisle and then crossing to the right bank you can see something of both. The D1 climbs away from the river, and just before Grand Brassac turn left on to the D103 and continue past Montagrier on the D104e to Ribérac. There are fine views over the Dronne Valley from this road.

From Ribérac, a not very exciting country town which, however, does have a colourful **market** on Friday mornings, take the D709 south as far as the crossroads at La Garde, and there turn left on to the D43 which takes you by a pretty route back to the Valley of the Isle at St Astier. This is a route through typical countryside of the White Périgord.

Forest of the Double   On your right and ahead of you as you come down the D709 from Ribérac lies the wild, lonely and mysterious Forest of the Double. With its many lakes and streams it can be very attractive on fine summer days, but for much of the year, except for the massing of the chestnut blossom in spring, it is rather dank and sinister, a place where it is easy to believe – as the people do – in evil spirits and witches.

Like the Green Périgord north of Brantôme, the White Périgord is an ideal region for those who are looking for a quiet country holiday with opportunities for walking, fishing, photography, bird watching and other country pursuits.

Villars   Excursions to the east and north of Périgord are on the whole more interesting than those to the west. The D78 and the D83 from Brantôme lead via Champagnac de Belair to Villars, where you will find one of the finest early Renaissance castles in Dordogne, the **Château de Puyguilhem**. It was built in the early part of the sixteenth century by a successful politician of the day, Mondot de la Marthonie, and, contemporary with several of the châteaux of the Loire Valley, it resembles them. When it was bought by the state in 1939 it had long been abandoned and was almost a ruin, but the excellent restoration which took place, partly during the war but mainly in the 1950s, is a credit to the Office of Historical Monuments. The rooms were furnished with antiques of the correct period given by national museums, and the château still has its original monumental fireplaces, the best of which has carvings showing the Labours of Hercules. The castle, which now belongs to the department of Dordogne, is open daily during the high season, morning and afternoon. For the rest of the year it is closed on Tuesdays, and is closed altogether in midwinter.

What to see

Near Puyguilhem, at the hamlet of Le Cluzeau, are the **Grottes de Villars**, caves with stalactite formations and a number of prehistoric paintings. They are open to the public from 15 June to 15 September, in the mornings until 11.30 and in the afternoons until 6.30.

St Jean de Côle

From the caves return to Villars and take the D98 to the village of St Jean de Côle. Although there is nothing of dramatic interest, the whole village, with its curious church, its two-tier Renaissance cloister, its Renaissance castle and its Périgord houses with a varied reddish-brown roofscape, creates an altogether charming effect. Some medieval houses from the twelfth to the fourteenth centuries have been well restored. It is a good place for a photo stop.

Thiviers

From St Jean de Côle it is only a few kilometres of pretty road on the D707 to the small town of Thiviers, situated just off the N21 on a promontory which marks the limits between the Green and the White Périgords. North of Thiviers, there are granite plateaux, really an outlying part of the Massif Central cut by deep river valleys. To the south lie the broader valleys of the White Périgord.

Thiviers, although without important attractions, has the charm of a genuine small country town still cloaked in the past and almost untouched by tourism or mass-production industry. It is a famous centre for **truffles** and **walnuts**, and its **Saturday markets**, where the peasants use a dialect that makes French seem a foreign language, are lively and full of interest.

Where to stay

Hôtel de France et de Russie, 51 Rue du Général-Lamy, 24800 Thiviers, tel. (53) 55 17 80, is a modest hotel with eleven rooms and no restaurant.

Château de Mavaleix, Mavaleix, 24800 Thiviers, tel. (53) 52 82 01, in the village of this name on the N21, 12 km north of Thiviers. It is a comfortable château-hotel in a castle dating from the sixteenth century, with twenty-two bedrooms and a good restaurant. Fairly expensive.

Jumilhac le Grand

There are two interesting castles within comfortable reach of Thiviers. Follow the N21 north for 4 km and then take the right fork, the D78, to Jumilhac le Grand. The splendid, many-towered castle dominates the town from a rocky height above the ravine through which the River Isle flows. It was once the property of the Knights Templar, but was given by Henri IV to an iron-founder, Antoine Chapelle, whose cannons he had found useful. The new owner improved the castle and it was further added to by his descendants, each in his own way.

Legend

This fairy-tale castle has its own legend. In the interior a spiral staircase leads to a room, built within the thickness of the walls, on the door of which is a portrait of Louise de Hautefort, the châtelaine of the castle, a flirtatious lady whose infidelities led to her being locked up in this room by her jealous husband. It is known as the 'spinner's room', as she is said to have passed her days spinning woollen thread and making tapestries to decorate the walls. It is also said that the man who brought her the wool was her lover, who had disguised himself in order to obtain work as shepherd to the castle. No one knows how long she was kept there or how the situation was resolved: one account says that the lover was caught by the husband and killed on the spot. Another version records that Louise and her husband were reconciled and that the disappointed lover became a monk.

The great hall of the château has a huge chimney-piece decorated with sculptures representing the four seasons, and one of the towers has a massive stone staircase with Louis XV balusters. The castle is floodlit at weekends from July to September, and is open daily morning and afternoon during the high season, in the afternoons only in spring and autumn, and is closed in winter.

Hautefort

From Jumilhac take the D80 to Angoisse, and just after the village turn south on the D704 to Lanouaille, continuing south for 17 km before turning left for the village of Hautefort, where there is another remarkable **château**.

This seventeenth-century château was built on the ruins of a twelfth-century fortress, which was the home of a famous troubadour, Bertrand de Born, an unusual man who was both a poet and a soldier, and became a monk at the end of his life. He was a man who glorified war and perhaps for this reason was placed among the damned by Dante in his *Inferno*.

History

The seventeenth-century château was built by a man of a different kind, Jacques François de Hautefort, whose ambitions were not hindered by the fact that his sister, Marie, was lady-in-waiting to the Queen, Anne of Austria, and was so beautiful that she troubled King Louis XIII. This was no mean achievement, for Louis was a man of strange character, pious, apprehensive, with little or no interest in women, though capable of infatuations with beauty in either sex. He was said to have been impotent for long periods, and though he managed a platonic friendship with Marie de Hautefort, it was certainly twenty-two years before he had a child by Anne of Austria, who was also renowned for her beauty. The child made up for the delay somewhat by reigning for seventy-two years as Louis XIV, the Sun King.

The château

Despite its great size – and majestic is not too grand a word for it – Hautefort is a well-proportioned, even elegant building, surrounded by a lovely park of 30 hectares and superb gardens in the French style.

In 1929 the then rather dilapidated castle became the property of the baronial de Bastard family who carefully restored it over the years, only to have it very seriously damaged by fire in 1968. Once again, at considerable expense and with state aid, the château was restored. The interior has some fine seventeenth- and eighteenth-century furniture, Flemish and Brussels tapestries, the altar which was used for the coronation of Charles X at Reims, and some admirable carved woodwork in the south-east tower.

Hautefort is in the same class as the great châteaux of the Loire Valley and is as well worth visiting. It is open to the public daily, morning and afternoon, from Palm Sunday to All Saints' Day. At other times of the year it is open only on Sunday afternoons and public holidays, and is closed for a month in midwinter.

Tourtoirac

On the banks of one of Dordogne's prettiest but least known rivers, the Auvézère, and 10 km west of Hautefort by the D62, is the small market town of Tourtoirac. Here, at the **Hôtel des Voyageurs**, Tourtoirac, 24390 Hautefort, tel. (53) 51 12 29, you can have a good lunch of regional dishes at a very moderate price.

What to see

In the village you can see the remains of a former **Benedictine Abbey**, including a part-Romanesque part-Gothic church which has been much restored, the Abbey living quarters, and some fourteenth-century fortifications.

Antoine Orélie de Tounens

An extraordinary man is buried in the local cemetery. He was a not-too-successful lawyer in Périgueux, called Antoine Orélie de Tounens, and he did what many men have done since they were first obliged hundreds of years ago to work in offices: he sat at his desk dreaming of other things, of adventure and faraway places. In 1858 it all became too much for him and, borrowing a large sum of money, he abandoned the legal life and took off for the extreme south of South America, intending to form his own kingdom and attach it to France. He did succeed in persuading local Patagonian Indian tribes to recognise him as their chief, and in 1860 proclaimed himself King of Auracania, Orélie Antoine I. It is still rough country down there, and in 1860 it was even rougher, so news travelled slowly, but when the Chilean authorities heard it they weren't impressed. In fact, they took umbrage and expelled him.

However, Orélie Antoine I had a touch of kingly stubbornness in his nature, and in 1869 he sailed off again to Patagonia to have another go. He had many adventures but no success, and was unceremoniously returned to France. He tried twice more to rejoin his 'kingdom', but eventually 'abdicated'. He settled down in Tourtoirac, where he died in 1878, aged fifty-three, a classic case of a man born before his time. A hundred years later the Sunday papers might have paid him a fortune for serialisation rights.

Montignac and Caves of Lascaux

From Hautefort the D704 leads you south into the land of prehistory, the Black Périgord. At La Bachellerie carry on south by the D65 and the D67 to Montignac.

This pleasant little town, unknown fifty years ago, is famous today because of its association with the nearby **Caves of Lascaux**, the most important prehistoric discovery in Europe.

Discovery

The caves were found in September 1940 by four teenage boys, looking for their dog. They saw the remarkable paintings on the walls and told the village schoolmaster, who in turn reported the discovery to the Abbé Breuil, a specialist in prehistory.

The paintings

The paintings were in such a fine state of preservation that many experts refused at first to believe that they were genuine, until it was found that an impermeable layer of rock above the roof of the caves had kept them perfectly dry, while a layer of vitreous calcite had formed on the walls, having the effect of placing the paintings behind a thin layer of natural glass. The authenticity of these prehistoric works of art was thus established beyond any doubt. After prolonged study it was found that there were many hundreds of paintings, covering a very long period, from about 25,000 years ago to 13,000 years ago. All the animals hunted by prehistoric man were shown, and there were also many signs and symbols which have not yet been conclusively interpreted. But the symbols, together with the fact that no tools, weapons or utensils have been found in the cave, suggest that it was used only as a kind of temple and was never lived in.

Closure of the caves

The caves were opened to the public, but in the early 1960s it was noticed that the paintings were becoming obscured by a green mould, caused by the carbon dioxide breathed out by the large numbers of visitors, which altered the humidity level and caused condensation. This, together with the light used to illuminate the drawings, produced conditions favourable to the growth of microscopic algae, so in 1963 the caves were closed to the public and have remained closed ever since. At present only two groups of five specialists each are allowed to visit Lascaux each week. To preserve the paintings so that scholars can continue to study them, it was found necessary to close the cave with special doors which seal it off from the outside atmosphere, and to install technical equipment which maintains a constant temperature of 13°C (55°F) and a constant level of humidity, to hold the carbon dioxide content at no more than 1 per cent.

The artists

During the long period in which prehistoric artists used the caves, technical skill in drawing and painting developed, so that scholars are now able to recognise several different styles. Because of the limited area of suitable surfaces, drawings were often painted over and the space used again, or drawings were superimposed on one another without painting out. The artists built wooden scaffolds, and even lowered themselves on cords into deep holes to reach suitable surfaces to paint on, working by the light of animal fat lamps.

In Lascaux, most of the animals depicted are female and pregnant, showing the wish of the hunters that the species they lived on should continue to thrive. Some of the drawings show animals pierced by arrows or spears, or surrounded by symbols which may represent traps or snares. Scholars have interpreted this as a kind of sympathetic magic, meant to cast a spell on the animals, making them easier to catch.

Lascaux II   Despite the closing of the Lascaux caves, it is possible for tourists to see copies of these drawings in identical surroundings because, at great expense, the main Bull Chamber and an adjoining recess, with all their paintings, have been exactly reproduced in another scene nearby, known as Lascaux II. Though done by modern artists, the paintings have been reproduced with the same materials as the originals, and to the millimetre. It was appreciated that the artists of the past were also hunters and that their wonderful draughtsmanship was due to their having studied every bone, every muscle, every strength and weakness of the animals on which they depended for survival. The same certainty of line can be seen today in modern works of the best Eskimo sculptors, also hunters whose lives depended on exact knowledge of their prey.

How to visit   A special system has been set up to avoid queues and long delays for
the caves   the people who want to see Lascaux II. Entrance is by ticket which can be bought only at a special ticket office in Montignac, with no tickets available at the site itself. Groups are limited to forty people at a time, and tickets are stamped with a particular time of day, being valid only for the group which enters the cave at that time. Provided you are there five minutes before the time stamped on your ticket you will not have to queue. When you go to the ticket office in Montignac (opposite the *Syndicat d'Initiative*) you may choose a ticket for the next available time, or any time after that which suits you.

The Valley of the Vézère from Montignac to Les Eyzies and the surrounding countryside is full of prehistoric sites and other places worth visiting. One reason for starting at Montignac is that if you do want to visit Lascaux II you can buy your ticket first thing in the morning for whatever time suits you, and then go off to see other things, returning to Lascaux just before you are due to go in.

Museum   The ticket that you buy for Lascaux also has a portion which entitles you to visit the **Prehistoric Research and Art Centre** at Le Thot 7 km away. This includes a museum illustrating all aspects of the life of prehistoric man, including a film and audio-visual presentations, and an exhibition showing the stages in the preparation of Lascaux II. There is also a park with animals of the types hunted by prehistoric men and shown in their drawings, including European bison, deer and Prszalski horses. The part of the ticket for Le Thot can be used at any time, and the visit offers an easy introduction to prehistory which will certainly be helpful to the non-specialist.

Prehistoric men, savage as they were, nevertheless had a sense of beauty. Even 30,000 years ago they made jewellery and gave their women delicately arranged ivory necklaces made from the teeth and claws of the animals they hunted. No doubt they were to some extent impressed by the beauty of the Valley of the Vézère and the feeling of shelter which it offers, but there were also practical reasons for settling there. The river water attracted animals, while the thick chestnut and oak forest offered cover for them. Caves provided the comfort of primitive homes, and the hunters could find plenty of flint from which to make tools and weapons.

Other caves

There is far more in and around the Valley of the Vézère than can be seen in one visit – there are, for example, more than fifty caves with some form of prehistoric art, but not everything worth seeing relates to prehistory.

Near the village of Thonac, 5 km from Montignac on the D706, the **Château de Losse** occupies a delightful site on a low cliff above the Vézère. On its other three sides it is surrounded by deep moats. The fortified entrance is fourteenth century, around the inner courtyard the living quarters are in an L-shaped Renaissance building started in 1576, and there is a splendid terrace beside the Vézère.

The château was the home and headquarters of Jean II of Losse, Governor of Guyenne, at the time of the first Bourbon kings. The rooms are furnished with sixteenth-century furniture and tapestries and contemporary weapons. The château is open to the public morning and afternoon from 1 July to 15 September.

This is a region where travellers must make their own choice of what to see. Two of the most interesting of the prehistoric sites within easy reach of Montignac are **La Grotte de Font de Gaume** and **La Grotte des Combarelles**. Font de Gaume is a corridor-like cave with side passages with drawings of animals which include reindeer, mammoths, rhinoceros and a wolf, and magic symbols like those at Lascaux. In addition, as this cave has been known since the eighteenth century, there are some later inscriptions of the 'Flintstone was here' variety. Some of the bison have their own names, such as Alain or Noel, acquired from the authors of the various graffiti cut into them in days when prehistory was less respected.

La Grotte des Combarelles, where guided visits of not more than ten people at a time take place, is another magnificent gallery of prehistoric art, with more than 300 drawings of animals.

Where to stay

Although there is no shortage of hotels in the region of the Vézère Valley, they are very well-occupied in summer so that it is advisable to book in advance, especially so if you have a particular hotel in mind.

Château De Puy Robert, 24920 Montignac, tel. (53) 51 92 13, is a small upmarket hotel, with twelve bedrooms, spacious grounds and a swimming pool. Rooms and restaurant are both expensive.

Relais Du Soleil D'Or, 16 Rue du 4 Septembre, 24920 Montignac, tel. (53) 51 80 22, with twenty-nine bedrooms, has a heated pool in the grounds. Rooms are moderately expensive but the three-room restaurant with menus starting at 75 fr (cheaper for children) is reasonably priced, with a good wine list.

Hôtel Le Lascaux, 109 Avenue Jean Jaures, 24920 Montignac, tel.

(53) 51 82 81, is a small hotel with moderate prices for both rooms and restaurant.

Terrasson-la-Villedieu

Rush Hôtel, 91 Avenue Victor Hugo, 24120 Terrasson-la-Villedieu, tel. (53) 50 03 74, is 17 km north-east of Montignac by the D704 and N89. While not offering anything of great historical interest itself, this little town is beautifully situated above the left bank of the Vézère, and is a suitable alternative to Montignac as a base from which to explore the region. In a quiet situation, despite its name, the Rush Hôtel is modern with a high degree of comfort and fair prices for the standards offered.

Les Eyzies-de-Tayac

Capital of prehistory

A short but lovely drive through the Vézère Valley on the D706 from Montignac, Les Eyzies-de-Tayac calls itself the capital of prehistory, and with good reason. A great deal of all that is known of prehistoric man derives from discoveries made within a few miles of Les Eyzies towards the end of the nineteenth century and at intervals since then.

Its position at the confluence of the Beune and the Vézère is unusual rather than picturesque; it huddles below an impressive but dark and overhanging limestone cliff, but is cheered up on Mondays by a colourful street market.

What to see

The village has a first-class museum of prehistory installed in the restored thirteenth-century château, halfway up the heights above the village, which once belonged to the barons of Beynac. Outside it stands the much-photographed **Statue of Primitive Man**, so convincing that it would not surprise you to hear it grunt. The **National Museum of Prehistory** may seem an off-putting title, but the collections are neat, clear and well-presented, and there can be few visitors who leave without some sense of awe at the length, patience and persistence of man's struggle to learn and to do better. It took many thousands of years to progress from bone to iron needles, yet the development from horse transport to space flight has been achieved in less than a hundred years. The great flywheel of human intelligence has continually gathered speed since, as this museum shows, it first began to turn so heavily and slowly in the minds of prehistoric men.

To understand it all more deeply would require visits to at least ten of the major sites around Les Eyzies, for which few people have the time and, possibly, not many the inclination. But **Font de Gaume**, mentioned on p. 112, which after Lascaux has the finest examples of prehistoric art, should be visited. Also important are the sites of **Laugerie Haute** and **Laugerie Basse**, which were inhabited by primitive men for more than 20,000 years and where more than 600 items from their daily lives have been found, including awls, harpoons, needles, flints, arrowheads, lamps and pottery. No other sites illustrate better how stubbornly man evolved through the ages.

Next to Laugerie Basse there is a splendid natural cave, the **Grotte du Grand Roc** which, for a change, has no associations with primitive man but does have an impressive display of stalactites and stalagmites, as well as crystalline formations which seem to defy the law of gravity. It is a pity that some of the formations have had to be protected from vandals with wire grilles.

Another cave, impressive by its sheer size, as well as by the large number of prehistoric engravings on the walls, is **Rouffignac**. This is 18 km from Les Eyzies by the D47 to Miremont, and then the D32. The galleries and chambers extend for more than 8 km, but a 4 km tour by electric railway covers all the most important galleries. Rouffignac is famous for the large numbers of mammoths represented but there are also horses, ibex, rhinoceros, bison and a fine engraving of two stags locked in combat. In many places the works are cut into rather than drawn on the rock. As this cave has been known since the fifteenth century – though it was mostly ignored until this century – it has graffiti here and there. It is advisable to take something warm to wear while visiting any caves; the temperature inside is usually a constant 13°C (56°F).

Of a different kind of interest, there is a thirteenth-century fortified church at **Les Eyzies-de-Tayac**, near the station. There is also a small **Museum of Speleology** which will interest pot-holers.

Where to stay
Les Eyzies-de-Tayac

Hôtel Cro-Magnon, 24620 Les Eyzies-de-Tayac, tel. (53) 06 97 06, has twenty-nine rooms. It is a good hotel, under the cliff, with a pleasant garden, shady terraces and a swimming pool. It is one of the Mapotel group, whose hotels can be relied on to be satisfactory and often very good. The restaurant (with one Michelin star) is worth a mention, being one of the few in the region which make an effort towards variety and lightness, in addition to the usual rich Périgord dishes. Above average prices.

Hôtel Centenaire, 24620 Les Eyzies-de-Tayac, tel. (53) 06 97 18, with twenty-six rooms, was built in 1963 when Les Eyzies was celebrating the centenary of the discovery of its prehistoric sites. It has high standards, with a two-star Michelin restaurant and a heated swimming pool in a small but pleasant garden. Above average prices. Light sleepers should note that it stands at the junction of two important roads.

Les Glycines, 24620 Les Eyzies-de-Tayac, tel. (53) 06 97 07, with twenty-five rooms, is a good hotel outside the village on the Périgord road, with a swimming pool and pleasant grounds. Rooms are above average price, but the restaurant is reasonably priced.

Hôtel Le Moulin De La Beune, 24620 Les Eyzies-de-Tayac, tel. (53) 06 94 33, has twenty rooms and is moderately priced, but with no restaurant. It is situated by the side of the Beune near the main road through Les Eyzies, but about 10 m below it, so that you look down on it from the road.

Le Bugue

Le Bugue, about 10 km from Les Eyzies on the D706, is an agreeable little town which can be used as an alternative base for exploring the sites already mentioned.

Hôtel Royal Vézère, Place Hôtel de Ville, 24260 Le Bugue, tel. (53) 07 20 01, another in the Mapotel group, is a good modern hotel with forty-nine rooms. It has a riverside terrace where meals can be taken, a swimming pool and disco.

Campagne

Château Hôtel, Campagne, 24260 Le Bugue, tel. (53) 07 23 50, is in the little village about 4 km from Le Bugue and the same distance from Les Eyzies. It is a modern building in traditional style, with eighteen rooms and a good restaurant with menus from 60 fr. Excellent value at the prices asked.

Where to eat

Almost without exception the best restaurants are those in the hotels, although there are tourist snack bars and café restaurants for cheap or hurried meals.

L'Albuca, Place Hôtel de Ville, 24260 Le Bugue, tel. (53) 07 23 50, in Le Bugue is what the French call 'serious' and has a terrace by the Vézère. Above average prices but special menu for children. Closed at lunch-time on Mondays and Tuesdays.

Sarlat

Situated 21 km from Les Eyzies-de-Tayac by the D47 and 25 km from Montignac by the D704, Sarlat is the capital of the Black Périgord and a *sous-préfecture* of the Dordogne department. If you drive through it on the dead-straight Rue de la Republique (known in the town as the Traverse), you will see nothing of one of the most interesting towns in the whole of France. It has to be seen on foot and it needs time.

There are more medieval, Renaissance, and seventeenth-century façades, and more turrets, gables, carved doorways, fountains and strange roofscapes than you can possibly hope to photograph or remember.

History

Founded in the eighth century around a Benedictine Abbey, Sarlat became a bishopric in the fourteenth century and remained one until the French Revolution. Often attacked during the Hundred Years War, it was assigned to the English by the Treaty of Brétigny, following the Black Prince's capture of the French king, Jean le Bon, at the Battle of Poitiers in 1356. It became French again before the end of the Hundred Years War. The town suffered in the sixteenth-century Wars of Religion, but since then has lived in peace, if not always prosperity.

Restoration

Although many medieval buildings had almost miraculously survived, they were often in an abused or dilapidated condition, and the town always considered itself too poor to do anything about them. In August 1962 a law was passed (*la loi Malraux*) with the object of conserving the best historical quarters of old towns, and Sarlat was one of the first four towns to benefit. Grants and loans made it possible to restore completely seventy buildings in the heart of the old town, even to the extent of installing modern comfort and drainage. The restoration programme continues, but more slowly now as grants to owners have been much reduced.

Sarlat is a town without any really outstanding monuments, even the Cathedral is of only passing interest, yet so many façades and details from the past create an ensemble which is a monument in itself, and the overall effect is so impressive that it attracts half-a-million tourists a year. Visitors who prefer not to compete with thousands of other tourists in the same small place at the same time may well enjoy Sarlat more outside the July/August high season.

Parking the car

The first problem to solve in Sarlat in the high season is where to park. As you come down the hill from the north to Sarlat, you will notice cars parked side by side down the slope of the hill on the right. If you are lucky enough to see a space there, take it, for you are unlikely to get closer to the old town, which lies in front of you to the left, starting on the lower slopes of the hill. If you arrive from the south, you will find two squares on the right with public parking. The first of these, the Place Pasteur, is sometimes a good bet, but really in Sarlat in the high season it is all a matter of luck and persistence, though it helps a lot if you follow the golden rule of sightseeing anywhere in the tourist world: 'Get there early!'

While there is no doubt that Sarlat is a very pleasant place to wander through, there are those who find that there is something unconvincing about it. The large number of façades and exterior details to be seen, contrasted with the very few interiors, can give the impression that it is a film set rather than a real town. The knowledge that there are modern bathrooms and fitted kitchens behind the medieval façades does not help.

Guided tours

It is a good idea to join one of the guided tours, which leave at regular intervals on weekdays (once on Sundays) during the June/September season, from the *Office du Tourisme*, Place Liberté, 24200 Sarlat, tel. (53) 59 27 67. Even if you do not follow all the French, the tour will take you by the shortest route to all the important points.

What to see

The most impressive feature of the **Cathedral** is the spacious and balanced interior typical of the late Gothic style. Outside the south doorway there is a courtyard closed on the south side by the **Chapel of the Blue Penitents**, a twelfth-century building which was part of the original abbey around which Sarlat developed. Societies of voluntary penitents were formed in the fourteenth century after the Church abandoned the imposition of public penance. The members of these groups took it upon themselves to absolve the sins of others, which they did by practising charity and carrying out such disagreeable tasks as the burial of the dead during epidemics. If you walk around the back of this chapel by way of the **Fountain Courtyard** and up the stone steps climbing the hill behind the Cathedral, you will come to the strange and graceless tower known as the **Lantern of the Dead**. No satisfactory explanation has been put forward for either its design or use, and no similar structure is known elsewhere.

If you look back from the steps as you approach this tower, you have a good view of the *chevet* of the Cathedral and of the roofscape of the old town.

Among the most interesting parts of the old quarter are the **Place de la Liberté** – surrounded by old mansions and medieval houses, and the site of a market on Saturday mornings – and the **Rue des Consuls**. Almost every house in this street has something of interest about it. The **Plamon Mansion** belongs originally to the fourteenth century, but as the fortunes of the Selves de Plamon family, who were cloth merchants, rose, so did their house, as additional floors and features were added by succeeding and successful generations. Also in the Rue des Consuls, at No. 8, is the fifteenth-century **Tapinois de Betou Mansion**, which has a great seventeenth-century staircase with wooden balusters. Everywhere in this street you can see intricate details of medieval and Renaissance architecture in the doorways, window frames, roofs and gables.

The square in front of the Cathedral, the **Place du Peyrou**, is a suitable point at which to interrupt your wanderings through Sarlat to sit on a café terrace and watch the world go by. The square includes the house, in the corner facing the Cathedral, where the writer **Étienne de la Boétie** was born in 1530. La Boétie, who came from a distinguished legal family and was himself a magistrate and member of the Bordeaux parliament, is remembered today less for his poems and essays than for his close friendship with the great essayist and philosopher, Montaigne. Their friendship began when they met at Bordeaux when Montaigne was twenty-three and La Boétie twenty-six, and continued until La Boétie died seven years later.

Entertainment

Sarlat has an active and varied programme of musical and theatrical events annually throughout the summer season. On a more mundane level, its Saturday market is famous.

Where to stay

Although Sarlat is an excellent base for excursions in the Black Périgord, in addition to being an interesting destination in itself, its hotel accommodation is relatively limited.

Hôtel St Albert, 10 Place Pasteur, 24200 Sarlat, tel. (53) 59 01 09, is the largest with fifty-seven rooms and is something of a 'tourist factory', but it has a well-run and moderately priced restaurant which gives good value for money.

Hôtel De La Madeleine, 1 Place Petite Rigaudie, 24200 Sarlat, tel. (53) 59 10 41, with nineteen rooms, is a good hotel with a good restaurant. Prices slightly higher than the St Albert.

Hôtel La Couleuvrine, 1 Place de la Bouquerie, 24200 Sarlat, tel. (53) 59 27 80, is installed in the modernised interior of a medieval and Renaissance building in the old quarter near the Town Hall.

These hotels do not offer private parking space; a possible solution to this problem would be to book in advance and arrive in the evening at a time when most visitors may have already departed in search of their own evening meal. An alternative is to stay outside the town and drive in early before all parking space has been taken.

Hotels within easy reach of the town include the following.

La Hoirie, 24200 Sarlat, tel. (53) 59 05 62, with fifteen rooms, is about 2 km south of the town by the D704 and C1. A small, comfortable hotel in country surroundings, with a swimming pool and a restaurant offering dinner only. Moderate prices.

Hostellerie de Meysset, Lieu-dit Argentouleau, 24200 Sarlat, tel. (53) 59 08 29, 3 km on the road to Les Eyzies, is a modern hotel with twenty-six rooms, on the expensive side but pleasant and comfortable.

Where to eat

In addition to the restaurants of the **St Albert** and **La Madeleine** (see p. 117), which are both recommendable, the **Restaurant Marcel**, 8 Avenue Selvès, 24200 Sarlat, tel. (53) 59 21 98, is a welcoming place where the owner is also the chef. He offers a variety of generous menus, including regional dishes, at fair prices. There are also a few moderately priced rooms, but it is a restaurant first and a hotel second.

Riverside villages and châteaux of the Dordogne

Domme

Sarlat is only 10 km from the Dordogne in its middle reaches. From Domme westwards almost to Bergerac there is a succession of picturesque riverside villages and dramatically sited castles. Going south from Sarlat, keep left on to the D46, and cross the river at Cénac. A road to the left winds up in hairpin bends to the remarkable *bastide* village of Domme.

History

Founded by Philip the Bold in 1281, it was captured by the English during the Hundred Years War and held for twenty years. The old walls as well as three of the ancient fortified gateways are still in existence.

What to see

The village as a whole has been very well restored, and still retains many interesting architectural details from the past. Among the most impressive buildings are the **Governor's House** and the **Town Hall**. Domme does not follow the normal rectangular pattern of a *bastide*, owing to the irregular nature of the ground. One side of the spectacular site falls in a sheer cliff to the river, and there is an esplanade which gives magnificent views over the river valley as far as Beynac in the west and the **Montfort loop** in the east. As you admire this, the most celebrated view in Dordogne, give a thought to the remarkable Protestant soldier, Geoffroi de Vivans, who during the Wars of Religion captured the town by making a night assault with picked men up the steepest part of the 150 m cliff. Thought to be unassailable, it was not defended, so the town was completely taken by surprise and captured without a fight.

Where to stay   **Hôtel L'Esplanade**, 24260 Domme, tel. (58) 28 31 41. Impeccable hotel, nineteen rooms and fine restaurant (one Michelin star). Wonderful views over Dordogne Valley. Prices a bit above average.

Return to Cénac, recross the river and turn left almost at once along the right bank to La Roque-Gageac, 3 km away.

La Roque-   The village of La Roque-Gageac, which in the past has won the title
Gageac   of the most beautiful village in France, is built immediately beside the river on a series of ledges in the steep cliff face, so that its golden stone houses seem from a distance to be piled one on top of the other. At the western end of the village there is an impressive-looking **château** in white stone. It looks to be early Renaissance but was in fact rebuilt in that style during the nineteenth century.

Although La Roque-Gageac has been much restored, its mixture of fine old houses, craftsmen's workshops and narrow alleys with views down to the river well repays a walk around. The quays here and at Beynac-Cazenac are reminders that there was once important one-way barge traffic on the river, particularly for the transport of wine.

Where to stay   **Hôtel La Belle Étoile**, La Roque-Gageac, 24250 Domme, tel. (53) 29 51 44, is a small flower-decked hotel with sixteen rooms and moderate prices for both rooms and restaurant.

Beynac-et-   Going west on the riverside road, soon after leaving La Roque-
Cazenac   Gageac, you see a magnificent castle crowning another great cliff ahead of you with a village below it. The village of Beynac, which was originally troglodytic, is also built, though somewhat less steeply than La Roque-Gageac, on shelves in the cliff, finishing in a group of old houses around the skirts of the castle.

Getting there   By car the castle has to be approached by a road which sweeps round behind the village for a couple of kilometres before turning back to the castle. There is a charge for parking.

There can be few places that have retained until today such a feeling of the medieval past as is created by this great feudal **castle**, frowning down on the few humble houses around it. Not even the car park and a tourist restaurant can destroy the impression that in this spot you come face to face with the Middle Ages.

History   It is not known for how long there has been a fortress in this place, but it is no doubt one of the oldest in Dordogne. There was certainly one here in the twelfth century, because it was captured by Richard the Lionheart and given to one of his captains, Mercadier, who used it as a base to terrorise the countryside to such effect that it became known as 'the house of Satan'. This earlier fortress was retaken and destroyed in 1214 by Simon de Montfort (father of the rebellious Simon de Montfort who features in English history books), and most of what you see today was built in the thirteenth and fourteenth centuries by the Barons of Beynac. During the Hundred Years War there were constant affrays between the French, based at Beynac, and the English, who held the castle of Castelnaud just across the river.

What to see

The main building was enlarged by a manor-house wing in the fifteenth century, but it is the feudal part which is open to the public; the château is still in private hands and is being slowly restored. There is little to see in the interior apart from the vast, vaulted state room – in which the Council of Périgord met from time to time until the seventeenth century – as well as a huge Renaissance chimney-piece, and a small oratory with some fifteenth-century frescoes, including the Last Supper. The visit to the interior is therefore perhaps not worth the 20 fr entrance fee asked (on top of 6 fr for parking).

A path around the base of the castle on the right leads up to a natural terrace with a fine view of the river valley as far as Domme. As you follow it, you can be certain that almost a thousand years ago Richard the Lionheart must have followed the same path with Mercadier, to stand at that same point, indicating the natural advantages of the position as they both looked down the valley and pondered what they should capture next.

Where to stay

Hôtel Bonnet, Beynac-et-Cazenac, 24220 St-Cyprien, tel. (53) 29 50 01, with twenty-two bedrooms, is a long-established and well-respected hotel on the riverside road, charging average prices for rooms and restaurant, which has a good reputation. It is a popular centre for local functions, on which occasions its normal peaceful atmosphere is somewhat disturbed.

Castelnaud

To reach the imposing ruins of the **fortress** of Castelnaud, the great rival of Beynac in the Hundred Years War, cross the river at Vézac. The original twelfth-century castle was knocked down by the order of Charles VII, but was rebuilt in red ironstone in the fifteenth century by the Caumont family. They left it to move to the less grim Château of Les Milandes, which they had built nearby. After the Caumonts ceased to maintain Castelnaud in the eighteenth century, the castle gradually fell to ruin until its restoration began in 1967. It is fitting that this castle should now house a museum of medieval siege warfare, for during the Wars of Religion it was the headquarters of the great Protestant soldier, Geoffroi de Vivans – the one who captured Domme – who was born at Castelnaud. Even if you do not go inside, Castelnaud is worth visiting for the **panoramic views** of the Dordogne Valley from the east end of the terrace.

Les Milandes

This château, used as a home by the Caumonts until the time of the

Revolution, is a short distance from Castelnaud. Josephine Baker, the great star of the French stage in the post-war years, bought Les Milandes with the idea of creating a home where abandoned children of different races and religions could grow up in mutual understanding. But despite the fact that her magnetism and beauty had brought her a fortune, this generous experiment ruined her, so that she was obliged to sell the château, its farmland and the leisure centre she had established there, and return to the stage.

The fifteenth-century **château**, restored at the end of the nineteenth century, is in very good condition and contains souvenirs of Josephine Baker, as well as the original owners, the Caumonts.

Cadouin

From Les Milandes turn away from the river on the D53 and then turn right down the D50 to Siorac-en-Périgord. This is an attractive route with views of the river. From Siorac take the D25 to Le Buisson and then to Cadouin.

Situated away from the river in a wooded valley on the edge of the Bessède Forest, Cadouin is renowned for its **Cistercian Abbey**, which has a splendid cloister in the flamboyant Gothic style. Two years after the abbey was founded in 1115, the Bishop of Le Puy made a present to the abbey of what was said to be the cloth which had bound the head of Christ on the cross. This piece of linen, decorated with bands of gold thread, had been found at Antioch during the Crusades. It assured the fame of Cadouin for centuries. Eleanor of Aquitaine, Richard the Lionheart, St Louis, Charles V and countless pilgrims on their way to St James of Compostella went to Cadouin to kneel reverently before it.

In 1934 it was examined by experts who declared it to be a piece of oriental cloth of the twelfth century with Kufic inscriptions of that time: in other words it was new when it was given to the abbey, so it seems that in the Middle Ages even the bishops were either untrustworthy or gullible.

The abbey's massive **Romanesque church**, consecrated in 1154, is typical of neither Périgord nor Cistercian style, but its simple strength provides an interesting architectural contrast with the intricate grace and elegance of the cloister, which dates from a much later period.

Where to stay

Hôtel Beauregard, Route de Trémolat, 24510 Limeuil, tel. (53) 22 03 15, with ten rooms, is a quiet little hotel in Limeuil, a village in a lovely situation at the confluence of the Vézère and the Dordogne. It is a good base for visiting Cadouin and, in the other direction, Les Eyzies.

Château de Regagnac, Cadouin, 24440 Beaumont, tel. (53) 22 42 98, is a private château – really more of a fortified manor house than a true château – with only five guest rooms. To reach it, take the D2 from Cadouin and fork left after about 5 km. An oasis of calm in the Bessède Forest, it is better described as a country house which accepts paying guests rather than a hotel. Rooms are quite expensive, and children under thirteen are not taken. It is unusual – just right for some, although others may find a degree of pretension.

Where to eat

The **Restaurant du Périgord**, 24480 Cadouin, where I lunched a few years ago, remains in my memory as an experience. It was the kind of place not listed by anyone, but which turns out to be sensational, inexpensive, copious and good. The meal started with the *patron* putting a bottle of red wine on the table. 'That's just for the soup', he said. 'I'll bring the real stuff later.' In fact all the wine, plus an aperitif and a walnut liqueur, was included in the price of the menu. When I last passed by, having already lunched, nothing seemed to have changed, so it might still be worth prospecting the Restaurant du Périgord if you fancy a true country lunch or dinner.

Trémolat
Where to stay

Le Vieux Logis, Trémolat, 24510 St-Alvère, tel. (53) 33 80 06, with sixteen rooms, is for those who like their country holidays with more than a touch of luxury. In pleasant grounds in Trémolat, near the picturesque **Cingle de Trémolat**, a great loop in the Dordogne, the Vieux Logis is a very comfortable and well-equipped hotel. Prices are a good deal higher than one would normally expect in the provinces but fair for what is offered. Trémolat is only about 20 km from Les Eyzies, via the D706, D703 and D30, and is a practical base for visiting both the prehistoric sites and the châteaux and villages of the Dordogne Valley.

Beaumont du Périgord

From Cadouin the D25 continues to Beaumont du Périgord, 12 km away, so that these two places can be combined in the course of one morning or afternoon visit.

Where to eat

There are two good reasons for visiting Beaumont du Périgord. One is the restaurant called **Chez Popaul**, in the **Hôtel Les Voyageurs**, 24440 Beaumont du Périgord, tel. (53) 22 30 11. This restaurant is well-known throughout the northern part of Aquitaine and is unlike any other in the region. It offers a choice of menus, but its individuality is in the second course, at which you serve yourself from a central table containing forty-five different *hors d'oeuvres*. You may take whatever you want, as often as you want, but it is essential to bear in mind that there are other normal courses to follow. The owners are Dutch, and this course is inspired by the famous Indonesian rice table (*rijstaffel*). While the cuisine is unpretentious, and quantity takes slight precedence over quality, it is satisfactory in every way, and prices are moderate. In season it is essential to book in advance. The hotel has ten inexpensive bedrooms.

What to see

The other interest in Beaumont is simply that it is a pleasant little *bastide* town built by the English in 1272. It was constructed in an 'H' shape as a mark of respect for Henry III, and has an unusual **fortified church**.

Couze St Front

From Beaumont the D660 leads by a pretty road through the Valley of the Couze back to the Dordogne and the village of Couze St Front. It is a place once well-known for the making of high-quality paper, although the industry has very much declined and the dozen or so old mills still standing produce little apart from some blotting- and filter-papers. In the past the high-quality paper produced here was marketed all over Europe by paper merchants of Amsterdam, and it may be that this association was the beginning of the popularity of this region with the Dutch, who now come here in large numbers every summer.

Lanquais

Near Couze, and still on the left bank of the Dordogne, is the **château** and village of Lanquais. It is well worth a visit, being a remarkably successful blend of a fourteenth-century Gothic castle with a Renaissance palace. This extension was made towards the end of the sixteenth century by Galiot de la Tour d'Auvergne, a member of one of France's most illustrious families.

History

The de la Tour d'Auvergne family supplied the country with a long succession of cardinals, bishops, counts, dukes, marshals and admirals, as well as the mistresses, wives and mothers of princes and the great, including Madeleine de la Tour, mother of Catherine de Médici, Queen of France.

Following the death of her husband, Henri II, in a friendly joust with an English soldier, Catherine ruled as regent during the minority of her sons. She reigned effectively if in somewhat unorthodox style, one of her political weapons consisting of a group of beautiful and noble young ladies whose work was to influence important men. The group, known as the Queen's *escadron volant* (flying squad), was required to seduce but not to be seduced – certainly not to the point of becoming pregnant. One of them was Isabel de Limeuil – known as Sweet Limeuil and the sister of Galiot de la Tour d'Auvergne – who lived at Lanquais when she was not at court. Unfortunately, she did her work too enthusiastically with the Prince de Condé and had a child by him, whereupon Catherine banished her from the court. The Prince de Condé is said to have recognised the child, which had been sent to him by Isabel in a basket lined with straw and a cloth discreetly embroidered with the arms of Condé. Catherine soon forgave her and found her a rich Italian banker as a husband.

The interior of Lanquais has some magnificent sculpted chimney-pieces and fine antique furniture.

Cross the Dordogne at Couze and follow the D660 towards Bergerac. To begin with it runs beside a tree-lined canal, built at a time when there was busy river traffic towards Bordeaux and this part of the river was difficult to navigate safely.

Bergerac

A few years ago Bergerac might fairly have been described as busy but nondescript, though graced by a wide and attractive reach of the river. Today it is a good deal more interesting, following the successful renovation, still in progress, of the old town next to the river. This area, now almost entirely pedestrianised, includes some charming old

What to see

squares and medieval houses, notably **La Vieille Auberge**, 27 Rue des Fontaines, which dates from the fourteenth century.

Bergerac is the chief centre for tobacco production in France, and the early seventeenth-century **Maison Peyrarade** now includes the excellent **Museum of Tobacco**, as well as a **Museum of the Town's History**. Close by, the Protestant church is a reminder that Bergerac is and always was one of the great strongholds of Protestantism in France. Near the statue of Cyrano de Bergerac and the Place de la Myrpe is the **Museum of Regional Ethnography**, which has a fascinating collection of the tools and early machines of the farmers and artisans of the region – equipment which might be forgotten as new machines, tools, technology and methods are introduced.

Cyrano de Bergerac

They won't like it in Bergerac, but I must tell you that Cyrano de Bergerac – the great swordsman and relentless duellist with the prodigiously long nose, who was the hero, overflowing with Gascon bravado, of Edmond Rostand's ever popular comedy, *Cyrano de Bergerac* – was not a Gascon, had nothing to do with Bergerac and almost certainly never went there. At least not this Bergerac.

Rostand's hero was based on a real-life character whose name was Savinien Cyrano and who was born in Paris. After becoming a soldier, he was posted to a company, commanded by Monsieur Carbon de Casteljaloux, consisting almost entirely of Gascons. To fit in better Cyrano added 'de Bergerac' to his name, it being the name of a property which his family owned in the country near Paris. He died in 1655, never even having acquired a Gascon accent.

But in Rostand's play, written nearly 250 years later, he was a full-blooded, touchy, swaggering Gascon, and has been ever since. In Bergerac they are proud of him, and are not at all interested in knowing that he was really a Parisian of Italian extraction.

Wine

Bergerac is at the centre of an important wine-producing region which has eleven *Appellation Contrôlée* wines, the best of which are the reds of Pécharmant and those with the plain Bergerac *appellation*. South of the river, the Monbazillac vineyards produce a sweet white wine second only to Sauternes. It is a heavy wine, which in good years can reach 18 degrees of alcohol. It can be tasted at the **Château of Monbazillac**, which is owned by the local co-operative of wine producers and has a good restaurant.

Bergerac is really a town more suited to a stopover or a halt for lunch, combined with a look at the old quarter, than a tourist destination in itself.

Where to stay

Hôtel de France, 18 Rue Gambetta, 24100 Bergerac, tel. (53) 57 11 61, with twenty rooms, is a good inexpensive modern hotel, but has no restaurant.

Hôtel de Bordeaux, 38 Place Gambetta, 24100 Bergerac, tel. (53) 57 12 83, has thirty-two rooms. It is comfortable and moderately priced with a good restaurant.

Relais De La Flambée, Route Périgueux-Pombonne, 24100 Bergerac, tel. (53) 57 52 33, with twenty-one rooms, is a pleasant hotel with gardens and a swimming pool, situated 3 km north of Bergerac on the N21 Périgueux road. Above average restaurant.

Manoir Le Grand Vignoble, 24140 Villamblard, tel. (53) 24 23 18, with twenty-six rooms, is a fine country hotel in a seventeenth-century manor surrounded by a park of 73 hectares at St Julien de Crempse on the outskirts of Bergerac. With a swimming pool, tennis, riding school and golf practice, it is rather expensive.

Where to eat

Brasserie Royal Périgord, Rue de la Résistance, 24100 Bergerac, tel. (53) 57 24 90, offers sound *à la carte* meals at average prices.

Le Cyrano, 2 Blvd Montaigne, 24100 Bergerac, tel. (53) 57 02 76, is a first-class restaurant (one Michelin star), but rather lacking in atmosphere. Menus at middle-of-the-range prices. The Cyrano also has ten bedrooms.

Closerie St Jacques, Monbazillac, 24240 Sigoulès, tel. (53) 58 37 77, 7 km from Bergerac by the D13, is another very good restaurant with one Michelin star (try the fricassee of pigeon with Monbazillac and red beans).

Lot

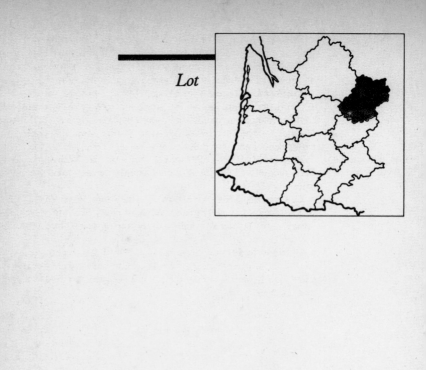

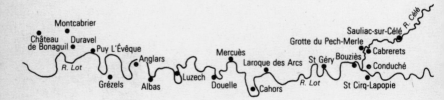

Montcabrier

Château
de Bonaguil ● Duravel ●
● Puy L'Évêque

R. Lot

Anglars

Grézels

Albas

Luzech

Mercuès

Douelle

Laroque des Arcs

Cahors

R. Lot

St Géry

St Cirq-Lapopie

Grotte du Pech-Merle

Bouziès

Sauliac-sur-Célé

R. Célé

Cabrerets

Conduché

Lot

Introduction

Lot is a department which in situation, topography and vegetation belongs more to the fringes of the Massif Central than it does to the south-west. However, its chief town, Cahors, is included in this gazetteer because it lies on the N20, one of the natural routes from the eastern Channel ports to the south, and is one of the main gateways to the south-west.

Cahors

As well as being an interesting place in itself, Cahors (which is pronounced Ka-or, with no 'h') is convenient for a stopover and as a base for excursions into the lovely valleys of the Lot and the Célé.

Situation   Surrounded on all sides by limestone hills, Cahors is built on an isthmus formed by a U-bend in the River Lot, which runs parallel to itself on each side of the town. It owed its foundation in pre-Roman times both to this natural fortress position and to the existence of a **sacred spring**, Divona, at the base of a cliff just across the river. It is now called the *fontaine des Chartreux*, because the Carthusian monks first piped the water to the town, which it still supplies with drinking water.

History   Cahors is a town with an unusual history. Despite what must have been, in its early days, a very remote position, it prospered and was known throughout the Roman Empire for its export of fine linen cloth.

In the Middle Ages, Cahors became one of the most important and prosperous towns in France. This rise in its fortunes began by chance. After the death in 1314 of Pope Clement V, who had made Avignon the seat of the Papacy, the College of Cardinals was unable to agree on a successor. In desperation, when the problem remained unsettled after two years of bitter bitter argument, they chose a man of seventy-two who appeared to be in poor health, hoping that he would give them time to find a proper successor, but not last too long.

Pope Jean XXII   The new Pope, Jacques Arnaud Duèze, who called himself Jean XXII, confounded the cardinals by living another eighteen years, during which time he showed himself to be a remarkably efficient administrator and a financial genius. He instituted a taxation system of which the subtlest brains of today could have been proud, and money poured into the Church's coffers, so that when he died, having outlived many of the cardinals who had thought of him as a stop-gap, he left a balance of more than twenty million gold francs in the treasury.

Jean XXII was born in 1244 in Cahors, the son of a bourgeois. As Pope, he developed a paternal friendship with the King of France, Philip the Tall, to whom he wrote letters full of fatherly advice, telling him to pay attention during church services, not to be shaved on Sundays, to watch the royal budget carefully, not to eat too much, and to take the advice of his doctors. Philip was no doubt happy with this correspondence, since Jean XXII was always ready to lend him money when he needed it. In fact, the Pope lent money all round Europe, to the Emperor Charles IV and to the kings of Aragon, Castile, Majorca, Naples, Hungary, Norway and England. In addition, he was always ready to help capable men from his home town, supporting them in business or finding them work, either as dignitaries of the Church throughout Europe, or as diplomats, scribes or just kitchen boys, according to their abilities.

Banking centre So men of Cahors, and Cahors itself, became known in many countries; Lombard bankers and merchants were attracted to this town, feeling that if Jean XXII was someone to judge by, the people would have a strong sense of finance. The local inhabitants soon proved the bankers right, quickly learning their skills, to the extent that Cahors became the most important banking centre in early fourteenth-century Europe.

The wars This enviable position was lost during the Hundred Years War, when Cahors, like all the other towns in the area, was repeatedly attacked by the English. Unlike the others, though, it was never captured, and even when it was ceded to the English following the Treaty of Brétigny in 1360 the town remained defiant.

Cahors also suffered in the course of the sixteenth-century Wars of Religion, being attacked in 1580 by a Protestant army led by Henri III of Navarre, later to become Henri IV of France. The town was eventually sacked after a battle lasting three days and nights.

The seventeenth and eighteenth centuries were times of comparative calm, during which Cahors expanded. When the Revolution came in 1789 it was accepted with no great enthusiasm, the townspeople even saving from the guillotine their former mayor, Louis Durfort-Léobard, who had been well-liked for his fairness and generosity. They snatched him from the scaffold, destroyed it and carried him back home in triumph.

Leon Gambetta In 1838, a son, Leon, was born to a grocer called Gambetta, who kept a shop in the market place near the Cathedral. As a boy, Leon Gambetta thought of becoming a sea-captain, but at eighteen he was sent to Paris to study law. He became first a successful lawyer, then a successful politician, and finally Président du Conseil (President of the Council of Ministers). Famous for his patriotic oratory and his republicanism, he became head of the Republican Union after the Franco-Prussian War, and promoted laws which enabled the Third Republic to be formed. He is often described as the Father of the Third Republic. Not surprisingly the main street in Cahors (and a good many other towns) is called the Avenue Gambetta.

Wine

Cahors is no longer known for the manufacture of linen, nor for international banking, but its dark red wine is exported far and wide. Cahors wines are full-bodied and reliable, sometimes so dark that they were called Black Cahors. There are still some which include the word *noir* in their names, although the local vintners are trying to promote a less heavy image. Most of the vineyards are in the Valley of the Lot west of the town.

Parking the car

As you enter Cahors from the north on the N20, a one-way system takes you briefly to the right and then, after a couple of hundred metres, to the left and back to the N20. On your right before you reach the N20 there is a large square, the Place Général de Gaulle, which is used for parking (not marked in the Red Michelin). Cahors is not a large town and this is a convenient place to leave the car and explore the old town on foot, or find a restaurant for lunch.

What to see

Not far from this parking area, you can still see some **remains of the ramparts** built in the fourteenth century to seal off Cahors on its isthmus. The Barbacane and the Tour St Jean, which formed part of these defences, are adjacent to the road near the point where you enter the one-way system. The Church of St Barthelemy, just across the road from the parking place, has a terrace from which there is an excellent view of the Lot Valley.

The main road runs downhill through the town, with the old part, known as the **Badernes quarter**, on the left, so that any of the turnings to the left leading down to the river immediately brings you into the old town.

The **Cathedral of St Etienne**, in the heart of the old quarter, is from the outside a grim, fortress-like building dating from the eleventh and twelfth centuries, but with a fourteenth-century façade. On the north side of the Cathedral, there is a Romanesque doorway, which used to be in this façade but was moved during the renovation. The **tympanum** of this doorway, illustrating the Ascension, is one of the best examples remaining of twelfth-century carving in the Languedoc style.

The vast, open nave, impressive in its simplicity, has a domed roof like many of the larger churches in the south-west. This part of the Cathedral remains as it was when built, though the ceiling of one of the domes has some fourteenth-century paintings, which were discovered during the nineteenth century beneath an old coat of whitewash.

A door on the right of the chancel leads to a fine cloister, which was added in the early sixteenth century in the flamboyant Gothic style, and though much of it is damaged, some superb carving remains.

Of other buildings in the old quarter, the most important is the **Maison Roaldes**, also known as the Maison Henri IV, because that is where the then King of Navarre is said to have stayed after the siege of Cahors in 1580. This late fifteenth-century house was restored early this century (at the time of writing it is temporarily closed to the public).

In other parts of the old town, although there is nothing quite as grand as the Roaldes mansion, there are many reminders of the past, in the form of elegantly-carved mullioned windows, stone shields with coats of arms, busts of former notables, iron-studded doors, and neglected corners yet to be restored. Perhaps because there is less of a fairground atmosphere than in Sarlat (see p. 115), and despite the fact that there are fewer impressive old houses, I find Cahors somehow more convincing and easier to believe in as an important medieval town.

The bridge

The **Pont Valentre** is without doubt the finest medieval bridge in the world, and should not be missed. It is at the other end of the town from the car park mentioned on p. 129, so you may prefer to rejoin your car and park again as close to the bridge as you can.

This bridge, a fortress guarding the town against attack from the river, is a good example of French medieval military architecture. The central of its three towers served as an observation post, while the outer towers could be closed by gates and portcullises. The defences were strengthened by a barbican, since demolished, at the town end of the bridge.

Local tradition has it that the bridge took so long to build that the architect made a bargain with the Devil to speed up the work. The Devil was to bring him all the materials he required, as instructed, in return for the architect's soul. The Devil not being without resources, the work did indeed begin to progress more rapidly, to the concern of the architect. Craftily, he asked the Devil to bring water in a sieve, which was, of course, impossible. In revenge at being outwitted, the Devil angrily knocked a corner off the central tower, which remained in this damaged condition throughout the Middle Ages. Eventually the bridge was restored, with the missing stone securely fixed in position, though with a small carving of the Devil trying to dislodge it.

In the early part of the nineteenth century Cahors still had two other medieval bridges – another one from the fourteenth century and one even older, with five towers – but these were pulled down and replaced, the first by the unlovely Pont Louis Philippe and the other by the ugly iron bridge, the Pont Neuf. The town councillors were proud of this, for iron was the latest thing. The people who used it daily were also pleased, as it was much easier to get their laden carts across its level road than up and down the donkey-back of the old bridge. If both these old bridges had survived, Cahors would no doubt have become one of the most famous tourist attractions in Europe.

One of the best views of the Pont Valentre is from the other side of the river near the Fontaine des Chartreux.

Cahors is a good base for excursions but as many of them cannot properly be said to relate to the south-west, I mention only a couple which are so easy it would be a pity to miss them.

Excursions St Cirq-Lapopie

This village (pronounced St Seer Lapopie) is one of the prettiest in France, standing on an escarpment high above the Lot, crowned by its fortified church and facing the towering limestone cliffs of the opposite bank. The narrow streets have old houses with corbels, exposed beams and Gothic and Renaissance features, many now restored and used as studios by artists and artisans. In the past St Cirq-Lapopie was an important centre for wood turning, but there are now only two artisans left who practise this old craft, making spigots and stoppers for wine barrels.

To get there, take the D653 to Vers, then turn right along the D662 to St Géry, cross the river at Bouziès and follow the D40 to St Cirq-Lapopie. Above the village there is a flat parking area called La Bancorel, which is also a good place for photographs of the village and the river.

La Grotte du Pech-Merle

From the D662 at Conduché, take the D41 to Cabrerets and the cave of Pech-Merle, one of the most interesting of all the prehistoric caves in France. It consists of several large intercommunicating chambers, which are full of impressive stalactites and stalagmites, with curious concretions in different colours, ranging from a frosty sparkle to a deep red. It may well have been the eerie beauty of these vast subterranean rooms that led primitive man to use Pech-Merle as a kind of temple: there is no evidence that it was ever inhabited. To the natural beauty of the cave man added his own superb drawings of bison, mammoths, horses and other animals.

In one place there is a single frieze of bison and mammoths, 10 m long and 3 m high, believed to have been drawn about 25,000 years ago. In other places there are mysterious signs and the marks of what are called 'negative' hands, made by placing the open-fingered hand against the wall and filling in the spaces and the outline with colour.

The tour of Pech-Merle covers about 1.6 kilometres inside the cave and takes about an hour and three-quarters. Of the many interesting sights, the most moving are the footprints of one of our far-distant ancestors which have been petrified for ever in the floor of the cave. They are said to be those of a woman walking with a stick, perhaps to help her find her way in the darkness of the cave, and accompanied by a child who, like small children of all times, did not stand still when told to.

131

'One can imagine', wrote Canon Lemozi, the priest who first explored the cave scientifically, 'that she stopped suddenly, disturbed by some distant noise, while the little one continued to play around her with all the unconcern of childhood.'

Pech-Merle can also be easily reached from St Cirq-Lapopie, so it is quite practical to see both these places in the course of one day's outing.

Sauliac-sur-Célé

Very close to Pech-Merle is an interesting **Open Air Museum**, the Domaine de Cuzals at Sauliac-sur-Célé, with examples of farm buildings as they were before the French Revolution and just before the First World War, as well as agricultural implements of all ages. There are wagons and tractors, both ancient and modern, and a museum of childhood and old toys, with something different demonstrated every day. The museum is open daily, except Saturdays, from 10 a.m. to 7 p.m. You can take your own picnic, or have a regional meal in the château restaurant.

Where to Stay
Cahors

Hôtel de France, 252 Avenue Jean-Jaures, 46000 Cahors, tel. (65) 35 16 76, is an Inter Hotel with seventy-nine rooms but no restaurant, in a relatively quiet situation not far from the Pont Valentre. Middle-of-range prices.

Hôtel Wilson, 72 Rue Pres. Wilson, 46000 Cahors, tel. (65) 35 41 80, has thirty-five rooms, and is a comfortably furnished but slightly more expensive hotel in a busier part of town, with no restaurant.

Hôtel La Chartreuse, Rue St-Georges, 46000 Cahors, tel. (65) 35 17 37, has thirty-four rooms, most of which overlook the river. To find it, cross the river by the Pont Louis Philippe and turn right. It is a moderately-priced functional hotel, with a large, ordinary restaurant but fair prices.

Hôtel Terminus, 5 Avenue Charles de Freycinet, 46000 Cahors, tel. (65) 35 24 50, is a good average hotel, with thirty-one bedrooms, not far from the station, and is inexpensive for the standards offered. The restaurant, **Le Balandre**, is under separate management and reservations should be made to (65) 35 01 97. It has kept its turn of the century decor and some of the waiters seemed old enough to go with it. The *patron* is the chef and offers the solid cuisine of Quercy, with menus starting at 80 fr.

Outside Cahors

Hôtel Beau Rivage, Laroque des Arcs, 46090 Cahors, tel. (65) 35 30 58, 5 km from Cahors on the D653, has sixteen bedrooms. It is moderately priced, agreeable and quiet, with a garden beside the Lot. Good regional restaurant.

Hôtel Château De Mercuès, Mercuès, 46090 Cahors, tel. (65) 20 00 01, 9 km north-west of Cahors by the D911, is at the other end of the scale, being one of the most expensive provincial hotels in France. It has sixteen very expensive rooms, seven even more expensive apartments in the château, and a further twenty-two rooms in its annexe, Les Cèdres. It is an attractive château, redecorated in the past few years, with splendid views and grounds including swimming pool and tennis. Restaurant menus start at 165 fr. Meals can be taken on the terrace.

Des Grottes, 46330 Cabrerets, tel. (65) 31 27 02, is a charming small hotel in Cabrerets, with seventeen rooms, a swimming pool and riverside terrace. Moderate prices.

At La Fontaine de la Péscalerie, where an underground stream emerges from a cliff face in a waterfall, 2.5 km from Cabrerets, the **Hôtel La Péscalerie**, La Fontaine de la Péscalerie, 46330 Cabrerets, tel. (65) 31 22 55, is a small country house hotel, with ten bedrooms, a high degree of comfort and a good restaurant. The rooms and the restaurant, with menus at 195 fr and 225 fr, are both expensive but reasonable for the high standards.

Where to eat
Cahors

In the heart of the old town near the *Mairie*, is **La Taverne**, 1 Rue J. B. Delpech, 46000 Cahors, tel. (65) 35 28 66, one of the best restaurants in the region. It is strongly influenced by the traditions of Périgord and Quercy cuisine, although menus change according to what the chef has found in the market. This is one of the places where, if you do not mind the expense, you can savour the real taste of truffles – *Truffes en Croustade* costs 300 fr. Menus start at 92 fr.

Le Balandre, tel. (65) 35 01 97. See Hôtel Terminus on p. 132. Menus from 80 fr.

Outside Cahors

Auberge du Sombral, Place du Sombral, St Cirq-Lapopie, 46330 Cabrerets, tel. (65) 31 26 08, is a little inn with a restaurant which serves regional specialities at modest prices. There are ten simple rooms.

Hôtel Restaurant Les Falaises, Bouziès, 46330 Cabrerets, tel. (65) 31 26 83, is an attractive little place, with nine rooms, a sun terrace, a garden down to the Lot and impressive views of the limestone cliffs opposite. A few km from St Cirq-Lapopie by the D40, it can also be reached by a narrow bridge over the Lot from the D662 on the opposite side, so it is within easy reach of Pech-Merle as well.

From Cahors to Bonaguil

Beside the River Lot

As it flows westward from Cahors towards Lot-et-Garonne, the River Lot becomes very serpentine with one great loop after another. The direct road from Cahors to Villeneuve-sur-Lot is the D911, which passes the Château de Mercuès, but unless you are in a desperate hurry the D8, a minor road on the opposite bank of the river, offers a more attractive drive. It takes you through a series of pretty villages – Douelle, Luzech, Albas, Anglars and Grézels – along some picturesque stretches beside the river, and through an important part of the Cahors vineyards, where many properties advertise *dégustation* – wine-tasting.

Puy L'Évêque

After Grézels, cross the river to Puy L'Évêque, a south-facing town whose houses climb the slopes above the river. It is a nice enough place but there is no special reason to stop unless you are thinking of lunch. Having crossed the river by the single-lane bridge you will quickly arrive at a road junction, with a spacious parking area in front of you and, to the right, the **Restaurant Henry**, 46700 Puy L'Évêque (tel. [65] 21 32 24). This is a non-tourist regional restaurant used by local businessmen and commercial travellers, a sure sign that it offers good value, and is to be preferred to the restaurants in the upper town on the D911, which trade rather on their view over the Lot than on the seriousness of their cooking.

Where to eat

Duravel

From Puy L'Évêque carry on by the D911 to Duravel, another sunny, south-facing village, cosily situated with its back against the hills. It has a **Romanesque church** with an even older crypt. The chancel has some good historiated capitals and behind the altar there is a sarcophagus, said to contain the remains of St Hilarion, St Piemont and St Agathon, brought back at the time of the Crusades. They may equally well be some insignificant old bones sold to a gullible knight by a street trader in Damascus, but then, as now, a good enough story would sell anything, and the bones are exposed to the faithful every five years in October.

Montcabrier

From Duravel take the D58 to Montcabrier, a small village which has a nice little hotel, the **Relais De La Dolce**, Montcabrier, 46700 Puy L'Évêque, tel. (65) 36 53 42, with twelve rooms, grounds with a swimming pool, and a good but rather expensive restaurant. From Montcabrier continue by the D673 to the pretty village of St Martin le Redon, and there turn right for the Château de Bonaguil, just over the border in Lot-et-Garonne. There is a point on this road which gives superb views of the castle across the valley.

Château de Bonaguil

History

This extraordinary feudal fortress, which has mellowed into one of the most romantic medieval ruins to be seen anywhere, was the work of Berenger de Roquefeuil, a brutal, spiteful, hunch-backed, liverish little man with grandiose ideas. Sensitive about his nobility and authority, he liked to proclaim himself 'the noble, magnificent and most powerful lord of the baronies of Roquefeuil, Blanquefort, Castelnaud, Comprey and Roqueferre, Count of Naut'.

When he was fined by King Charles VII for his brutality towards his vassals, he reacted by strengthening his castle, which was originally built in the thirteenth century. He worked on it for forty years, determined to build a castle that his ungrateful subjects would be unable to capture – nor even the English if they dared to return, nor even the most powerful regiments of the King of France. All this despite the fact that Charles VII had published edicts forbidding private defence works. While everyone else had given up feudalism and was building *châteaux de plaisance* on the Loire and throughout France, Berenger stubbornly went on with his fortress, until in 1520 he had completed the last feudal castle built in France. It was a masterpiece of military architecture, presenting difficult angles to all possible lines of cannon fire, with an inexhaustible water supply and enormous storage capacity for food, powder and weapons – and it was always fully garrisoned.

Yet it was all in vain, for there was never an attack, never a siege, never a blow struck with military intent at Bonaguil. The Lord of Bonaguil waited and waited to prove his point, living on to eighty-two, despite his weakly constitution, before dying within its walls. It was not until the Revolution that the castle was partly dismantled, and it stands today a monument to the vindictive spirit of one man, but is also a magnificently impressive ruin. How Turner would have loved to paint it!

The castle, which now belongs to the municipality of Fumel, is open to the public, and from 1 June to 31 August there are guided tours (some in English) at 10.00 and 11.00 in the morning, and at 3.00, 4.00, 5.00 and 6.00 in the afternoon. Musical evenings at Bonaguil during the summer season attract high-level international performers. Details can be obtained from the *Syndicat d'Initiative*, Pl. G-Escande, 47500 Fumel, tel. (53) 71 13 70.

Where to eat

Restaurant Les Bons Enfants, Bonaguil, 47500 Fumel, tel. (53) 71 23 52, is pleasantly situated below the castle, offering good regional food at moderate prices.

Le Cellier, Bonaguil, 47500 Fumel, tel. (53) 71 23 50, at the entry to the village, offers menus from 50 fr (70 fr on Sundays). A little less 'atmosphere' but good food.

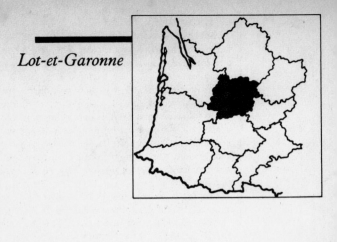

Lot-et-Garonne

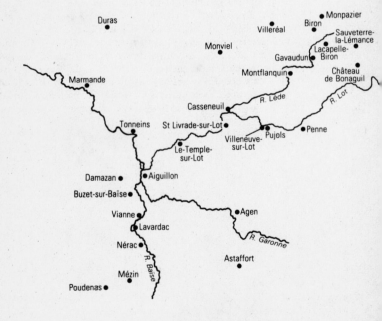

Duras

Monpazier

Villeréal Biron

Sauveterre-la-Lémance

Monviel

Lacapelle-Biron

Gavaudun

Montflanquin

Château de Bonaguil

Marmande

R. Lède

R. Lot

Casseneuil

Tonneins

St Livrade-sur-Lot

Penne

Villeneuve-sur-Lot Pujols

Le-Temple-sur-Lot

Damazan Aiguillon

Buzet-sur-Baïse

Agen

Vianne

Lavardac

R. Garonne

Nérac

Astaffort

Mézin

R. Baïse

Poudenas

Lot-et-Garonne

Introduction

At Bonaguil you are in the department of Lot-et-Garonne, named after the two great rivers that water it. Away from their broad valleys, intensely cultivated and carrying the main roads, this department is inexhaustible in its variety and charm. It has often been called the Tuscany of France since the great French writer, Stendhal, first described it in this way, no doubt thinking of its golden summer light, the red-roofed farms, the hilltop villages and castles, the chestnut woods, cypresses and tall poplars that are to be seen everywhere in the landscape.

It is a symphonic countryside in which the same themes and the same notes recur, ingeniously varied but always harmonious – vineyards and orchards, fields of corn and tobacco, leafy woods and pine forests, green and secret valleys, rolling hills crowned here and there with *bastide* villages. Its seductive charm leads you on from one little valley to another, each with its own inviting river or lake, a wooded hillside, an old church or stone-built manor, each different but with a family resemblance.

Bonaguil is a good place to begin a tour of the *bastide* villages in the north of the department and those just across the border in southern Dordogne.

Monpazier

Follow the road north from Bonaguil to Sauveterre-la-Lémance where you join the D710; continue north on this road, ignoring a right fork to Villefranche du Périgord, but after a further 5 km take the road to the left, the D660, signposted Monpazier.

Construction of *Bastides* The village is a *bastide*, another form of the word *bastille*, originally signifying an outlying fort which defended the approaches to a town. *Bastides* like Monpazier came into existence as villages all at once, each one being founded, built and inhabited within a year.

It was Alphonse de Poitiers, brother of King Louis IX (St Louis), who first thought of them. Through his marriage to the heiress of the Count of Toulouse, he became overlord of a large part of Aquitaine,

137

but when he drew up his inventory he found that all he had was an empty title, for every place of importance was already in the hands of a lord who paid him homage, but gave nothing else.

New rights

So he decided to provide himself with what he lacked, and in 1253 he founded Villeneuve-sur-Lot (to the west of Cahors) and Villefranche de Rouergue (to the east). People were encouraged to come and live in the *bastides* by being given the right of self-government and new freedoms which feudalism had not permitted. They were allowed to elect their own councillors; they were given a free flour mill and a free oven, so that they could make their own flour and bake their own bread without having to pay a tax to a lord; they could marry their daughters to whom they wished, and dispose of their property as they chose. In addition they were excused many taxes, and although guaranteed protection by their lord, they were not obliged to do military service.

When it was quickly realised that the construction of the *bastides* had important economic, military and political advantages, other powerful lords, including the King of France, and the King of England – who was also Duke of Aquitaine – promptly followed the example set by Alphonse de Poitiers.

Structure

Monpazier, which was founded in 1289 by Edward I of England, Duke of Aquitaine, has survived almost unchanged from the Middle Ages and is a classic example of a *bastide*. It is a parallelogram, 400 m long by 220 m wide, with two pairs of main streets of equal width at right angles to each other, dividing the town into eight blocks around a central square, which was kept as a market and meeting place. The square is surrounded by a covered arcade wide enough – 8 m – to allow carts to pass. Parallel to the main streets are narrower streets, all of the same width. All the houses were the same size – 8 m wide by 20 m deep – and were separated from each other by a narrow space, which served in theory as a fire-break and in practice as a rubbish dump. There was always a church in the centre of the *bastide* close to the market place.

The repetitious architecture and uniformity must have made the *bastides* dull and boring but, scarred by the passage of time, ruined and rebuilt here and there in individual fashion, with different roof lines, varying doors and windows, they have become today very picturesque – and none more so than Monpazier.

History

Most of the later *bastides* were built on heights and played an important part in the Hundred Years War. Monpazier, founded by the English, was captured by the French in 1312, retaken by the English in 1316, again taken by the French in 1327, recaptured by the English in 1347, taken back by the French in 1360, and handed to the English under the Treaty of Brétigny shortly afterwards.

Monpazier's troubles continued during the Wars of Religion when it was taken by the Protestant captain, Geoffroi de Vivans.

In 1637 there was a peasant revolt when 8,000 people banded

together to ravage the countryside and plunder the castles. They were led by a weaver named Buffarot, who was eventually captured, taken to Monpazier, and broken on the wheel in the main square.

It is astonishing that a place with such a violent and chequered history should have survived almost unchanged into the present century. Today it is a quiet and charming village, disturbed only twice a year during the spring and autumn mushroom markets, for which Monpazier is now famous and which bring restaurateurs from all over France.

Where to stay   **Hôtel de France**, 24540 Monpazier, tel. (53) 61 60 06, is a typical French small country town hotel in an old house near the main square. It has ten bedrooms and a sound but undistinguished restaurant, at moderate prices.

Biron

History   From Monpazier take the D2 towards Villeréal, but turn off after 5 km on to the D53 to the château and village of Biron. This great castle was built between the twelfth and seventeenth centuries by fourteen generations of the Gontaut-Biron family, the premier barons of Périgord. Whenever fortune favoured them, they added something to their stronghold, so that there are now fifteen different buildings joined to each other around courtyards and galleries, with a profusion of towers, keeps, turrets, gables, Gothic arches and crenellations, Renaissance windows and doorways, all of which are outdone by the unique chapel. This remarkable building owes its conception to the unmatched self-importance of the Gontaut-Birons who were both big- and pig-headed. Deciding that they must have their own private place of worship, they built it on top of the existing parish church, so that there are two naves – the upper one for the family, reached from the castle courtyard, and the lower one at the level of the village street, used as the parish church.

The Castle of Biron is on a height and dominates the surrounding countryside over a radius of 30 km, offering an impressive panorama. Not long after the first fortress was built it was captured, in 1211, by Captain Algais, a mercenary fighting for the Albigensians. A year later it was retaken by the first Simon de Montfort, which was bad luck for Algais, who had been one of de Montfort's men but sold his services to the other side. De Montfort had him tied to the tail of a horse and driven over the stony land until he was torn to pieces.

Biron changed hands often during the Hundred Years War but came back to the Gontaut-Birons in 1451. Another treacherous episode in its history occurred in the seventeenth century, at the time of Charles de Gontaut-Biron, a friend of Henri IV who received many favours, being made first an admiral and then a marshal of France. When in 1598 he was created a duke, put in charge of the French army and made Governor of Burgundy, he repaid these favours by launching a plot which would have broken up France and given him a kingdom of his own. His treachery was discovered and Henri IV generously pardoned him, but de Gontaut-Biron was not repentant, continuing to plot and again being exposed. Henri IV again promised to pardon him if he would confess his crime. However, true to the nature of his family he proudly and stubbornly refused and, there being a limit to Henri's indulgence, de Gontaut-Biron was executed in the Bastille in 1602.

Visiting the castle

The castle, owned by the de Gontaut-Biron family for nearly 800 years, is now the property of the department of Dordogne and is being slowly restored. It is open daily throughout the year (except 15 December to 1 February) morning and afternoon, Tuesdays excepted, and every day from 1 July to 7 September. Among the many things in the interior worth seeing are the largest **vaulted kitchens** in France.

Excursions Lacapelle-Biron

From Biron take the road south to Lacapelle-Biron, a village which owes its existence to the fact that an eighteenth-century Marquis of Biron found the noise of the market held beneath the castle walls more than he could bear, and ordered the stallholders to move further away. They chose the site which has become Lacapelle-Biron.

Where to eat

Restaurant Chez André, Lacapelle-Biron, 47150 Monflanquin, tel. (53) 71 64 50, is a nice country restaurant where the owner/chef specialises in good regional food at moderate prices.

Gavaudun

Carry on south on the D150 through the very picturesque Valley of the Lède to Gavaudun, a once-fortified village of which the **old gateway** remains, with the **great keep** of the ruined castle high on the cliff above it. Just inside the gateway there is a café restaurant, which is a good place to stop for coffee or a light meal.

Monflanquin

From Gavaudun the D150 carries on to Monflanquin, another *bastide* village sited on a conical hill and visible for miles around. It was founded by Alphonse de Poitiers in 1256, and has a **central square** on the slope of the hill. Still with all its arcades, the square is surrounded by fine medieval houses, now well restored. The **church** at the top of the hill is in southern Gothic style. The nave and the choir, destroyed during the Wars of Religion, were rebuilt in 1673, and the fifteenth-century fortified façade has also been renovated. Near the church there is a square with a terrace giving extensive views to the east, where the Château of Biron can be picked out easily.

Where to stay and eat

Hôtel Restaurant La Tonnelle, Place Foirail, 47150 Monflanquin, tel. (53) 36 40 16, is a modest hotel with twenty rooms at very reasonable prices, and a good restaurant specialising in regional recipes.

Auberge Le Bossu, 47150 Monflanquin, tel. (53) 36 40 61, is 2 km outside Monflanquin on the D253, the road to Savignac-sur-Leyze. A small but very good regional restaurant, where it is advisable to book in advance. Menus from 60 fr to 150 fr. Closed on Sunday evenings and Mondays. The inn also has seven bedrooms.

Villeneuve-sur-Lot

Background

This small town has the distinction of being the first *bastide* and therefore the first place in Europe to sever the chains of feudalism. While most of the later *bastides* were built on heights, this first one was built in the valley and on both sides of the river. The original fortifications, of which only two of the gates remain – the **Porte de Paris** and the **Porte de Pujols** – formed a rough circle cut in half by the River Lot and joined by a fortified bridge with three towers, similar to the Pont Valentre at Cahors. Unfortunately, two of the towers and two of the four arches of the bridge collapsed. It was rebuilt without towers and with one arch replacing the two that had fallen, so that it now presents an odd asymmetrical appearance.

Villeneuve is encircled by gently sloping hills, crested with woods and with orchards, farm fields and vineyards on the lower slopes. It is an important fruit and vegetable centre, whose orchards produce most of the plums to make the prunes known throughout France as *prunes d'Agen*.

Villeneuve is now a town of about 35,000 people, with the old *bastide*, most of which is on the north side of the river, now a pedestrian shopping area. The market is still held (Tuesday and Saturday mornings) in the old central square, the Place Lafayette, which has kept its arcades and has an attractive fountain in the middle. It is surrounded by old houses, some of them timbered and most of them restored during the seventeenth and eighteenth centuries. One of the oldest houses, just off the square, is the **Maison de Viguerie**, an old court house dating from 1369.

The church

The town has an unusual church, the **Église St Catherine**, which would stand a fair chance in any competition for the ugliest modern church in Europe. It was built at the turn of the century in bright red brick in a style which has been described variously as Romanesque-Byzantine and Neo-Greek-Gothic. In other words nobody is quite sure what it is. But although the exterior is unprepossessing, the stained-glass windows from the old Gothic church which it replaced were saved and built into the new church, so that it has a set of twenty-three fifteenth- and sixteenth-century stained-glass windows, unmatched anywhere else in Aquitaine.

The building of this church was arranged by Villeneuve's most distinguished citizen, Georges Leygues, who became a member of the French Assembly in 1882 when he was twenty-eight, and remained in

Parliament for more than fifty years until his death in 1933. He was several times a government minister, and as Minister of the Marine, was responsible for the rebuilding of the French navy, which in 1939 was one of the most modern in the world.

Villeneuve, with its shady squares, flower gardens and café terraces, is an attractive town but one which, until recently, has taken little interest in tourism, though a few Dutch and British visitors have discovered it. However, thanks to the enterprise of a few of its influential **Leisure** citizens it now has a **golf and holiday complex** in the hills about 10 km north of the town at Castelnaud de Gratecambe. There are eighteen- and nine-hole courses and a practice range, set in lovely countryside. There is also a new hotel (see page 143), a good restaurant and forty-eight holiday flats.

Excursions A few kilometres to the east of Villeneuve lies the village of Penne, **Penne** which is easily recognised by the **modern basilica** on top of its 150 m height, although Penne is, in fact, an old village, chosen by Richard the Lionheart as a key strongpoint in the Lot Valley. Vestiges of his **castle** and **fortifications** remain, as well as a number of old houses which have seen a violent past, for it was the scene of massacres and so much carnage that it was known as *Penne la sanglante* – Bloody Penne. Now restored, it is a centre for potters, glassblowers and other artisans. It is worth making the climb from the village, past the basilica, Notre Dame de Peyrehugade, to the highest point where there is a tremendous view of the Lot Valley and far to the north.

Casseneuil Ten km to the north-west of Villeneuve by the D242 is the interesting old village of Casseneuil, situated at the confluence of the Lot and the Lède, where a Celtic town stood before the Romans arrived and made it their area capital. Some authorities claim that Charlemagne, liking Casseneuil, built a summer palace in which his son Louis and his daughter Radegonde were born, but no trace of it remains. The village is a maze of narrow streets and alleys, with many timbered medieval houses. Those backing on to the River Lède make an attractive picture from the opposite bank. The **church** has some unusual features including a triple nave and an octagonal tower, with some Romanesque and Gothic capitals and a restored sixteenth-century doorway.

Where to Villeneuve-sur-Lot is rather lacking in good hotel accommodation, **stay** although there are several good hotels in the surrounding countryside.

Hôtel La Residence, 17 Avenue Lazare-Carnot, 47300 *Villeneuve* Villeneuve-sur-Lot, tel. (53) 40 17 03, has eighteen bedrooms and is quietly situated. Unpretentious but comfortable, it has changed hands recently and the moderate prices are a little higher than those quoted in the current Red Michelin. No restaurant.

Hôtel Les Platanes, 40 Blvd de la Marine, 47300 Villeneuve-sur-Lot, tel. (53) 40 11 40, has twenty-one bedrooms at moderate prices.

Grand Hôtel du Parc, 13 Blvd de la Marine, tel. (53) 70 01 68, has forty bedrooms at middle-of-the-range prices. It is part of the Mapotel group.

Outside Villeneuve

Auberge La Résidence, Route de Villeneuve, 47440 Casseneuil, tel. (53) 41 08 08, is a straightforward village hotel with twelve bedrooms at reasonable prices. It has a good regional restaurant with menus from 50 fr, where meals can be taken outside on a shady terrace.

Hôtel Les Chênes, Pujols, 47300 Villeneuve-sur-Lot, tel. (53) 49 04 55, is a comfortable modern hotel with twenty bedrooms and a swimming pool, just outside the picturesque old village of Pujols, 4 km south of Villeneuve.

Golf Hôtel du Périgord Agenais, La Menuisière, Castelnaud de Gratecambe, 47290 Cancon, tel. (53) 01 60 19, is near Castelnaud de Gratecambe, 9 km along the N21 north of Villeneuve, on the edge of the golf course. It has forty bedrooms and a high degree of comfort, with a first-class restaurant. Middle of range for price.

Where to eat

Restaurant Du Parc, tel. (53) 70 07 64, is in the same building as Hôtel du Parc (p. 142) but under different management. It is an efficient restaurant which maintains high standards at fair prices.

La Toque Blanche, Pujols, 47300 Villeneuve-sur-Lot, tel. (53) 49 00 30, is next door to the Hôtel des Chênes (above). The reception does not match the very high standard of cooking and presentation. One Michelin star. Menus start at 95 fr, 160 fr on Sundays.

Auberge Lou Calell, Pujols, 47300 Villeneuve-sur-Lot, tel. (53) 70 46 14, was recently acquired by Monsieur Lebrun, the chef/owner of La Toque Blanche (above). The dining room has fine views over the Valley of the Lot and Villeneuve. It is simpler and slightly cheaper than its sister restaurant.

Hostellerie De La Source, Route de Bordeaux, 47110 St Livrade-sur-Lot, tel. (53) 01 04 64, lies on the main Bordeaux road (D911) between St Livrade-sur-Lot and Le Temple-sur-Lot. Menus from 65 fr, with average cuisine, but worth making the short journey on fine summer evenings for the pleasure of dining on a terrace above the Lot with fine views in both directions.

Agen

The *préfecture* of Lot-et-Garonne, about 30 km south of Villeneuve and situated on the Garonne halfway between Bordeaux and Toulouse, is the main business and trade centre of the mid-Garonne.

History

According to legend, the city was founded by a friend of Hercules fifty years before the outbreak of the Trojan War, that is to say about 1200 BC. It is just as likely that it was founded a few years after the Trojan War, as another legend says some remnants of the Trojans made their way to Britain, which they found inhabited by only a few giants, and where they founded the city which became London. They might well have passed up the Garonne Valley on the way, and a few may have stayed behind to found Agen. There was certainly a town here long before the Romans arrived and made it their capital of the mid-Garonne area.

Agen is a prosperous modern town which has retained little evidence of its long past; there can be few people in its streets today who have heard the legend of its foundation and fewer still who believe it. They are more interested in rugby football and their team, which has several times won the French championship.

What to see

Pleasant as it is, Agen is not a town which need detain the tourist long. Its **Cathedral**, St Caprais, is of limited interest compared with most other French cathedrals. On the other hand, the **Agen Museum** is of above average interest and well worth a visit. It occupies four splendid sixteenth- and seventeenth-century mansions, which have been restored and are now intercommunicating. The most important single item is a lovely marble statue from the first century BC, known as the **Venus de Mas** because it was found in the last century in a farm field near the small town of Mas d'Agen. The statue, which has lost the head and one arm, is more girlish than the Venus de Milo but is sculpted with equal mastery. There is another Venus, with the body made in alabaster and the head in marble, which is said to represent an empress of the second century AD. It was found at Tayac not far from Agen. Among many other interesting exhibits there are some notable paintings, including five Goyas and works by Corot, Courbet, Boudin, Watteau and Sisley.

Where to stay

Agen itself has a number of not-very-large and not-very-exciting hotels.

Hôtel Ibis, 105 Blvd Carnot, Agen 47000, tel. (53) 47 31 23, is one of the large modern chain, with thirty-eight bedrooms at average prices. The restaurant, as is usual in Ibis hotels, offers a limited but inexpensive menu.

Hôtel Restaurant La Corne d'Or, 47450 Colayrac St Cirq, tel. (53) 47 02 76, on the edge of town on the Bordeaux road, has fourteen average-price rooms and a good restaurant with menus starting at 90 fr (50 fr for children).

Château St Marcel, Boé, Agen 47240, tel. (53) 96 61 30, is about 3 km from the centre of Agen on the N113, the Toulouse road. Recently renovated by a new proprietor, it is now a rather expensive hotel with a good restaurant.

Château St Philippe, St Nicholas de la Balerme, 47220 Astaffort, tel. (53) 87 31 73. Follow the N113 for about 12 km south-east of Agen and turn right on to the D114. A fifteenth-century manor restored and extended during the nineteenth century and recently redecorated, it is set in spacious grounds with garden and terrace beside the Garonne, achieving luxury without ostentation. It has well-furnished bed-rooms, some with four-poster beds. The restaurant is difficult to fault, with superb food, charming and efficient service. Menus from 100 fr. Rooms are expensive but not excessively so.

Where to eat

L'Ours Blanc, 14 Rue Cailles, Agen 47000, tel. (53) 66 14 93, near to Agen's daily covered market (in itself worth looking at for gourmets – the fishmongers' stalls are works of art). This is a typical market res-taurant where the business of the day is serious eating, with generous portions of well-prepared regional dishes at bargain prices.

L'Absinthe, 29 bis Rue Voltaire, Agen 47000, tel. (53) 66 16 94, is not easy to find – just off the Blvd de la République on the left as you approach the river. A gastronomic restaurant they claim, and on the whole they may be right. Prices are above average.

Hostellerie De La Rigalette, Vallon de Vérone, Agen 47000, tel. (53) 47 37 44, is about 2 km from Agen – take the Bordeaux road and turn right on the D302 signposted Villeneuve-sur-Lot. The restaurant is good but rather expensive, with menus from 125 fr. There are also seven moderately priced bedrooms, recently decorated.

Nérac

Thirty km west of Agen by the D656, Nérac is today a quiet little town with a glorious past of great significance in the history of France. It lies on the banks of the River Baïse (pronounced By-ease), at the limits of the Agenais and the pine forests of the Landes and close to the Armagnac country.

History

It was the seat of the D'Albret family, Gascon princes who, with grim determination, constantly increased the size of their domains, and who by inheritance became Kings of Navarre, although most of Navarre lay on the other side of the Pyrenees and they soon lost that part to the King of Spain.

Marguerite D'Angoulême

In the sixteenth century, Marguerite D'Angoulême, sister of the King of France, married Henri, King of Navarre. As Queen she wel-comed philosophers, poets and religious reformers, including Jean Calvin to the court, which became an important source of Protestant thought and action. Marguerite de Navarre was herself an accom-plished writer and is still remembered for her *Heptameron*, a book of seventy-two short stories, gathered when a royal party told each other stories to pass the time, while they were trapped by swollen rivers and broken bridges in a remote Pyrenean abbey.

Her daughter, Jeanne D'Albret, was an active and indomitable Protestant, as a result of whose efforts the whole of Béarn and most of the Agenais became Protestant. She and her husband, Antoine de Bourbon, made their home in their Renaissance château at Nérac, and at the older castle in Pau. Their son, Henri, was born at Pau, but spent most of his youth at Nérac, making war on Catholics and making love to any woman he could lay his hands on. In 1572 he married Marguerite de Valois, daughter of Catherine de Médici and sister of the King of France.

Henri, the first Bourbon king

He was thus heir to the throne when Henri III, Catherine de Médici's youngest and childless son, was assassinated in 1589. He overcame the strong Catholic opposition by the simple expedient of abandoning Protestantism and becoming a Catholic, saying, in effect, that the crown of France was well worth the change.

So this rustic Gascon, whose wife described him as a 'peasant', complaining that he smelled – which was undoubtedly true, as he himself was proud of saying that he took a bath only once a year – became the first of the Bourbon line, which was to rule France until the Revolution and again after it. His personal bravery as a soldier, his relentless gallantry and his concern for ordinary people endeared him to the masses and made him the most well-loved of all France's kings. When you see a restaurant – and they exist in many parts of the world – called *La Poule au Pot*, it is a reminder of Henri IV's declaration that he wanted to see a chicken in the pot for everyone on Sundays. In Gascony, they still call him affectionately 'our Henri'.

Marguerite De Valois

His wife, Marguerite De Valois, who is still warmly remembered as Queen Margot, was the most beautiful and the best-loved of all France's queens. She was as famous for her love affairs as he was for his, but, human nature being what it is, they could not abide each other. Margot was a cultured woman who spoke Spanish, Italian and Latin as well as French, wrote poetry, and liked to surround herself with men who had no objection to regular close acquaintance with soap and water.

Queen Margot was also brave and daring. She once rode five days and nights, sleeping where she found shelter, to escape Henri's soldiers, who had been ordered to bring her home after she had let a weekend in pleasant company in Agen drag on for three months. She was a lovable character and when, from time to time, her amorous inclinations led to her being placed under house arrest in remote castles, there were always men ready to give their lives to help her escape, or who were happy to share her imprisonment. No wonder Alexandre Dumas wrote a 'cloak and dagger' novel about her life.

What to see

Of the square **Renaissance château**, where Henri IV spent much of his youth and the first years of this first marriage, only the north side remains. It has been restored and now houses the town's **museum**. Most of the old town is on the opposite side of the river, its narrow streets still containing a number of sixteenth- and seventeenth-century houses. On this bank of the Baïse there is also an attractive park with several fountains, called **La Garenne**, which was laid out by Henri's father, Antoine de Bourbon. Next to the

Fontaine St Jean there is a sculpture representing *Fleurette Noyée* – Drowned Fleurette – which recalls an old story that Fleurette, daughter of the King of Navarre's gardener and Henri's first love, drowned herself in despair when she was abandoned by him.

In modern Nérac it is somehow easier to believe this old legend than it is to accept that it was here, in this quiet little town of farmers and fruit growers, that the bloody and bitter struggle between Catholics and Protestants was engendered. The Wars of Religion tore the whole of France apart, starting in 1562, and finishing in 1598 when Henri signed the Edict of Nantes, bringing to an end, at least temporarily, what his mother had been instrumental in starting.

Where to eat

There is a restaurant in the main street almost opposite the château but it is of little interest.

Restaurant D'Albret, 42 Allée D'Albret, tel. (53) 65 01 47, is a representative provincial restaurant, with good cooking at reasonable prices.

Poudenas

Anyone looking for a lunch to remember should make the short drive to Poudenas to one of the best restaurants in Gascony. Follow the D656 from Nérac to **Mézin**, a red-roofed village almost Provençale in aspect, with the distinction of being the birthplace of Armand Fallières, the only Lot-et-Garonnais ever to be President of France (1906–13). Continue on the D656 to Poudenas.

This is a delightful old village on the banks of the Gélise. Until recently it consisted of an Italianate château, a village street, a row of galleried houses, two restaurants and a ruined mill. But the owner/chef of La Belle Gasconne, a restaurant well-known all over Gascony, bought the mill and has converted it into a tiny but luxurious hotel (same address and telephone number as the restaurant). It has only six bedrooms, each with bathroom *en suite*. The original flour-mill machinery has been retained, the sluices and the fabric of the mill have been restored, and huge picture windows look out directly on to the mill pond and the ancient stone bridge of the village. The mill race still passes in a hush (double glazing) beneath the building which has, as its garden and park, a green and shady island in the Gélise. It is an altogether delightful place worthy of the reputation of its restaurant.

La Belle Gasconne, Poudenas, Mézin 47170, tel. (53) 65 71 58, is a small restaurant, much in demand in summer, so it is advisable to book in advance. The dining room is charming and the welcome is warm. Madame Gracia's talent is always to treat the rich raw materials of the region, which in the wrong hands can make heavy meals, with incredible lightness and often with originality. Menus are from 115 fr to 210 fr. Good as they are, the desserts *à la carte* are overpriced.

The **Château de Poudenas** is open to the public every day from 3 p.m. to 6 p.m. including Sundays. It produces the local sweet aperitif called Floc de Gascogne, made from Armagnac and grape juice, which can be tasted and bought on the premises.

Vianne   From Poudenas return to Mézin on the D656, continuing until the road forks – right for Nérac, left for Lavardac. Keep left on the D408, which is a very pretty road through the Valley of the Gélise. At Lavardac turn left on to the D642 to Vianne. This 1,000-year-old village has retained its walls and its two turreted gateways, and has a thirteenth-century church, renovated in the fourteenth and sixteenth centuries. If, by chance, you have not had lunch, you will find in the small central square a rather tatty-looking restaurant where you can have a far-from-tatty meal at almost medieval prices. It is the **Bar Au Relais**, Place des Maronniers, Vianne 47230, tel. (53) 97 57 18.

From Vianne it is a few kilometres to Damazan, where you can join the autoroute for Bordeaux and its vineyards.

Wine   However, those really interested in wine may like to take a longer route across country which crosses some of the excellent vineyards of Lot-et-Garonne. Only a few kilometres from Vianne is Buzet-sur-

Buzet-sur- Baïse, which produces good red wines similar to those of the Médoc.
Baïse   There is a well-organised cooperative, which offers interesting guided tours of the wine museum and cellars on Tuesday and Thursday mornings in the summer season. The best of the Buzet wines is Château de Gueyze, which in good years compares with the lesser classified growths of Bordeaux.

Duras   Further north in Lot-et-Garonne, by way of Aiguillon, Tonneins and Marmande, on the N113 and D708, the little town of Duras is the centre of another area producing some good *Appellation Contrôlée* reds and some even better dry whites from the Sauvignon grape. Of a number of good wines, Château de Boussinet and Domaine de Durand have been produced at St Jean de Duras for 300 years. (Tasting daily: tel. [53] 89 02 04.)

From Duras, carry on north by the D708 to Ste Foy la Grande, where you can join the D936 for Bordeaux.

Country holidays

The department of Lot-et-Garonne with its lovely and fertile countryside is the perfect area for a country holiday with the full flavour of France. There is a great variety of things to do and places to see, as and when you want to, without pressure or obligation. There are scores of country cottages (*gîtes ruraux*) to let in summer, many on working farms. Numerous facilities exist for fishing, boating, canoeing, cycling, riding and walking (there are 800 km of signposted footpaths for horse-riding and walking, including the GR652, which was one of the old pilgrim routes to St James of Compostella).

Anyone who draws or paints or takes a keen interest in photography will find an endless variety of subjects. If you are staying in a farm cottage in late September, you may well find yourself invited to give a hand with the grape harvest, an occasion which collects together relatives and friends of the farmer on the old principle that many hands make light work. Afterwards you may be asked to join in the *vendaison* lunch in the farm kitchen or on trestle tables outside. There are still many farms and vineyards where this old tradition is maintained.

As a change from the leisure activities mentioned above and many others, there are many *bastide* villages, castles and old churches to visit, and small country towns where the markets are a delight. In summer you are always within easy reach of a good music festival, or events like the international folk dance festival held every year in Casseneuil, which brings groups of dancers from the five continents to this ancient town.

It is a place for individual holidays where you will occasionally see other tourists in the restaurants or on the café terraces in the small towns, but they, like you, will be almost unnoticed in the stream of local life.

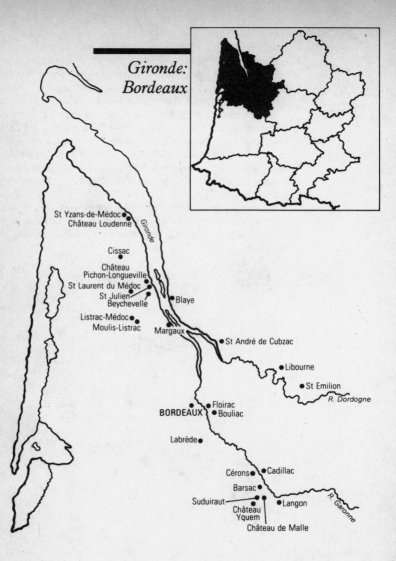

Gironde:
Bordeaux

St Yzans-de-Médoc
Château Loudenne

Gironde

Cissac

Château
Pichon-Longueville
St Laurent du Médoc
St Julien-
Beychevelle ● Blaye

Listrac-Médoc
Moulis-Listrac
Margaux

● St André de Cubzac

● Libourne

● St Emilion
R. Dordogne

Floirac
BORDEAUX ● Bouliac

Labrède●

Cérons ● Cadillac

Barsac ●
Suduiraut ● *R. Garonne*
Château ● Langon
Yquem
Château de Malle

Gironde: Bordeaux

Introduction

Named after the estuary, 75 km long and up to 10 km wide, which is formed by the meeting of the Rivers Dordogne and Garonne, Gironde is the largest department in France. Though not a scenic wonderland, it has a coastline with enormous sandy beaches, and also includes the charming countryside of Entre Deux Mers, between the two great rivers. This is a landscape of gentle hills, rarely more than a hundred metres in height, shared between oak and chestnut woods and the neat, lineal patterns of vineyards. From the central backbone, many streams run either north to the Dordogne, or south to the Garonne.

From the sea inland the southern part of the department is covered by pine forest, which stretches further south through the Landes and contains a number of large lakes near the ocean coast. Gironde also includes the triangular peninsular of Médoc, bordered on its western side by more pine forests and the ocean, and sloping on its north-eastern flank towards the river in plain, uninviting country. However, it is just right for producing the finest red wines in the world.

It is these wines which for hundreds of years have brought visitors to Gironde and to the Bordeaux region in particular.

Bordeaux

History
The Romans
The history of Gironde is the history of Bordeaux. Originally, 300 years or more before Christ, it was a little Celtic port which traded with the Phoenicians, but under the Romans, who called it Burdigala, Bordeaux became prosperous, for it was during the Roman occupation that wine was first produced in the Bordeaux region.

An English town
There is no doubt that its position would have made Bordeaux an important port in any circumstances, but its prosperity was very much enhanced by the marriage in 1152 of Eleanor of Aquitaine to

Henry Plantagenet, who became Henry II, King of England. As a result of this alliance, Bordeaux became an English town, remaining so until the end of the Hundred Years War in 1453. During this long period Bordeaux thrived on its steadily increasing commerce with London, based on the wine trade.

When Bordeaux ceased to be English, its commercial life declined, but the city continued to grow, becoming a place of dirty, tortuous streets, cramped in by its fortifications and surrounded by insanitary marshes.

Montaigne

In 1581, Montaigne, known to posterity as an essayist, was appointed Mayor of Bordeaux. He did the job well, succeeding in pacifying the rival religious factions in the city; but when in June 1585 there was an outbreak of plague, Montaigne judged it prudent to remain in his castle in the country until the danger was over. This conduct tarnished his reputation.

Despite outbreaks of plague and worsening conditions, no improvements were made for over a hundred years, until in the eighteenth century a succession of competent governors transformed Bordeaux.

Boucher

The work was begun by Claude Boucher, governor from 1720 to 1743. At first he made himself very unpopular with the Bordeaux wine merchants and with Montesquieu, who was not only a famous writer but also President of the Bordeaux Parliament and a vineyard owner. Boucher tried to put through a law obliging owners to uproot most of their vines, because he was afraid that the great expansion in the planting of vines at the expense of other crops would lead to economic imbalance and perhaps starvation in bad years. Fortunately for Bordeaux, no such law was ever enforced.

Though he had little faith in Bordeaux's commerce in wine, Boucher did have the energy and vision to demolish the worst parts of the city and start again. The work was continued by Louis Urbain Aubert, Marquis de Tourny and governor from 1743 to 1757, and by his successor, Dupré de St Maur.

Eighteenth century

The Marquis de Tourny did for Bordeaux what Baron Haussmann was to do for Paris a hundred years later, bringing light and air into a dirty, crowded city by laying out wide avenues and spacious squares. Today the old part of Bordeaux between the Chartrons and the St Michel quarter has more than 5,000 eighteenth-century buildings, many of which have been restored in the past few years.

It was during this eighteenth-century rebuilding that Bordeaux was given its splendid façade along the Garonne, including the Place de la Bourse. In the same period the 'magic triangle' of the Allées de Tourny, the Cours Clemenceau and the Cours de l'Intendance was laid out, as well as the stately Cours du Chapeau Rouge, the Place de Tourny and the Place Dauphine (since renamed the Place Gambetta).

It was a mark of Tourny's genius that, in addition to providing Bordeaux with one of the finest riverside façades of any European city, he also created a public garden, saying, 'In a commercial city one should regard a public garden as extremely useful. Businessmen will often meet each other there, and in conversation many deals will be done. It will be a second stock exchange . . .' He was careful to place it close to the port and the offices of the leading wine merchants.

In those days a *negociant* would live on the site of his business. Their houses were built with the offices on the ground floor, splendid reception rooms on the first, bedrooms on the second, and domestic quarters on the third floor. The *chais* or wine cellars were placed behind the house. The chief area where the merchants lived, near the Quai des Chartrons, is today one of Bordeaux's smart residential areas, most of the merchants' houses having been converted into comfortable flats.

Prosperity

In the second half of the eighteenth century, Bordeaux enjoyed great prosperity, the trade in sugar and slaves with the West Indies having been added to the exports of wine. It became the most important port in France, such affluence giving rise to more improvements to the city, notably the building of the Grand Théâtre, which was opened in 1780.

Decline

In 1789 the Revolution put an end to the golden age of Bordeaux. The city's economy was further ruined by blockades during the Napoleonic Wars, and it was not until the restoration of the Bourbons in 1815 that recovery began. In this period the first bridge across the Garonne, the Pont de Pierre, was built, and the Esplanade des Quinconces, the largest square in Europe, covering 12 hectares, was laid out.

Nineteenth century

During the whole of the nineteenth century, work had been carried out on securing the sand dunes of the Landes, and planting pine forest on what had been barren land. In the second half of the century the drainage of huge areas of the Landes was undertaken, getting rid of unhealthy swamps and enabling the forest to be further extended. As a result the Landes changed from being one of the poorest departments in France to one that was made rich from the export of wood and resin. This new prosperity benefited Bordeaux, the nearest city, which continued to expand and increase its economic importance.

The prosperity of Bordeaux was built on wine, which is still the most important factor in its commerce. However, the cultivation of the vine is a form of farming, and like all farming it is subject to ups and downs. Almost every year in the 1930s was a bad one for Bordeaux wine, and times became so depressed that just prior to the Second World War many of the wine estates were sold.

Recent development

After the war things changed in Bordeaux. Under the leadership of its go-ahead Mayor, Jacques Chaban Delmas, new industries were set up. In addition to the ever-present wine, the city now has important space and aviation industries, as well as electronic and automobile plants, food, clothing, construction, medical goods and paper-making factories. With this rapid expansion greatly increasing traffic to Bor-

153

deaux, a second bridge, the Pont St Jean, was opened in 1965. This was followed only two years later by the great suspension bridge, the Pont d'Aquitaine, which carries *autoroute* traffic between Bordeaux and the north of France.

In the same period the Bordeaux Lac complex was developed. This is a modern business section built in ideal conditions around a spacious lake with sailing and water sports facilities, together with a clutch of new hotels to suit every level of expense account from junior executive to international director level. All of it is within easy reach of the Pont d'Aquitaine and the *autoroute*. In the town centre the worst slums were torn down and replaced by another business, administrative and hotel section.

Bordeaux today

Bordeaux, with a population of 618,000 in the urban area, is now the eighth-largest town in France, but after the convulsions of the 1950s and 1960s it has almost ceased to grow, and has entered a difficult period. Although it is 98 km from the open sea, Bordeaux has always been a sea town, but in the past few years the activity of the port, like that of most of the other great ports of Europe, has been in sharp decline. In the 1950s, for example, all the wine exported from Bordeaux went by ship, while today almost every drop of it goes by road. As tankers become bigger, some of the oil refineries, which were constructed on the Gironde to the accompaniment of great fuss and opposition – because they were near some of the finest Médoc vineyards – have now moved away to Port Verdon at the mouth of the estuary, or they have been closed with even greater fuss – because of the loss of employment.

So Bordeaux is busy trying to find a way of compensating for the falling off of so much of its profitable sea trade. This is not a problem faced by Toulouse, the only other large town in the south-west, which is about the same size as Bordeaux and growing. It is not near the sea.

Unlike most major riverside cities, Bordeaux does not have, and has never had, any promenades or tree-lined walks beside the Garonne. For the Bordelais it is a strictly functional river to which they give hardly a glance except when crossing one of the bridges, or when actually involved in the dock trade. It is a fact that the Garonne adds little to the attractions of Bordeaux, apart from a sense of space. This is because the city is very one-sided, nine-tenths of it being on the west bank, with almost nothing to look at on the opposite side.

What to see
Parking the car

Bordeaux is one large town where parking is not usually a problem for the visitor. A large part of the Quinconces Esplanade is given over to parking, and there is a large multi-level underground car park beneath the Allées de Tourny. Both the Quinconces and the Allées de Tourny are within easy walking distance of most of the important points of interest in the city. (At the time of writing the famous Bordeaux market, normally in the Place des Grands Hommes, has been transferred to the nearby Allées de Tourny, where it will stay until the

154

BORDEAUX STREET MAP

PLACES OF INTEREST

1. Tourist Office
2. Grand Théâtre
3. Église St Pierre
4. Cathedral of St André
5. Town Hall
6. Museum of Fine Arts
7. Museum of Decorative Arts
8. Meriadeck Complex
9. Église St Michel
10. Girondins Monument
11. Porte d'Aquitaine
12. La Grosse Cloche

autumn of 1990, while another underground car park is built beneath its usual site.)

The Allées de Tourny run at one end into the Place de la Comédie, on the east side of which stands the **Grand Théâtre**. This is a building for which the word splendid is an understatement, if not miserly. Built in 1773–80, it is the best theatre in France, and one of the finest in the world.

The masterpiece of the architect Victor Louis, who also built the Théâtre Français in Paris, it faces the square with a Corinthian colonnade of twelve columns supporting a balcony, with statues of nine muses and three goddesses, one above each of the columns. Not surprisingly, the building suggests a miraculously preserved temple from the ancient world. The colonnade has a splendidly carved ceiling which, like the whole building, is beautifully illuminated at night.

The interior of the theatre is one of unrelenting boldness and luxury, from the magnificent staircase which mounts and then divides into two flights right and left – and which was imitated by Garnier when he designed the Paris Opera House nearly a century later – to the gilded pillars and carvings of the auditorium, its domed and painted ceiling, and the great crystal chandelier made up of 14,000 pieces of glass.

It is a short stroll from the theatre across the busy road junction to the **Rue St Catherine** and the old quarter of Bordeaux, the part that used to lie within the city walls.

Once the main street of Bordeaux running from one city gate to another (one of them, the Porte d'Aquitaine, still exists at the far end), the long Rue St Catherine is now a pedestrianised shopping street, always crowded. Its shops may not match the elegance of the Cours de l'Intendance or the Cours Clemenceau, as Oxford Street does not match Bond Street in London, and as Lexington Avenue does not match Fifth Avenue in New York, but this is where Mr and Mrs Everyman of Bordeaux do their shopping, especially for clothes. There is little in it now to make you think of it as an old street, but it was almost certainly laid out by the Romans, and if you take the third turning on the left, the Rue Parlement St Catherine, you soon find yourself in the **Place du Parlement** in the old town.

Over the past few years this conservation area has been systematically restored and is now one vast museum of eighteenth-century architecture. Modern café terraces blend well with the serenity of the old streets and squares, and the whole quarter has an atmosphere that will appeal to most people. Those interested in architecture will find dozens of buildings and hundreds of structural details worth noting. The **Église St Pierre** was largely rebuilt last century and is of no great interest.

From the Place St Pierre it is a short walk via the Place de la Bourse and the Cours du Chapeau Rouge back to the Allées de Tourny. If you want to see the Cathedral of St André, leave the Place St Pierre in the opposite direction by the Rue des Bahutiers (a *bahut* is a sideboard, and a *bahutier* the man who makes them), and then turn right into the **Rue du Loup**. This street, which has some good seventeenth- and eighteenth-century houses, crosses the Rue St Catherine and leads you to the Cathedral.

The Cathedral of St André is very large, almost as big as Notre Dame in Paris, but apart from that it is of only average interest, somewhere in the middle of the league as far as French cathedrals go. It was first built towards the end of the eleventh century, but was entirely rebuilt between the thirteenth and fifteenth centuries. During the Revolution it was used for storing cattle fodder.

There is a fine Gothic transept and choir, and on the north side there are two superbly carved doorways – the thirteenth-century Porte Royale, so called because it was the entrance used by several kings of France, and, on its left, the slightly later north door.

The bell tower, known as the **Tour Pey Berland** after the archbishop at the time when it was built in 1440, is separate from the Cathedral. This was to avoid putting too much weight in one place on the marshy ground. During the Revolution it was sold and converted into a tower for making lead shot, but it was bought back by the Church in 1850 and restored.

Next to the Cathedral is the Bordeaux **Town Hall**, the finest in France. Originally an episcopal palace, the Palais Rohan, it has been the Town Hall for the past 150 years, having been in succession an Imperial palace, the *préfecture*, and a Royal palace. It was built towards the end of the eighteenth century as the intended palace of Archbishop Ferdinand Maximilien de Meriadeck de Rohan Guemenée. He was a man as proud and pretentious as his name, and also extremely rich. He felt the existing Archbishop's residence was beneath his notice, so he ordered a new one, obtaining the king's permission to demolish part of the old town to make room for it.

He gave the architect detailed instructions of what the palace should contain: among many other things a library, a laboratory, a circular salon, an octagonal room and a courtyard large enough to entertain an entire regiment, as well as gardens and orangeries. He spent a great deal of money to ensure that he got what he wanted, but alas, life being what it is even for the great, he was appointed to the Archbishopric of Cambrai, in the north of France, before the building was completed, so he never lived there. It was his successor who enjoyed it.

The Museum of Fine Arts is approached through the gardens of the Town Hall. Its collections include works by Titian, Rubens, Van Dyck, Reynolds, Delacroix, Corot, Matisse and many Impressionist works, including several by the Bordelais artist, Albert Marquet.

The Museum of Decorative Arts, almost next to the Town Hall in the Rue Bouffard, has a good and interesting collection of household objects and period furniture, including sixteenth- and seventeenth-century glass, old pewter, ivories and enamels and a finely panelled salon furnished in the style of a merchant's house of the early nineteenth century. This collection, well arranged in the eighteenth-century Lalande Mansion, is well worth a visit.

The new Bordeaux. For the sake of contrast with the old quarter, it is interesting to look at the new Meriadeck complex, named after the Archbishop, just behind the Town Hall and the Fine Arts Museum.

The renewal of this dirty, dilapidated and unhealthy quarter, once dear to junk merchants and prostitutes past retirement age, was begun in 1954 on the initiative of the then Mayor of Bordeaux, Monsieur Chaban Delmas.

Around the central Esplanade Charles de Gaulle, whose ponds and fountains reflect the mirror-panelled walls of the *Préfecture*, it presents today 27 hectares of modern office buildings, hotels, administrative blocks, a skating rink and a public library, interspersed with greenery and spacious water gardens.

La Porte St Eloi, more commonly known to the Bordelais as **La Grosse Cloche**, is a thirteenth-century gate, which was rebuilt in the fifteenth century, over the Rue St James. Its two round towers, 41 m high, support the bell, which was rung in former times to signal important events in the city, such as the starting of the grape harvest.

The **Église St Michel** is not far from the river and the Pont de Pierre. Although begun in the middle of the fourteenth century, it was not completed for nearly 200 years. The triple-naved interior is impressive by its size alone, and contains a fine reredos in the St Joseph Chapel. The church has some unusual modern stained glass which replaces the medieval windows ruined by bomb blast during the Second World War. Some of the designs are abstract and do not sit easily in the ancient stone of their frames, but there are a number of traditional biblical subjects treated in a pleasing and colourful manner.

The bell tower, which the Bordelais call La Flèche (the arrow) because of its height, is separate from the church, as in the case of the Cathedral, and for the same reason. At 114 m it is the tallest spire in the whole of southern France.

The Girondins Monument, which stands in the Place des Quinconces, was erected at the end of the nineteenth century to the memory of the Girondins executed at the time of the Revolution. It consists of a 50-m column surmounted by a Statue of Liberty breaking her chains. At the base there is a fountain basin, remarkable for two quartets of superbly sculpted bronze horses charging convincingly from the water. You can almost hear them snort.

Where to stay

There are numerous hotels of all levels in Bordeaux. What follows is a selection of those most convenient for the main points of tourist interest and the vineyards.

158

Town centre

Grand Hôtel et Café de Bordeaux, 2 Place Comédie, 33000 Bordeaux, (opposite the Grand Théâtre), tel. (56) 90 93 44, has ninety-five rooms, and is Bordeaux's equivalent of *the* Café de Paris – great for watching the world go by. Prices slightly above average.

Royal Médoc, 3 Rue de Sèze, 33000 Bordeaux, tel. (56) 81 72 42, with forty-five rooms, is a pleasantly run hotel, recently redecorated, and in a convenient situation. Average prices. No restaurant.

Hôtel de Sèze, 23 Allées de Tourny, 33000 Bordeaux, tel. (56) 52 65 54, next door to the Royal Médoc, has twenty-five rooms. Moderate prices. No restaurant.

Normandie, 7 Cours 30 juillet, 33000 Bordeaux, tel. (56) 52 16 80, is just off the Allées de Tourny, near the Grand Théâtre. It has a hundred rooms at average prices, but no restaurant.

Bordeaux Le Lac

Convenient for excursions to Médoc vineyards, and with relatively easy access to the town centre.

Sofitel Aquitaine, Parc des Expositions, Bordeaux Le Lac 33300, tel. (56) 50 83 80, is a luxury hotel, with 212 rooms and swimming pool. Room prices are high. Two restaurants, one expensive, one average.

Novotel Bordeaux Le Lac, Parc des Expositions, Bordeaux Le Lac 33300, tel. (56) 50 99 70, has 173 rooms to the usual predictable and reliable Novotel standards. No charge for children in parents' room; children's menu in restaurant. Swimming pool. Prices slightly above average.

In Médoc vineyards

Relais de Margaux, Margaux 33460, Gironde, tel. (56) 88 38 30, is a luxury hotel in every way, with twenty-eight rooms at sky-high prices, and is haunted by American and Japanese wine buyers anxious to impress each other. Good restaurant with special menu for children of well-to-do parents.

Hôtel Restaurant de France, Listrac-Médoc, 33480 Castelnau, tel. (56) 58 03 68, has a pleasant little restaurant with six rooms at very reasonable prices.

Where to eat

Bordeaux is one of the best towns in France for eating out and it would take several pages to list half of the dozens of good restaurants. Here is a representative selection:

Town centre
Expensive

Le Chapon Fin, 5 Rue Montesquieu, 33000 Bordeaux (near Place des Grands Homme), tel. (56) 79 10 10, serves superb food in splendid surroundings and is the oldest established restaurant in Bordeaux, a favourite with Toulouse-Lautrec, Sarah Bernhardt and Edward VII. One Michelin star. Closed from 10–30 July.

La Chamade, 20 Rue Piliers de Tutelle, 33000 Bordeaux (behind Place de la Bourse), tel. (56) 48 13 74, has one Michelin star and cuisine and service well up to it. Tables are discreetly arranged in alcoves in eighteenth-century vaulted rooms.

Dubern, 42 Allées de Tourny, 33000 Bordeaux, tel. (56) 48 03 44, is another of the long-established traditional restaurants of Bordeaux, although the decor and cuisine were modernised a couple of years ago. Recipes are often original.

Moderate

Bistrot Clavel, 44 Rue Charles Domercq, 33000 Bordeaux (opposite railway station, Gare St Jean), tel. (56) 92 91 52, has the same owner as Le Chapon Fin, and is managed by his daughter. It serves first-class meals at reasonable prices, and very good wines.

Le Vieux Bordeaux, 27 Rue Buhan, 33000 Bordeaux (near La Grosse Cloche), tel. (56) 52 84 36. Despite its name and position, it is a restaurant with modern decor of mirrors, spotlights and what some call animation and others noise, but tasty food is well presented and at fair prices.

Le Loup, 66 Rue du Loup, 33000 Bordeaux (between Place St Pierre and the Cathedral), tel. (56) 48 20 21, is a pleasant reasonably priced restaurant, with menus for children. It is closed from 15 to 29 August.

Brasserie Noailles, 12 Allées de Tourny, 33000 Bordeaux (no need to phone) is situated diagonally opposite Le Grand Théâtre. I include this because it is utterly French, utterly Bordelais, completely traditional – *nouvelle cuisine* came and went and they never noticed it here – where the local business people lunch, and expect their food the way *grand'mère* does it. Not *haute cuisine* but good and reasonably priced.

Outside the town centre

Le St James, 3 Pl. C. Holstein, Bouliac, 33270 Florac, tel. (56) 20 52 19, is near the church in Bouliac. Cross the river by the Pont de Pierre or the Pont St Jean and in either case keep right on the D936 and under the railway bridge, then turn right on to D10 for Florac and Bouliac, about 3 km. The best restaurant in the Bordeaux area has two Michelin stars, and a shady terrace with a view across the Garonne of Bordeaux. Jean-Marie Amat is a remarkable chef, whose discerning clientele have followed him here from the Cours de l'Intendance where this restaurant used to be. You can enjoy good Bordeaux wines, and this is also the place to discover what the best Armagnac is all about. Menus begin at very reasonable prices for cuisine of this level, and take off for the sky.

In the vineyards

Auberge Le Savoie, 33460 Margaux, tel. (56) 88 31 76, in the village of Margaux 16 km north of Bordeaux on the D2, is a sound restaurant where you will find the best regional cooking at pleasingly low prices.

Night life

Like all French towns, Bordeaux has its fair share of night clubs and cabarets, some erotic, some more so. Many of the bars and clubs have hostesses, some of whom are not averse to making money for themselves as well as the club, and there are clubs for homosexuals of both sexes, which are cheerfully advertised as such. You will also find a number of standard non-specialised discos.

Do not expect French night life to be cheaper than it is anywhere else, for they aim to take as much and give as little as possible – and it's up to you to take an opposite view. As the night scene changes often, it can be helpful to ask your hotel for recommendations.

Alternatively, there is a give-away monthly in Bordeaux called *Plein-Feux*, often to be found on ordinary bar and brasserie counters, in which night clubs and discos advertise, together with restaurants, saunas, shops and even the zoo. If you read French you may well be surprised by an article which sometimes appears in this magazine under the title '*Points Chauds*'. It describes the private enterprise side of Bordeaux night life, including the localities preferred by the best-looking prostitutes – male and female – transvestites, and which car parks in the Bordeaux Lac area are currently popular with exhibitionist couples who like to make love in public, and which are used by *échangistes* – couples who like to change partners, but will be happy with one if they cannot find two.

You may well prefer to keep to the clubs, which are closely watched by the police, and are mostly well run.

Some possibilities:

Night club   **Club Le Mexico**, 82 Rue François de Sourdis, 33000 Bordeaux, tel. (56) 96 69 16. Night club and cabaret.

Discos   **Le Paradise**, 34 Rue Judaïque, 33000 Bordeaux, tel. (56) 44 22 80.

Le Colony, 13 Rue Georges Bonnac, 33000 Bordeaux, tel. (56) 81 40 97.

The vineyards

The vineyards of Bordeaux cover more than 1,000 sq km, stretching along the banks of the Dordogne and the Garonne and on both sides of the Gironde, the common estuary of the two rivers. They are the most extensive in the world producing high-quality wines – ten times the size of those of Burgundy and five times those of Champagne. With an annual production of about 500 million bottles, they alone produce half the fine wines of France.

Conditions   The temperate ocean climate, sunshine, and a soil which varies from limestone hills to pebbles and sand combine to produce wines of quality which nevertheless vary considerably in character from place to place. Although people tend to think of Bordeaux as a red wine area, total production is roughly half red, half white.

Leading wines   The Bordeaux region includes nineteen sub-regions, each making a wine with a character of its own. The most important of them are Haut Médoc, Graves, Sauternes and Saint-Emilion. Within these nineteen sub-regions there are numerous different *Appellations Contrôlées*. Haut Médoc, for example, is an *Appellation Contrôlée*, but includes Saint Estèphe, Pauillac, Saint-Julien and Margaux, each of which has its own *Appellation Contrôlée*. No guarantee of quality goes

Classification

with the term *Appellation Contrôlée*, except that it is given only to districts which produce sound wine. The AOC label guarantees only where the wine was made, but conveys no information about the methods by which it was made. For example, nothing states that AOC wines must be aged in wood, and many are not.

Other divisions of Bordeaux wine include the 1855 classification of the great growths (crus) of Médoc which named fifty-eight wines, four first, twelve second, fourteen third, eleven fourth and seventeen fifth growths. Although in 1973 Château Mouton-Rothschild was moved up from a second to a first growth, there have been no other official changes, and as 1855 was a long time ago there is no doubt that if the classifications were redone objectively today, a number of wines would be downgraded and others upgraded by at least one class. The American wine writer, Robert Parker, suggests that about thirty of the fifty-eight are now in the wrong class.

Apart from Château Lafite (now Château Lafite-Rothschild), which was placed first in the 1855 classification, the other Grands Crus Classés include these words on their labels.

Another label statement which you will see is *Cru Bourgeois*. This classification, first made in 1932, refers to wines which are well above average, though not pretending to be the equal of classified growths, although some are. In 1978 the *Syndicat* of Bourgeois Growths – there are 150 member vineyards – recognised three categories, Cru Grand Bourgeois Exceptionel, Cru Grand Bourgeois and Cru Bourgeois, but the EEC did not follow suit and allows only the optional use of Cru Bourgeois.

Wine labels   The reading of wine labels is more subtle than it may seem to the uninitiated but, while it is not possible to write about Bordeaux without saying something about wine, I will not say too much about labels. However, it may be useful to mention that apart from châteaux there are also numerous co-operatives which produce countless thousands of bottles. Some of their names are a little misleading. There is, for example, no Marquis de Saint Estèphe, except on the wine labels of this co-operative. Others may have encouraging pictures resembling châteaux, though the word château is not used in the name. They may also say *Mise en bouteille à la Propriété*, or words to that effect, which means at the co-operative bottling plant.

These marketing ploys in no way detract from the wine, which is often AOC and made to high standards by a *Groupe de Viniculteurs* or a *Co-opérative de Vinification*, who will be named in small print on the label. It simply means that the wine is made from grapes supplied by many different growers and carefully blended, rather than a wine from one château vineyard.

Making wine   The making of wine is a traditional business, but although traditions die hard, changes do take place. Visitors can no longer see the juice being extracted from the grapes by treading them in wooden tubs, for this is a thing of the past in Bordeaux. Anthony Barton, owner of Château Langoa-Barton and Château Léoville-Barton – third and second Grand Cru respectively – and a member of an Anglo-Irish family prominent in the Bordeaux wine trade for more than 250 years, says that his father remembered seeing the workers jigging about on the grapes to the music of a fiddler. Nowadays the object is to damage the grapes as little as possible before they go into the vats, simply stripping them from the stalks in an *égrappoir*.

There was a time when all the red wine was made initially in wooden vats, before going into barrels and eventually into bottles, but today some of the greatest wines start off in stainless steel vats, others in oak vats.

Tannins

Important discoveries have been made recently about the nature of tannins, the substances found in Bordeaux wines which enable them to keep and improve over a great many years. Some vintages of some wines took as long as forty years to reach their best, the great disadvantage being that such wines were often almost undrinkably harsh when they were young. The new knowledge of tannins will enable wines to be made which will mature quite young but hold their quality for many years.

Harvesting

Some vineyards have introduced machines which pick the grapes. One such machine will replace forty pickers, but the great estates still pick by hand. In the traditional manner, the workers often come back from the last picking on trailers loaded with jovial men and women, students and children, singing old harvest songs, to a Bacchanalian feast on trestle tables in the sun. The days when robot drivers of grape picking machines face each other across an empty table and, computer operated, of course, raise empty glasses to each other in salutation at harvest end are, happily, still some way in the future.

Châteaux

Although there are some very fine period châteaux among the four thousand or so making their own wine, the majority of the properties are just country houses, some impressive, some modest, some simple farmhouses. The quality of the buildings bears no relation to the quality of the estate's wine.

Visitors are welcome at most of the châteaux, so if you want to see where and how your favourite wine is made, it is perfectly possible to do so. But there is a correct way to go about it.

Visiting the châteaux

The first thing to do is to call in at the local tourist office, *Syndicat d'Initiative*, or *Maison du Vin*, to find out which châteaux in their particular region can be visited. The Maison du Tourisme et du Vin de Médoc at La Verrerie, 33250 Pauillac, tel. (56) 59 03 08, for example, has a publication *Découverte du Médoc* which not only lists all the wine châteaux and locates them on maps, with full information about visiting, but also gives details about nearby coastal resorts.

Having chosen the château you wish to visit, it is best to telephone, asking if it will be convenient to arrive at a particular time. Many properties are closed to visitors during the grape harvest and the making of the wine, because they have no staff to spare. Some are open morning and afternoon, others only in the afternoon, while Saturday and Sunday hours may differ from those of weekdays, and many are open only at certain periods of the year. It is advisable, therefore, to avoid disappointment by telephoning in advance.

The châteaux do not operate like stately homes, so do not expect to see anything of the owner's house, except in a few cases where a reception room is kept for visitors to the wine-making side, which is all the proprietors expect to show you. On the better estates you are not likely to be offered anything to taste, except possibly the first- or second-year wine maturing in the casks – rarely anything from a bottle.

Wine tasting

If the property is organised to allow you to taste wine which has already been bottled, you may well be expected, though not obliged to buy some. However, before you taste or buy, ask yourself why the property is keeping wine to sell to tourists when, if it were good value, it could have been sold much earlier through the normal channels.

Whether you buy wine at an estate, or at a local *Maison du Vin*, or at a small shop in the Bordeaux area, do not expect a bargain because you are on the spot. The market does not work like that. It may well be less expensive than at home, but you are likely to find it at a more advantageous price in any of the big hypermarkets elsewhere in France, or in the French Channel ports.

Here are a few of the more interesting châteaux in the Médoc region (English is spoken at all those listed):

Château Loudenne, 33340 St Yzans-de-Médoc, tel. (56) 09 05 03, in northern Médoc overlooking the Gironde, near St Yzans, has been British-owned for more than 100 years. Attractive buildings and courteous reception. (Cru Bourgeois.)

Château Cissac, 33250 Cissac, tel. (56) 59 58 13, in Cissac on the D104, has an eighteenth-century *chartreuse* built on Roman foundations by Victor Louis, architect of Bordeaux's Grand Théâtre. (Cru Bourgeois.)

Château Pichon-Longueville-Comtesse-de-Lalande, 33250 Pauillac, tel. (56) 59 19 40, off the D2 near Pauillac, has a reception room with panoramic views over the Gironde and the vineyards of Pauillac. Closed in August. (Second growth.)

Château Langoa-Barton/Léoville-Barton, 33250 St Julien Beychevelle, tel. (56) 59 06 05, is a beautifully kept traditional wine estate with immaculate *chais*. The Barton family has lived in the eighteenth-century Château Langoa since 1821. Courteous reception. (Second and third growths.)

Château Beychevelle, 33250 St Julien Beycheville, tel. (56) 59 23 00, on the D2 in St Julien commune, is a beautiful long, low fifteenth-century château with a central pavilion and wings on either side, lovely gardens and a terrace overlooking the river. (Fourth growth.)

Château La Tour-Carnet, 33112 St Laurent Médoc, tel. (56) 59 40 13, on the D101 near St Laurent du Médoc, has a thirteenth-century tower and seventeenth-century buildings. (Fourth growth.)

Château Maucaillou, 33480 Moulis, tel. (56) 58 01 23, near Moulis-Listrac, is a château where you pay for tasting but are given a commentary and explanation of the wines. It also has a **Museum of Arts and Crafts** of the vine and wine. Splendid *chais*. (Cru Bourgeois.)

These are just a few of the possibilities. Several other châteaux have exhibitions of various kinds, and lovely parks or gardens.

Excursions south from Bordeaux

Château de La Brède

The picturesque Château of La Brède is situated about 16 km south-east of Bordeaux by the *autoroute*, and 1 km outside the small town of Labrède (which is the modern spelling of the town). Surrounded by moats so wide that it seems to be floating in the middle of a small lake, it has a thirteenth-century keep, but was built mainly between the fifteenth and eighteenth centuries. It was the home of Montesquieu –

Montesquieu

Charles Louis de Secondat, Baron of La Brède. Although he travelled widely in Europe and often spent the winter in Paris, this great French writer and liberal thinker regarded La Brède, where he was born in 1689, as his real home.

A lawyer by profession, Montesquieu became a magistrate and later President of the Parliament of Bordeaux. As a writer he was elected first to the Academy of Bordeaux and then to the French Academy, gaining a reputation with his *Lettres Persanes*, a satire on French society of his day. More important was his learned work on the *Greatness and Decline of the Romans*, which preceded Gibbon by a hundred years. Most significant of all was *L'Esprit des Lois*, a work which is still topical today and which influenced the drawing up of the constitution for the First Republic in 1791, particularly in its recommendation that legislative power should be separate from executive power.

After visiting England, where he had many regular clients for his wine, Montesquieu laid out the park around La Brède like that of an English country house. It is one of the attractions of La Brède that the park and the château, still inhabited by his descendants, remain exactly as they were in his day.

Montesquieu was one of those fortunate people who seem to be born happy. He was of equable temperament, enjoyed all aspects of life, and was as contented in the country, where he took pride in the proper management of his vineyards, as he was in the literary salons of Paris.

Unlike that other great French essayist closely connected with Bordeaux, Michel de Montaigne, whose work was constantly interrupted by his inconsiderate and ill-humoured wife, Montesquieu was very happily married. This may have been due to the fact that although he was deeply fond of his wife and his three children, he preferred not to live with them. He installed them instead in his château of Rochemorin, at Martillac, within walking distance of La Brède, and visited them regularly.

The château is open to visitors on summer afternoons, every day except Tuesday from June to the end of September, and on Saturdays and Sundays at most other times of the year. Montesquieu's apartments and library are kept as they were in his lifetime.

Cadillac

The American town near the Great Lakes, which built the 'Rolls Royce' of American cars, was named after this *bastide* on the right bank of the Garonne about 30 km from Bordeaux, by the D10.

The castle

The thing to see here is the enormous castle, built between 1598 and 1620 by Jean Louis de Nogaret de la Valette, Duke of Épernon. This strange person had been the dear friend and favourite of the 'lady king', Henri III, whose depravity has already been mentioned.

It is said that King Henri IV, realising that this curious duke was tremendously rich, very ambitious and desirous of regaining the influence at court which he had enjoyed under Henri III, encouraged him to build this great castle, knowing that the more time and money the duke spent on it the less dangerous he would be.

The château was built on the site of a feudal castle whose ruins were first cleared away. The guided visit (it is closed on Mondays) takes about an hour. In the vast rooms there are eight magnificent chimney-pieces carved in coloured marble and a number of fine painted ceilings. The vaulted basement rooms were used as workshops by the weavers who made the seventeenth-century tapestries which hang in some of the salons. The château also has an unusual spiral staircase. Having been used as a women's prison for a hundred years from 1828 to 1928, the building was in poor condition when its restoration was undertaken in 1952.

Wine tasting

The **Maison du Vin de Cadillac** is installed in the west wing. Tasting of the wines made in the Cadillac region (Première Côtes de Bordeaux) is free.

Château de Malle and the Sauternais

The charming Château de Malle lies on the other side of the river from Cadillac and is reached via the villages of Cérons, Barsac and Preignac on the N113.

This is one of the nicest estates in the whole Bordeaux region. It is not too grand but everything about it is attractive – the superb wrought iron gates, the courtyards, the terraces, the lovely Italianate garden with huge trees and a small theatre. The residence was originally built for Jacques de Malle, a Bordeaux magistrate, in the early part of the seventeenth century, with the two-storey central pavilion being added about a hundred years later.

The château is still owned and lived in by members of the de Malle family, and is open to the public from mid-March to mid-October, except on Wednesdays outside July and August. The interior is beautifully furnished with antiques and pictures. The estate, lying at the limits of Sauternes and Graves, is unique in that it produces both the sweet white wines of Sauternes and a red Graves. Its white wines were classed as a second growth in the 1855 classification of white wines.

Château Suduiraut

Not far from the Château de Malle is the beautiful estate of Suduiraut, a fine seventeenth-century residence with a shady park laid out by France's most famous landscape gardener, Le Nôtre. Château Suduiraut is a first growth and its wines are among the greatest of Sauternes.

Château d'Yquem

Next door, however, are *the* greatest. Château d'Yquem was placed in a class of its own in the 1855 classification, Premier Grand Cru, and is considered by many to be the greatest sweet white wine in the world. The château, by the way, is called Château Yquem, and the wine Château d'Yquem. The building, a small fortified château around a central courtyard, dating from the fifteenth and sixteenth centuries, has belonged to the Lur Saluces family for the past 300 years or so. Before that it was owned by the family of the essayist, Montaigne, whose family name was Michel Eyquem.

Unfortunately, the château is not open to the public, although in its position on a low hill it can be easily seen, and one can walk round the outside. The courtyard of Château Yquem is one of the selected places used for concerts and musical events, which take place throughout the Bordeaux region during the month of May.

Where to eat

Barsac

Hostellerie Du Château De Rolland, 33720 Barsac, tel. (56) 27 15 75, is a pleasant restaurant surrounded by vineyards. It also has nine bedrooms, and is moderately expensive.

Cérons

Grillobois, Cérons, 33720 Podensac, tel. (56) 27 11 50, is a small hotel, with a swimming pool and a good restaurant at average prices.

Langon

There are several restaurants in Langon. The best, **Claude Darroze**, 95 Cours General Leclérc, 33210 Langon, tel. (56) 63 00 48, is a one star Michelin restaurant, which can offer you a superb lunch accompanied by the Graves and Sauternes wines of the region. Prices are above average but fair. There are also eighteen bedrooms at average prices.

Picnic place

If you are simply looking for somewhere to picnic, you could do worse than to take the road in Barsac signposted 'Port de Barsac'. You will find yourself in a pleasant spot beside the Garonne with no visible port in sight.

Excursions north and east from Bordeaux

Blaye

On the right bank of the Gironde, about 36 km from Bordeaux via St André de Cubzac and then the D669, is the old town of Blaye. It is situated on a rocky spur above the Gironde, at a point where the estuary was narrow enough to be defended against attacks from the sea. Three forts were built to form this line of defence, one on the Médoc side, one on the island of Pâté in the river, and the most important at Blaye.

The fort

This huge fort, which still stands intact, is one of the great defensive masterpieces of the world. Completed in 1689 by the military architect, Vauban, it completely encircles the old medieval town, with a frontage above the river almost a kilometre in length. There are good views across the estuary from the ramparts, 50 m above water level.

The interior of the citadel is a small town in itself, with barracks arranged in streets and squares, a church, a hospital and the commander's house, as well as the towers, bastions and gateways of the fort. The fort no longer has any military significance, and the commander's house has become a museum of the art and history of Blaye.

The Duchess of Berry

It was in this house that the glamorous Duchess of Berry was imprisoned in November 1832, after trying and failing to launch a revolt against King Louis-Philippe. Despite having been a widow for twelve years, she gave birth to a baby daughter in May 1833, a scandal which put an end to her political ambitions – her husband having been heir to the throne before his assassination, she had wanted to see her son as king. She had been born Marie Caroline de Bourbon-Sicile, grand-daughter of the King of Naples, and a month after the birth of her baby, she was shipped back to Sicily.

The citadel of Blaye is inhabited, and a number of artisans have workshops there.

Where to stay and eat

Hôtel La Citadelle, 33390 Blaye, Gironde, tel. (57) 42 17 10, is a pleasant hotel with views over the estuary, a swimming pool and a restaurant with a special menu for children. Average prices.

Plassac

At Plassac, 4 km south of Blaye by the D669, some interesting Roman remains have been excavated. Between the first and fifth centuries AD three Roman villas existed on the same site. Objects found there are exhibited in the **Gallo-Roman Museum** next to the site and include amphoras, plates, vases, iron tools and decorative bronzes as well as eighteen painted wall panels, which have been restored, from the first-century villa. The Museum is open mornings and afternoons from 1 June to 30 September.

Bourg

The D669 also passes through Bourg-sur-Gironde between Blaye and Bordeaux. The town is pleasant enough with an upper part and a port area down by the river, now used only by pleasure boats, but there is nothing of absorbing interest for the tourist. It is best known these days for the sound and very good value Côtes de Bourg red wines produced on the nearby hillsides.

Only 5 km to the east of Bourg, by the D669 and then a left fork on to the D113, is the **Grotte de Pair non Pair**, where you can visit a rock shelter with Stone Age drawings of horses, mammoths and bison. In the summer season it is open from 10 to 11.30 in the mornings and from 2.30 to 5 in the afternoons.

St Emilion

Situated on a hilltop facing south, overlooking the Valley of the Dordogne, St Emilion lies about 40 km east of Bordeaux by the N89 to Libourne and then the D243. Its red wines have been famous for centuries, and still enjoy a world-wide reputation, while the town itself is packed with interest.

History

The Romans cultivated vineyards on the slopes of the St Emilion hills; you can still see in places the lines of stones between which they planted their vines. The Roman poet, Ausonius, had a villa there, and Château Ausone, named after him and believed to be built on the same site, produces one of the most famous of the St Emilion wines.

The town itself had a much later origin when a Breton monk, Emilion, came to live there in the eighth century in a cave hollowed out of the rock. In time, other monks joined him and a community grew up.

The monks gradually hollowed out more caves and galleries. Part of these troglodytic works became the strange and ugly underground church now called the Église Monolithe.

Like other towns in Aquitaine, St Emilion was repeatedly attacked and changed hands several times during the Hundred Years War, and suffered again during the sixteenth-century Wars of Religion, when it was pillaged by both Catholics and Huguenots.

Although in 1789 the Bordeaux parliamentary party, the Girondins, supported the Revolution, Robespierre suspected them of planning some degree of independence from Paris and had twenty-one members arrested and executed. Eight others escaped to St Emilion, where Madame Bouquey, a relative of one of them, hid them in an underground gallery, reached through the side wall of a well in her garden. They stayed more than a month in this dark, damp hole, until, hearing that government officials were scouring the town to find them, they left of their own accord, hoping to avoid involving Madame Bouquey. But it was too late. Only one of the eight got away, the others being captured and guillotined in Bordeaux, together with six members of the Bouquey family.

What to see

The town has conserved its medieval ramparts, although they are now partly concealed by houses built upon them. A walk or drive round the outside gives a good idea of what it must have been like in medieval times.

The first thing that catches the eye on arriving by road from

Libourne is an isolated, ruined stone wall, pierced by arched windows, on the edge of the town. This is all that remains of a fourteenth-century **Dominican convent** destroyed during the Wars of Religion.

The famous **monolithic church** – really a misnomer since it is not built from one stone but dug out of a cliff face – must be admitted to be impressive, despite its ugliness and gloom. Its fourteenth-century steeple, extensively restored during the sixteenth century, rises directly from ground level at the top of the cliff in which the church is hollowed out – a curious and inelegant arrangement. Most of the underground work was done in the eleventh and twelfth centuries, creating the equivalent of three naves and leaving ten great pillars of rock supporting the cave roof.

This miserable interior was no doubt more attractive in the early days, when the walls were heavily painted and decorated. But this was all scraped off during the Revolution when the church was used to produce saltpetre.

In the twelfth century the canons of St Emilion showed sound judgement in deciding that the underground church was really too uncouth. They built instead a more civilised church above ground in the normal way. This **collegiate church** is in two distinct parts – a Romanesque nave, together with a Gothic choir and transept added in the fourteenth, fifteenth and sixteenth centuries. There is also a fine fourteenth-century cloister.

There is so much to see in St Emilion that an hour soon passes as you wander up and down through the narrow cobbled streets. There are several fifteenth- and sixteenth-century houses, even the shell of a fourteenth-century building, called the **Maison Gothique** on a corner in the Rue Guadet, opposite the Rue des Girondins. The **Maison Bouquey**, a seventeenth-century house, still stands just off this road, but neither the garden where the fugitives were hidden nor the house is open to the public.

The picturesque ivy-covered ruins of the **Couvent des Cordeliers** in the upper town are worth visiting, particularly what remains of the cloister.

In the middle of the town, the **Porte de la Cadène** (in Latin, catena means chain) marks the place where a chain could be stretched across the road to control cart traffic between the upper and lower towns, thus preventing medieval traffic jams.

The Jurade

First established by Richard the Lionheart and confirmed by King John, the Jurade of St Emilion was a form of municipal council, whose purpose was to administer the town in general, and in particular to supervise the quality of the wines it produced. This it did throughout medieval times, but later ceased to operate until being reformed in 1948, since when it has carried out its control of the wine as before. Every spring, members of the Jurade attend Mass together and then hold a ceremony at which they assess the wines of the previous year's harvest to ensure that they are up to the required standard. The Jurade also meets towards the end of September. On this occasion they pass in procession through the town in their scarlet robes to the Tour du Roi, where they climb the steps to the platform at the top, from which, to the accompaniment of a trumpet call which sounds out over vineyards and valley, they proclaim that the grape harvest can officially start. These spring and autumn occasions conclude with an official banquet, which is naturally accompanied by the best local wines.

The châteaux

There is a **Maison du Vin** in St Emilion where you can obtain full information on the wines and the châteaux which can be visited.

The châteaux in the St Emilion area are, for the most part, a good deal less grand than those of Médoc or Sauternes, an exception being the Château de St Georges at Montagne-St Emilion, 3 km to the north. This was built in the eighteenth century by Victor Louis, architect of the Grand Théâtre in Bordeaux.

The wines

The wines of St Emilion are sound and reliable, thoroughly deserving their reputation. In my opinion, the same cannot be said of the macaroons, which are also produced and sold in the town. I may well have been unlucky, but those I have tried seemed to have the texture of play-dough and to have been made in the dankest corner of the underground galleries.

Where to stay and eat

Auberge de la Commanderie, Rue Cordeliers, 33330 St Emilion, Gironde, tel. (57) 24 70 19, with fifteen rooms, is a good average hotel with a restaurant, charging average prices.

Hostellerie Plaisance, Place Clocher, 33330 St Emilion, Gironde, tel. (57) 24 72 32, has a very good restaurant at somewhat above-average prices. It also has twelve rather expensive bedrooms.

Logis de la Cadène, Place Marché au Bois, 33330 St Emilion, tel. (57) 24 71 40, has a straightforward, relaxed atmosphere, and features good Bordelais cooking at modest prices, with a half-price menu for children.

Côte D'Argent

Royan
Pointe de Grave
Soulac-sur-Mer
Gironde
Montalivet-les-Bains
Lesparre
Hourtin Plage
Hourtin
Lac d'Hourtin-Carcans
Maubuisson
de Médoc
Castelnau
Carcans
Lacanau
Brach
Lacanau Océan
Ste Hélène
Grand Crohot
Lac de Lacanau
St Medard
Arès
Andernos-les-Bains
Cap Ferret
Bassin d'Arcachon
Arcachon
Gujan Mestras
Pyla-sur-Mer
Dune du Pilat
La Hume
R. Eyre
Pilat Plage
Étang de Cazaux et de Sanguinet
Port Maguide
Ispes
Navarosse
Biscarosse-Plage
Biscarosse
Étang de Biscarosse et de Parentis
Mimizan-Plage
Étang d'Aureilhan
Mimizan
Bias
Mézos
St Julien-en-Born
Lit-et-Mixte
St Girons
Mont de Marsan
Étang de Léon
Moliets
Léon
Villeneuve-de-Marsan
Vieux-Boucau-les-Bains
Messanges
Magescq
Grenade-sur-L'Adour
Étang de Soustons
Soustons
Eugenie-les-Bains
Dax
Hossegor-Capbreton
Geaune
R. Adour
BIARRITZ

Côte D'Argent

Introduction

It was a Bordeaux journalist, Maurice Martin, who in 1905 first called the long, straight shoreline of Aquitaine between the sea and the forest 'the silver coast'. He wrote: 'On these 228 kilometres of beaches the eternal sea, sometimes gentle, sometimes angry, throws its silver fringe at the foot of the immaculate dunes.'

The beach is the longest, straightest and sandiest in all Europe. Facing the dark blue of Biscay and backed everywhere by the dark green of the pines, this strip of light golden sand, almost white in the blazing sun, offers a unique sense of space and freedom, stretching as much as a kilometre wide in places at low tide and vanishing into the distance north and south.

Behind the flat sands the dunes rise sharply. They vary in depth from 500 m to 8 km and reach their maximum height at the Dune du Pilat, at 114 m the highest in Europe and more than 3 km long. Looking inland from the top of the dunes you see a level expanse of pines, the largest forest in western Europe. It holds a chain of serene and spacious lakes – Lac d'Hourtin-Carcans is the largest in France – also with sandy beaches. Flowing from the lakes to the sea are hidden rivers called *courants*, which glide between the trees and whose rushy banks are the haunt of herons and wildfowl.

The main road to Spain crosses the forest from north to south, presenting to passing travellers speeding through Landes a monotonous and false picture of what is really a very individual region.

From Soulac to Arcachon

In the days when it was first called the silver coast, this shoreline was wild and almost completely deserted, apart from the one resort of Arcachon and its nearby fishing villages. Today, there are still empty stretches, as well as several modern beach resorts, which are listed from north to south.

Soulac-sur-Mer   Reached from Bordeaux via St Médard, taking the D1 to Castelnau de Médoc and then the N215 to Lesparre – or more slowly and with more to see by the D2 through the famous vineyards of Médoc to

173

Lesparre, and then the N215 – Soulac is a pleasant and popular resort not without interest.

The beach is protected by offshore sandbanks beneath which, according to an old local legend, lies the town of Noviomagus, which was engulfed by the sea and sands in the sixth century. Recent tests have, for once, confirmed the truth of an old legend.

Soulac is not far from the Pointe de Grave, the extreme tip of the Médoc, from which there is a ferry across the Gironde estuary to **Royan**, a large and lively resort with wide sandy beaches well protected from the open sea.

What to see

The basilica of **Notre Dame de la fin des Terres** is a twelfth-century Romanesque church, which was extended in later years but was gradually buried by the encroaching sands, until by the eighteenth century only the spire was visible. During the course of the nineteenth century, the sand was cleared away and the church was restored, so that it now stands in a sandy hollow, cosily encircled by dunes except on one side. The columns of the nave have some interesting capitals showing St Peter in prison and Daniel in the lion's den. The stained glass windows are modern, made by a craftsman in Limoges and put in place in 1954.

Port Bloc, where the ferries leave for Royan, is an attractive spot with an old oak wood, ideal for summer picnics.

Where to stay and eat

Soulac has a number of small tourist hotels, several holiday villages, some camp sites and a fair share of cafés and snack bars, but the best place to stay is in the small neighbouring resort of **L'Amélie** (named after a wrecked ship).

Hôtel Les Pins, L'Amélie, Soulac-sur-Mer 33780, tel. (56) 09 80 01, has thirty-five rooms and a reasonable restaurant with lower prices for children. Moderate rates.

Montalivet-les-Bains

Many towns in the south-west claim to be capital of something, and there is no doubt that Montalivet-les-Bains has long been established as the nudist capital of France (although the nearby village of Grayan-et-L'Hôpital also claims to have the largest naturist camp in Europe). Montalivet is a kind of United Nations of active, healthy, family naturism, and unlike many other resorts, where there are special beaches for nudists, in Montalivet the special beaches are for *textiles*. This is the French naturist word for those people who prefer to wear clothes, however minimal. *Textiles* are banned from the 1,500-m beach of the Centre Heliomarin, founded in 1950 by the French Naturist Federation for the exclusive use of nudists. This centre is very well equipped with sports and leisure facilities, among neatly laid-out bungalow villages, a large shopping centre and restaurants. It can receive up to 7,000 nudists and is especially popular with Germans. The address is: Centre Heliomarin, Montalivet-les-Bains, 33930 Vendays-Montalivet, tel. (56) 09 30 47.

Where to stay

Outside the Centre Heliomarin, **Motel Restaurant Grill Les**

Acacias, Vendays-Montalivet 33930, tel. (56) 41 73 23, is between Montalivet-les-Bains and the inland village of Vendays-Montalivet, with twenty-two rooms at average prices. The restaurant is open only from the beginning of July to the end of September, but the motel is open year round.

Hourtin Plage

Hourtin Plage is situated on the ocean beach near the northern end of Lac d'Hourtin-Carcans, called Lac d'Hourtin at the northern end and Lac de Carcans at the southern end. A beach resort, with the emphasis on beach, it is reached from Bordeaux via Salaunes, Ste Hélène, Brach and Carcans, a route which begins as the N215 and changes its number several times without really changing direction. There is a rough-terrain BMX course and an adventure island for children called the Ile aux Enfants. There are shops and restaurants, and the beach is supervised by lifeguards.

Where to stay

Airotel de la Côte D'Argent, Hourtin Plage 33990, tel. (56) 09 10 25, is one of several luxury caravan sites of this name in various places in France. It has 750 places, as well as bungalows, caravans and mobile homes to let.

Espacotel, Résidence Hôtelière, 33121 Carcans-Maubuisson, tel. (56) 44 23 11, lies on the shore of the lake itself, near the village of Hourtin, and is a tourist apartment complex with its own beach, bar, restaurant and swimming pool.

Maubuisson

At the southern end of the lake, Maubuisson is very much orientated towards sporting activities, offering twenty-six tennis courts (four covered), extensive sailing and windsurfing facilities on the 16 km-long lake, and 100 km of cycle paths through the forest, as well as archery, boules, and a choice of swimming in the lake, in swimming pools, or at the ocean beach at Carcans-Plage a few kilometres away.

Where to stay

Hôtel Restaurant du Lac, Maubuisson, 33121 Carcans-Maubuisson, tel. (56) 03 30 03, has thirty-nine rooms at average prices.

Espacotel, Résidence de Tourisme, 33990 Hourtin, tel. (56) 44 23 11, is a complex with 150 apartments for four to six people and a swimming pool. Same telephone number for booking as at Hourtin Plage.

Holiday villages and **gîtes villages** offer flats and chalets to let, as well as rooms. Full information from Maison de la Station, 33121 Carcans-Maubuisson, tel. (56) 03 34 94.

All the resorts mentioned above put the emphasis on active open air holidays in relatively basic and inexpensive accommodation, so visitors should not expect a high degree of comfort.

Lacanau-Océan

The pretty Lac de Lacanau, 8 km long, has the village of Lacanau on the land side, and the beach resort of Lacanau-Océan a few kilometres away on the sea side. The popular Lacanau-Océan is a larger version of the resorts mentioned above, having been developed considerably in the past ten years. It offers facilities for sports of all kinds, including golf, tennis, riding and cycling, while its big and reliable Biscay rollers have made it a mecca for surfers from all over the world. International stars of the sport are attracted to the surfing championships held there regularly.

Lacanau-Océan is essentially a camping and chalet resort, but there are several small tourist hotels.

Hôtel Étoile d'Argent, Place de l'Europe, Lacanau-Océan, 33680 Lacanau, tel. (56) 03 21 07, has nineteen rooms and a restaurant at average prices. There is another Hôtel Étoile d'Argent, much smaller, in Lacanau itself, tel. (56) 03 21 07. It has nine rooms at slightly lower prices.

Hôtel L'Oyat, Front de Mer, Lacanau-Océan, 33680 Lacanau, tel. (56) 03 11 11, is a modern hotel with thirty-three rooms at average prices, and an inexpensive restaurant.

Arcachon

Unlike the places mentioned above, Arcachon is an old-established resort, whose first bathing establishment was opened in 1823 by a Breton sailor named François Legallais. At the time Arcachon was just a fishing village with a few score inhabitants, but Legallais' example was followed by others and soon private villas began to be built. By 1857, when the railway reached Arcachon, the commune had 283 houses and was receiving a few thousand visitors a year. Arcachon has continued to expand ever since, and now has a permanent population of about 14,000, becoming during the summer one of the largest resorts in France, with about 200,000 visitors.

It enjoys an exceptional situation on the shores of what is almost an inland sea. This triangular land-locked bay, the **Bassin d'Arcachon**, covers 150,000 hectares, with a perimeter of 84 km, and an opening to the sea less than 3 km across. The narrow, navigable channel changes position frequently, but despite the ocean's efforts to block this entrance with sandbanks, it remains open because the Bassin is also the estuary of the 100 km-long River Eyre, whose current with the aid of the ebb tide washes out the sand brought in on the flood.

At low tide most of the Bassin is exposed as sandy mud flats, but Arcachon is near enough to the open sea for there always to be water on its beaches.

The long coast around the bay is backed almost everywhere by pine trees, but has a number of oyster ports and fishing villages, and a string of smaller holiday resorts.

The Bassin is protected from the rough seas of Biscay by the long arm of Cap Ferret, which has increased in length by 4 km in the past

200 years. It does, however, get some rough weather and this, together with the presence of strong currents at some states of the tide, as well as a large island, sandbanks and variable channels, calls for some skill when manoeuvring a boat. These conditions have made Arcachon a famous sailing centre, with frequent yacht races and international competitions. The marina has berths for more than 2,000 yachts and cabin cruisers.

The bay is always a pleasant sight, full of interest and activity. Yachts with sails of many colours tack to and fro, motor boats zoom about, canoes and rowing boats provide a slower note, and there are always water-skiers and windsurfers to demonstrate their skills or to fall over.

Quarters

When Arcachon was originally developed it was divided into four sections, each named after a season of the year. Of these spring and autumn have been forgotten, but the *Ville D'Été* and the *Ville D'Hiver* are still two distinct quarters. The *Ville D'Été* is centred on the two long boulevards that run parallel to the beach, with the shops and restaurants, the Casino and most of the hotels. In season it is smart, colourful and animated. The *Ville D'Hiver* is calmer, lying higher up in the forested dunes, with winding roads designed to lessen the effect of sea breezes and comfortable villas set back in spacious gardens.

Arcachon has always had a certain *cachet*. It was here that Alfonso XII of Spain became engaged to Archduchess Marie Christine of Austria. In the suburb of Le Moulleau the celebrated Italian poet and dramatist, Gabriele d'Annunzio, lived with his Russian mistress, Countess Goubouleff. The town has always been popular with the rich families of Bordeaux, who keep second homes there for weekends and the summer. A good many of these villas, particularly towards Les Abatilles and Le Moulleau, are still in existence, their large gardens thick with pines, mimosas, bamboos, palms and magnolias. Some owners, though, have sold to developers who have filled the gardens with blocks of flats, so that Arcachon now has a dual character, part modern, part period.

Parking the car

In the height of the summer season the town becomes very crowded and parking just where you want is almost impossible, although parking somewhere is not too difficult. The best bet for day visitors is the car park next to the railway station, which is within easy walking distance of the beach.

Oysters

Arcachon has long been noted for its oysters, which are cultivated in 'parks' in several parts of the Bassin, particularly around the island called Ile aux Oiseaux, which is a favourite halt for migrating birds. Altogether there are nearly 2,000 oyster 'farmers' around the Bassin and the industry is very important to the local economy.

Beaches

Including the adjacent suburbs of Le Moulleau and Les Abatilles, Arcachon has a frontage on the bay of about 12 km, all of it with sandy beaches. This gives holiday-makers a wide choice in finding their own favourite place on these calm beaches, with the added option of the completely different ocean beaches within easy reach.

The brothers Péreire, the financiers who developed Arcachon in the nineteenth century, retained a large estate for themselves at Les Abatilles. Some years ago the municipality bought part of this estate so that a section of the pine-covered dune frontage to the Bassin could be preserved, and an attractive tamarisk-lined garden promenade for pedestrians has been created at the foot of these dunes beside the beach.

Spa

At Les Abatilles a spa and mineral water source was discovered in 1922 when drilling for oil was taking place. Instead of oil they struck water 485 m beneath the surface, and when doctors declared it beneficial to health, a spa was set up. The water is still bottled and sold in many parts of France.

What to see

In the conventional tourist sense of sightseeing, there is not a lot. The most interesting building in Arcachon was the Casino Mauresque which, inspired by the Alhambra in Granada and built as a winter casino in 1863, had a kind of bizarre charm. Unfortunately, it was completely destroyed by fire in 1977, although its attractive park and gardens remain and give beautiful views over the bay.

Because Arcachon is not an old town, there is nothing of real historical interest; its oldest church, **Notre Dame**, dates from 1722, and although the **Église St Ferdinand** is in the Romanesque style, it is merely a copy built at the turn of the century.

There is a **museum/aquarium** which has an interesting collection of marine species and sea birds of the region. It is open from 30 March to 30 September.

Tourists who enjoy markets will find the **covered market** in Arcachon worth a visit. Its stalls have a wonderful display of fish and shellfish, and fruits and other produce of the region – in arrangements that are minor works of art.

What to do
Boat trips

In the summer, numerous boat trips are available on the Bassin. A regular half-hourly service runs between Arcachon and Cap Ferret (crossing time about thirty minutes), and an independent motor boat service goes from Le Moulleau to Cap Ferret. Or there is a daily two-hour trip around the Ile aux Oiseaux, and a two-and-a-half-hour trip past the Dune du Pilat to the Argouin sandbank at the entrance to the Bassin. Other trips enable people to stay on this sandbank from 11 a.m. to 5.30 p.m. for sunbathing and picnics. There is no shade, so take sun tan oil, a hat and light clothing to cover up when the sun gets too hot.

Guided visits to the oyster parks take place every day. On certain days, depending on the tides, there are boat trips up the River Eyre into the forest, and four-hour sea-fishing trips are also available.

Information on the above boat services can be obtained from the

Union des Bateliers d'Arcachon, Blvd Veyrier-Montagnères, 33120 Arcachon, tel. (56) 83 17 64.

Golf   Apart from swimming, sunbathing and boating, Arcachon has a good eighteen-hole golf course. When you are feeling less energetic there are scores of cafés where you can enjoy half a dozen of some of the world's freshest oysters with a glass of cool white wine, and watch the world go by.

Where to stay   There are at least twenty hotels in and around Arcachon, all heavily booked in the summer season. The following is a selection.

Arc Hôtel, 89 Blvd de la Plage, 33120 Arcachon, tel. (56) 83 06 85, is a modern functional hotel with direct access to the beach and its own swimming pool. It has thirty bedrooms and three flats with above average comfort and prices; no restaurant.

Grand Hôtel Richelieu, 185 Blvd de la Plage, 33120 Arcachon, tel. (56) 83 16 50, with forty-three bedrooms, is very centrally situated and next to the beach. Above average prices. No restaurant.

Hôtel Les Ormes, 1 Rue Hovy, 33120 Arcachon, tel. (56) 83 09 27, is set back from the road, beside the beach and not far from the marina. It has twenty-four rooms at slightly above-average prices, and good views across the Bassin. There is also a goodish restaurant with lower-price menus for children.

Roc Hôtel et Moderne, 200 Blvd de la Plage, 33120 Arcachon, tel. (56) 83 07 43, has fifty-four rooms, some of which are soundproofed. The hotel is open from 1 April to 15 October, and the restaurant from 15 May to 30 September only. Moderate rates.

Hôtel Les Vagues, 9 Blvd de l'Océan, 33120 Arcachon, tel. (56) 83 03 75, is pleasantly sited near the beach, and the dining room has panoramic views. It has twenty-nine rooms at a little above average prices. The restaurant offers dinner only, for residents only, also at above average prices.

Accommodation   In addition to hotels there are always numerous villas to let in Arcachon during the summer months. It is advisable to book well in advance for the July/August high season, but June and September are no problem. Addresses of agents with properties to let can be obtained from the *Office de Tourisme*, Place Franklyn Roosevelt, Arcachon, 33120, Gironde, tel. (56) 83 01 69.

Where to eat   **Chez Yvette**, 59 Blvd du General Leclerc, 33120 Arcachon (opposite railway station), tel. (56) 83 05 11, is a well-known and old-established restaurant specialising in sea food, with straightforward cuisine, serious but not fancy. The fish is fresh enough to jump off the plate.

Chez Boron, 15 Rue du Professeur Jolyet, 33120 Arcachon, tel. (56) 83 29 96, is a nice, civilised restaurant, unpretentious but professional, with slightly above average prices.

Bayonne, Cours Lamarque de Plaisance, 33120 Arcachon, tel. (56) 83 33 82, is a somewhat cheaper restaurant, open from Easter to the end of September, offering lower-price menus for children. It also has eighteen rooms at modest prices.

Le Patio, 10 Blvd de la Plage, 33120 Arcachon, tel. (56) 83 02 72, is a good restaurant not far from the marina, charging slightly above-average prices.

Les Abatilles

La Réserve du Parc, Parc Péreire, Les Abatilles, 33120 Arcachon, tel. (56) 83 24 01, near the promenade mentioned above, is an unambitious but perfectly sound restaurant very attractively situated near the beach with splendid views across the bay. Tables are inside (picture windows) or outside on the terrace, and there are no shocks with the bill.

This list by no means exhausts the better restaurants of Arcachon. If you want to be sure of a good meal, you may do better to avoid restaurants with a view of the sea, some, though not all, of which trade on this rather than their cuisine. **La Guitoune**, 95 Blvd de L'Océan, 33115 Pyla-sur-Mer, which once had a Michelin star, has been slipping for some years and is not what it was.

**Excursions
Dune du
Pilat**

Reached via Les Abatilles, Le Moulleau, Pyla-sur-Mer and Pilat Plage, the Dune du Pilat is about 8 km south of Arcachon, reached by turning off the coast road where the signpost indicates Biscarosse. About 2 km along this road on the right there is a metered and patrolled car park, from which you can climb the dune. Alternatively, carry straight on instead of turning left at the Biscarosse sign, following the road which climbs for about 1 km, with good views of the entrance to the Bassin, to another point from which the dune can be climbed.

All visitors to Arcachon should at least go to see the Dune du Pilat even if, understandably, they abstain from climbing it. This is one dune which it has not been possible to fix by planting grass, shrubs and pine trees, and it continues to move slowly inland, so that the café-restaurant at the foot on the land side has to move a little further away from it every year or two. The climb to the top has become a lot easier since a rough wooden staircase with 190 steps was installed a few years ago. This saves the lung-bursting business of sliding back one step, up to your ankles in sand, for every two steps up, but it is still not a climb to be undertaken by any other than those fit and in normal health. Once you get to the top there are splendid views in every direction, and in summer there are often hang-gliders enjoying their sport near the dune.

Petit Nice

If you carry on beyond the Dune du Pilat on the Biscarosse road, passing some large camp sites in the forest on the right hand side and then a camp site notice mentioning Petit Nice, you will see soon afterwards on the right, at the top of a rise, a road with a 'No Entry' sign. This is the exit from the parking for Petit Nice beach; the entrance is about 200 m further on. You drive down through the pines to a very large parking area with roads winding among the trees. There are excellent spots for picnics, with one or two snack bars and easy access to the beach. Here, as everywhere else on the Côte D'Argent, most of the girls go topless, and there is a good deal of nudity of both sexes and whole families, though these are not specifically naturist beaches.

There is room for about 700 cars, which seems a lot, but people soon disperse on the huge beach. Lifeguards supervise the bathing on certain stretches, but on all the ocean beaches it is very important to read the safety notices, and never to bathe when the red flag is flying.

Where to stay

Hôtel Haitza, Place Louis Gaume, Pilat Plage, tel. (56) 82 74 64, is situated among the pines, close to the beach. It has fifty rooms at reasonable rates.

Hôtel Beau Rivage, Blvd Océan, 33115 Pyla-sur-Mer, tel. (56) 54 01 82, has twenty-two rooms at average prices. It is near the beach, with a shady terrace and a restaurant of the same name next door.

Where to eat

Auberge Chez Tin Tin, tel. (56) 22 74 82, is situated near the Dune du Pilat on the road to Biscarosse. I remember this establishment when it was just a hut with a few tables under the pines, a swing and a see-saw for children, and would hardly have dared to call itself a restaurant. But it has moved with the times and become serious, with quite a reputation these days for regional dishes. There is also a crêperie.

La Hume and Gujan Mestras

Gujan Mestras is a fishing and oyster producing port and commune adjacent to Arcachon, reached by the D650 which follows the shore line. The waterside here looks, in parts, like a Mexican slum or one of the *favelas* of Rio de Janeiro, but nobody lives in the shacks – they are the stores and workshops of the oyster 'farmers'. La Hume is one of the seven little ports that make the commune of Gujan Mestras the oyster capital of the Bassin.

What to see

While the picturesque fishing cabins and the views across the bay make La Hume a popular spot with artists and photographers, its main attraction is a '**medieval village**' where, every summer, numbers of different craftsmen work in front of the public and explain the secrets of their particular craft. There are from thirty to forty of them including potters, metal workers, jewellers, basket makers, bookbinders, weavers and many others. The 'medieval village' may look like an old film set, but the craftsmen are real enough, often with some of the best in France among them. The village is open from 10 a.m. to 12 noon and 2 p.m. to 7 p.m., later on some evenings, from mid-June to mid-September.

Nearby, there is a children's (and adults') paradise called **Aquacity**. Covering 6 hectares, this was the first of these water parks in Europe (there are now two others in France) and is open to everyone. The entry ticket, valid for the whole day of issue, covers all the amenities except for the restaurant-snack bar, with special rates for families. There is also a picnic area. It offers a variety of swimming pools, paddling pools, boating areas, pools with artificial waves and several kinds of water chutes and tunnels – all with water at about 30°C (80°F).

Le Teich Ornitho- logical Park

Continuing east on the D650 a couple of kilometres from Gujan Mestras, you pass the Château de Ruat, just beyond which you will see a turning on the left, leading to the Wildfowl Reserve.

No serious ornithologist or birdwatcher visiting the Arcachon region should fail to visit it. Occupying part of the estuary of the Eyre and covering 120 hectares, it is a mixture of ponds, meadows, rushy areas and small woods, situated on one of the most important bird migration routes in Europe.

During the course of the year it is possible to see 260 different species of birds. Among these seventy-five nest regularly in the reserve, others halt and rest there during their migration, and others come down from northern Europe to spend the winter there.

The reserve is divided into four areas. The **Parc des Artigues** covers about 2 hectares, with numerous species of exotic ducks from all over the world at liberty on the water, as well as aviaries housing many of the local species, including birds of prey which have been injured and are being cared for. The **Parc de la Moulette**, covering 7 hectares with several small lakes, has practically the whole variety of swans, geese and ducks of Europe at liberty, with several other species of water birds.

The **Parc de Causseyre**, which forms the greater part of the reserve – about 100 hectares – is accessible to the public by a sign-posted footpath leading to the estuary of the Eyre. Four hides and an observation post make it easy to see and photograph birds. At the end of the path where the estuary joins the Bassin, the **Parc Claude Quancard**, is a haven for waders and other birds of the shoreline. Although the public are not allowed into this area, there are two hides which facilitate observation, the best time being during the incoming tide.

Youth hostel

The whole Reserve is open from 10 a.m. to sunset all year round. It has the equivalent of a **Youth Hostel**, which also has simple family accommodation, where it may be possible to spend the night. It has room for about forty people, and provides simple meals.

By road to Cap Ferret

As an alternative to crossing to Cap Ferret from Arcachon by boat, it is possible to make the circuit of the Bassin by car, passing through several smaller resorts on the way.

Andernos-les- Bains

Andernos-les-Bains is a lively summer resort with 4 km of sandy beaches, from which the tide recedes almost out of sight at low tide. It also has an important oyster port and a marina, an artificially deepened channel avoiding the necessity of waiting for full tide before getting afloat. There is a pleasant promenade lined with pines and tamarisks behind the beach. The town is also the setting for a popular jazz festival every summer. Many people from Bordeaux have second homes in Andernos, where the great actress Sarah Bernhardt once

182

had a villa. There is very limited hotel accommodation, most people staying in rented villas or in one of the very large camp sites such as **Camping Fontaine-Vieille**, 4 Blvd du Colonel Wurtz, 33510 Andernos-les-Bains, tel. (56) 82 01 67.

Arès

Next along the shore, Arès is a smaller resort and oyster port, nice enough but no cure for boredom.

As you approach Cap Ferret there is a group of little holiday resorts which enjoy access to the ocean beaches on one side – from Grand Crohot down to Cap Ferret – and to the more sheltered beaches on the Bassin on the other.

Le Canon, Le Grand Piquey – protected by a large sand dune – and Piraillan, a pretty place at the edge of the pines, are all pleasant.

L'Herbe

L'Herbe is a surprising little place with narrow alleys of tarred wooden houses overrun with vines. It was built in the seventeenth century at a time when a law forbade building in stone next to the beach, and the tradition has been maintained since then. It, too, is an oyster port.

Cap Ferret

This is a natural 'jetty' in sand which protects the Bassin from the rougher seas of the ocean. Inaccessible except by boat until 1928 when the first road was built, it at once became popular with rich Bordelais, who built spacious villas there and filled the gardens with mimosas. It has remained a rather exclusive little resort for those who like quiet weekends and peaceful holidays. In season a Heath Robinson-like or, if you prefer, Emmett-like train, converted from a horse-drawn tram, runs across the dunes to the ocean beaches.

Where to stay

Cap Ferret has several small hotels.

Hôtel La Fregate, Avenue de l'Océan, Cap Ferret 33970, tel. (56) 60 41 62, has twenty-four rooms at reasonable prices. No restaurant.

Where to eat

Quatre Saisons, 62 Avenue de l'Océan, Cap Ferret 33970, tel. (56) 60 38 13, is a sound restaurant charging modest prices. It also has simple rooms at inexpensive rates.

Biscarosse-Plage

About 40 km south of Arcachon, Biscarosse-Plage is another sun, sea and sand resort, which has developed from almost nothing in the past twenty years. It has no real character nor identity of its own, but it has an immensity of sandy beach and, for those who prefer to avoid the cool and rugged sea, both indoor and outdoor swimming pools.

The town of Biscarosse is about 10 km inland from the resort – pretty slow ones on summer evenings when everyone is leaving the beach. The town is attractively situated between two large lakes, the Étang de Biscarosse et de Parentis to the south and the Étang de

Cazaux et de Sanguinet to the north. As with the other lakes in this chain, they have sandy beaches and are excellent for fishing, sailing, windsurfing and water-skiing.

A pretty road leads from Biscarosse-Plage through the forest to the tiny sailing villages of Port Maguide, Ispes and Navarosse, all on the shores of the Étang de Cazaux et de Sanguinet, charming triplets in the sun, misty and mysterious in the early morning.

Where to stay

Biscarosse-Plage has about a dozen hotels of average standard.

Hôtel La Forestière, Avenue Pyla, 40600 Biscarosse, tel. (56) 78 24 12, has thirty-four rooms at average rates, and a restaurant with lower-price menus for children.

Navarosse

Hôtel Transaquitaine, Navarosse, 40600 Biscarosse, tel. (58) 78 13 13, is a small simple hotel, quietly situated, with no restaurant, and rooms at average prices.

Ispes

Hôtel La Caravelle, Ispes, 40600 Biscarosse, tel. (58) 78 02 67, is very pleasantly situated, with good views across the lake and rooms and restaurant cheaper than usual.

Mimizan and Mimizan-Plage

South of Biscarosse, parts of the coast and the forest are used by the government as a rocket research station, so this area is closed to the public. The road swings inland, following the east side of the Étang de Biscarosse et de Parentis and then turning south to Mimizan, about 35 km. Mimizan lies between the pretty lake of Aureilhan and the coast about 5 km away, where the resort of Mimizan-Plage has developed.

History

Between the wars, Mimizan was a favourite haunt of Winston Churchill, who used to stay at the Duke of Westminster's house by the lake, a building now in ruins. Like Biscarosse, Mimizan is essentially a sun, sand and sea resort, but it is older and has more character. In Roman times there was a port here, which they called Segosa, and in the Middle Ages Mimizan was quite an important town in the area. But the port and then much of the town was engulfed by the sands, and by the eighteenth century even most of the church had been buried.

An interesting thing about Mimizan is that during the Middle Ages it was a sanctuary town, quadrilateral in shape with sides 1,800 m long, marked by eight stone columns of which four still exist. The abbey and the town itself lay within these boundaries. Any fugitive, even a murderer, could claim the protection of the Church and live with impunity, so long as he stayed within these limits.

All the people living in the enclave, fugitives or not, had special rights relating to shipwrecks, which were frequent on that coast. They were allowed to drink until they could drink no more from any barrels of wine washed ashore, and were also permitted to make themselves clothes from any bales of cloth found on the shore. As the same ship often carried both, and they invariably drank first and made the clothes later, they were sometimes oddly dressed. All that remains of this old town is part of the ruins of the **Benedictine Abbey**, including a doorway with some fine Gothic carving. From Mimizan to Mimizan Plage is now almost one continuous town.

The beach   Mimizan Plage is divided by a small *courant* as the local rivers are called, so that there is a Plage Nord and a Plage Sud linked by one bridge over the stream, although it is the same huge sandy beach on both sides.

In addition to its beaches, Mimizan is a good centre for walking and cycling in the forest, which is particularly attractive in this area.

Where to stay   Mimizan has about a dozen hotels, varying from ordinary to above average in comfort.

Hôtel Côte d'Argent, 6 Avenue Maurice-Martin, Mimizan 40200, tel. (58) 09 15 22, is a comfortable hotel with forty rooms at somewhat above average prices, and a restaurant with panoramic views of the sea.

Hôtel Bellevue, 34 Avenue Maurice-Martin, Mimizan 40200, tel. (58) 09 05 23, has thirty-six rooms at very reasonable prices, and an inexpensive restaurant which offers dinner only.

Plage Sud   **Hôtel Parc**, 6 Rue de la Papeterie, Plage Sud, 40200 Landes, tel. (58) 09 13 88, in a pleasant and calm situation, has sixteen bedrooms. Rooms and restaurants are both modestly priced.

Au Bon Coin, Mimizan, Plage Sud, 40200 Landes, tel. (58) 09 01 55, nicely situated by the lake, has eight expensive bedrooms, but is really better known as a good, well-established restaurant (one Michelin star).

From Mimizan to Hossegor-Capbreton

From Mimizan the road runs south a few kilometres in from the coast to the next large resort, which is Hossegor-Capbreton – a distance of about 55 km. In between it passes through several villages from which there are roads to named beaches.

St Julien-en-Born   The D652 passes first through Bias, from which there is a narrow road to the beach about 8 km away, then comes to St Julien-en-Born, where the nearest beach is **Contis-Plage** (with two small hotels) on the north bank of the Courant de Contis. Inland from St Julien-en-Born is the old village of **Mézos**, which has a well-preserved Gothic church originally built by the Knights of Malta in the fourteenth century.

There are two good little restaurants in Mézos: **Boucau**, Mézos, 40170 St Julien-en-Born, tel. (58) 42 61 38 and **Verdier**, Mézos, 40170 St Julien-en-Born, tel. (58) 42 61 27. Both are inexpensive and offer a high standard of regional cooking.

The D652 continues south to Lit-et-Mixte, St Girons, Léon, Moliets, and Messanges, to Vieux-Boucau-les-Bains and Hossegor-Capbreton.

From each of these places, with the exception of Léon, a road runs directly to a sandy beach. From Lit-et-Mixte the D88 leads to Cap de L'Homy Plage, while from St Girons it is only 5 km to St Girons-Plage.

None of these small places is a full scale resort, coming alive only for a few weeks in summer. They are just superb beaches with the basic facilities of car parks, duckboards to cross the sand dunes, and some seasonal snack bars and restaurants. At most of them bathing is supervised, at least during the August high season. Any notices regarding bathing in the sea should be taken seriously.

Léon South of St Girons the D652 passes the Étang de Léon, an attractive lake popular with anglers, near the village of the same name.

Instead of a road to the sea, Léon has a *courant*. The Courant d'Huchet, the outfall from the Étang de Léon, is the prettiest of all those in the forest, and although boat trips are available on most of them, this one is the most fascinating.

Boat trips After being rowed across the lake, the flat-bottomed boat has to be punted along the narrow *courant*, which for 12 km meanders through the forest, bordered by alders, willows and pines, sometimes open to the sky, sometimes in a creeper-covered tunnel of green shade from overhanging branches, and with yellow and white water lilies in the still parts. Not far beyond the lake there is a small shelter for fishermen where, at certain times of the year, they wait night after night for the eels. Having swum upstream as elvers to grow to maturity in the lake these eels will now head back to their breeding grounds in the Atlantic. When the time comes, the fishermen hang nets from a timber framework permanently erected across the *courant*, sometimes catching as much as half a ton of eels in one night.

The further the boat goes down the *courant* the more exotic the vegetation becomes, with cypresses, tamarisks and wild hibiscus abounding. The shortest trip takes one and a half hours return, the longest – to the sea and back – four hours. Morning is considered the best time of day for this excursion.

Where to stay **Hôtel du Lac**, 40550 Léon, Landes, tel. (58) 48 73 11, is a simple but pleasing little hotel beside the lake at Léon. It has sixteen rooms and is inexpensive both in its good restaurant and in the accommodation.

Moliets and Messanges

South of Léon the D652 passes through Moliets (with two small hotels and holiday flats) and Messanges, both of which have roads to the sandy beach. Moliets Plage is the beach for Léon.

Vieux-Boucau-les-Bains

History

Vieux-Boucau-les-Bains, the next town on this road, has a curious history. Its name means 'the old river mouth', for from 907 to 1164, and again between the fourteenth and the sixteenth centuries, the important River Adour emptied into the sea here (see also p. 188), with the flourishing Port d'Albret at the mouth. However, as the old port of Bayonne, 40 km to the south, was silting up, King Charles IX sent an engineer to fix a permanent mouth for the river there, where it has now been since 1578. As Port d'Albret became silted up and forgotten, the town became known as Vieux-Boucau, 'the old river mouth', instead.

Modern development

Vieux-Boucau went to sleep for a couple of hundred years, but with the development of tourism since the war it has gradually come to life again. Behind the sand dunes which silted up the old harbour, the former bed of the Adour was marked by a swampy depression, flooded by the sea at the time of the year's highest tides. Deciding that it would be a simple matter to create an artificial lake by linking the depression to the open sea, engineers did just that, also building a barrage to regulate the level of the lake. Next a lakeside resort area was developed and called, once again, Port d'Albret. The resort includes a small island in the lake on which there is a 'fishing village' with restaurants, bars and discos, linked to the shores by water buses.

This artificial lake is connected by a stream to the much larger lake, the Étang de Soustons 8 km further inland, which also has tourist facilities and is a popular sailing centre.

Where to stay

Hôtel Côte D'Argent, Rue Principale, Vieux-Boucau-les-Bains, 40480 Landes, tel. (58) 48 13 17, has forty-seven rooms. The restaurant, offering typical Landais food, is more expensive for dinner than for lunch, but their rates all round are somewhat below average.

Hôtel La Bergerie, Avenue du Lac, Soustons 40140, tel. (58) 41 11 43, is a small hotel built in the Landais style, surrounded by pleasant grounds. It has twelve rooms at average prices, and a restaurant for residents only and dinner only, which is not cheap.

Château Bergeron, tel. (58) 41 58 14, an annexe of Hôtel La Bergerie (above), is another hotel in which the restaurant is reserved for clients only and dinner only at above average prices. This is a nineteenth-century property with seventeen rooms at unexceptional rates, which has been well modernised and has nice grounds and a swimming pool.

Where to eat

Pavilion Landais, 40140 Soustons, tel. (58) 41 14 49, enjoys a good view of the lake and offers value for money. It has one Michelin star and serves regional recipes, with game from the Landes during winter. There are also eight rooms at average prices.

Hostellerie Du Marensin, Place Sterling, 40140 Soustons, tel.

(58) 41 15 16, is a good regional restaurant near the lake, with a cheerful atmosphere, hearty portions and agreeably low prices. It also has fourteen inexpensive rooms.

Hossegor-Capbreton

Between Vieux-Boucau-les-Bains and Soustons the D79 turns off south for Hossegor-Capbreton.

Hossegor-Capbreton is one resort but two different communes, separated by the Bourret canal. Together these twin towns form the largest summer resort between Arcachon and Biarritz. Despite considerable development over the past ten years, it remains a very attractive place for a holiday because of the variety in its setting. It has a large tidal lake with sandy beaches, a canal, two rivers, the ocean beaches and the forest, with the backdrop of the Pyrenees in sight from any small elevation. Its attraction is increased because the seashore has not been much urbanised as yet, most of the development having been of villas tucked away on forest roads. There is variety, too, in the difference between the almost entirely new Hossegor, and Capbreton (originally Cap Breton), which has a long history.

History   Hossegor-Capbreton is another place which owes its lake to the temperamental Adour. During historical times this river has several times changed its course and the position of its estuary, alternating between Cap Breton, Port d'Albret and Bayonne. It was shifting sandbanks that caused this phenomenon. In the year AD 907 the river left Cap Breton to flow into the sea 20 km further north at what is now Vieux-Boucau – Port d'Albret as it was then – but in 1164 it left Port d'Albret, making its way into the sea at Bayonne, 20 km south of Cap Breton. Within a hundred years, though, the river mouth was back at Cap Breton, which became a maritime town of considerable importance, and was known as 'the port of a hundred captains'. Then in the fourteenth century a terrible storm blocked the estuary, causing the river to return to Port d'Albret, where it seemed inclined to stay. Meanwhile, the old port of Bayonne was silting up without the river, and King Charles IX sent an engineer, Louis de Foix, to try to fix a permanent mouth for the river. The work was completed successfully, and since 1578 the Adour has flowed into the sea at Bayonne, being kept there by constant dredging. Capbreton, like Port d'Albret, lost its maritime character, but the lake at Hossegor occupies the old bed of the Adour.

The days of the whalers and cod fishermen who sailed from Capbreton as far as Newfoundland are long forgotten but, with the growth of tourism, Capbreton is once again a port, this time for pleasure boats. It has a marina with more than 1,000 berths.

Sea bathing

Hossegor-Capbreton is one of the best places on the Côte D'Argent for sea bathing. Just off the coast there is a deep trench in the ocean bed, ten times as deep as the sea on either side of it. This valley, parallel with the shore and formed at the same time as the mountain chain of the Pyrenees, has the effect of calming the sea so that the waves reaching the beach at Hossegor are reduced in size. Bathers have the choice of a stimulating dip in the cool sea, or a swim in the warmer and shallower waters of the tidal lake.

Modern development

Capbreton's story is an old one, but at the turn of the century the present site of Hossegor was deserted. It was not until a small colony of writers and artists from Biarritz settled there in 1900 that a community began to grow up there, the charm of its situation making it steadily more popular. Today the 2.5 km-long lake is especially popular with dinghy sailors and yachtsmen. There are plenty of other facilities for outdoor activity, including an established eighteen-hole golf course.

Where to stay
Hossegor

Hôtel Beauséjour, Avenue Genets, off Avenue Tour du Lac, Hossegor 40150, tel. (58) 43 51 07, enjoys a calm situation between the lake and the ocean, with forty-six rooms and its own swimming pool. It charges somewhat above average rates and has a rather pricey restaurant.

Hôtel Ermitage, Allée des Pins Tranquilles, Hossegor 40150, tel. (58) 43 52 22, is a small hotel with twelve rooms at moderate prices. The restaurant for residents serves dinner only.

Hôtel de la Plage, Hossegor 40150, tel. (58) 43 50 12, on the sea front, has twenty-six rooms at slightly above average rates, but a reasonably priced restaurant.

Capbreton

Hôtel Ocean, Avenue G. Pompidou, Capbreton 40130, tel. (58) 72 10 22, has fifty-two rooms, many with views over the port and the ocean. Prices are very fair in both rooms and restaurant.

Hôtel Miramar, Blvd Front de Mer, Capbreton 40130, tel. (58) 72 12 82, on the sea front, has forty-two rooms at average prices. The restaurant is open evenings only.

Where to eat

Hossegor-Capbreton has plenty of seasonal cafés and restaurants but is not the easiest place in which to find a good one. One oasis is the **Huitrières du Lac**, 1187 Avenue de Touring Club, 40150 Hossegor, tel. (58) 43 51 48, a restaurant overlooking the lake and specialising in sea food at fair prices. It also has some rooms at average rates.

La Sardinière, Avenue G. Pompidou, 40130 Capbreton, tel. (58) 72 10 49, features prices which are a little above the norm but fair.

Labenne-Océan and Ondres-Plage

The Côte D'Argent ends south of Hossegor-Capbreton where the Adour flows into the sea, but between that point and Hossegor-Capbreton there are two more small beach resorts, Labenne-Océan and Ondres-Plage.

189

Inland from the Côte D'Argent

Nature Park

The Regional Nature Parks in France differ from the National Parks, the object of which is to preserve a particular environment, in that they are set up in scenic but underpopulated zones with the object of stimulating the local economy and attracting suitable activities. They are locally, not nationally, managed by a committee of regional politicians, landowners and representatives of various organisations and businesses.

This Parc Naturel Regional des Landes de Gascogne was set up in 1970 with the chief aim of attracting tourism to the interior, to counterbalance the large numbers visiting the coast, and to develop local crafts and small industries. It covers more than 206,000 hectares, the northern half in Gironde, the southern half in the Landes.

Geographically, the Park lies on both sides of the River Eyre and its two tributaries, the Grande Leyre and the Petite Leyre. The river flows into the Bassin d'Arcachon through the Ornithological Park of Le Teich (see p. 182).

Activities

The Park offers many attractions for the tourist. Both the Grande and the Petite Leyre, as well as Eyre itself, are suitable for canoes, kayaks and flat-bottomed boats, although motor boats are not allowed on these rivers. There are miles of signposted paths for riding and walking throughout the Park, and there is a circuit of 330 km of cycle track through the forest, all within the boundaries of the Nature Park. There are also five horse-riding centres, several canoeing bases and several picnic areas.

Museum

The Park's major attraction is the Open Air Museum (Ecomusée de Marquèze). This is reached by a small train (fare included in the entrance fee) which runs from the little town of Sabres and covers the 5 km through the forest to Marquèze in about ten minutes. There is no access by road.

This Open Air Museum has been established on the site of a deserted farming community, where some buildings have been restored and others have been taken piece by piece from other parts of the forest and re-erected. It is a complete reconstruction of a *quartier* – a typical agricultural community of the Landes as it would have been fifty to a hundred years ago. It includes the farmer's house (*maison de maître*) with its period country furniture, a servant's house, the homes of the farm labourers, a thatched barn, a mill and the miller's house, buildings for the storage of tools and farm carts and different buildings for different animals. The chickens, for example, were kept in raised coops as a protection against foxes. There is also an orchard which serves as an unusual living museum of old varieties of apples, pears, cherries and peaches, no longer grown commercially and becoming increasingly rare.

The Open Air Museum is open every day of the week from Palm Sunday to the end of October, and also on Saturdays, Sundays and public holidays at other times of the year. A guide leaflet in English is available so that you can wander around on your own, and there is a picnic area and a playground for children. You should allow the best part of a morning or an afternoon to see it properly, and to enjoy an interesting outing for the whole family.

Accommodation

The Regional Nature Park has accommodation in *gîtes ruraux* (country cottages) and in holiday villages, with their own leisure facilities, at Hostens and Sabres.

The Parc Naturel Regional des Landes de Gascogne, Préfecture des Landes, 4011 Mont de Marsan; tel. (58) 06 24 25.

Mont de Marsan

Mont de Marsan with a population of 31,000 is the *préfecture* of the Landes department, a quiet place of no special interest to tourists, although it is a good base for exploring the Landais forest. It is built around the junction of two minor rivers, the Douze and the Midou, which become the Midouze, a tributary of the Adour. There is an attractive park beside the Douze.

The town comes alive during the second half of July for a week of Spanish-style fiesta in honour of the local patron saint, Madeleine. There are bullfights (popular throughout the southern part of the south-west) and also the less cruel *Courses Landaises* (see p. 80). Star of the fiesta is the 'bull of fire', a full-sized model of a bull loaded with fireworks and rockets, which is set alight and paraded pyrotechnically through the streets, causing a good deal of 'explosive' excitement in the crowds. There are also sporting competitions of various kinds.

Where to stay

Hôtel Richelieu, Rue Wlérick, 40000 Mont de Marsan, tel. (58) 06 10 20, is a well-run hotel with seventy rooms and a very good restaurant with pleasant, efficient service. Prices are reasonable and there is a wide choice of menus in the restaurant.

Where to eat

Le Midou, 12 Place Porte Campet, 40000 Mont de Marsan, tel. (58) 75 24 26, is a restaurant in the true Landais style both in decor and cuisine, at average prices. It also has eleven inexpensive rooms.

Villeneuve-de-Marsan

The little town of Villeneuve-de-Marsan, 17 km east of Mont de Marsan by the D1, is another good base for excursions in the region and has two excellent establishments which are good hotels and even better known as restaurants.

Where to stay and eat

Restaurant Hôtel Francis Darroze, Grand Rue, 40190 Villeneuve-de-Marsan, tel. (58) 45 20 07, is a solid one star Michelin restaurant concentrating on regional recipes and produce, including game in season. It is quite expensive, but has a low-price menu for children. There are thirty comfortable bedrooms, and three suites at above average rates and a swimming pool.

Hôtel De L'Europe, Place de la Boiterie, 40190 Villeneuve-de-Marsan, tel. (58) 45 20 08, is a smaller hotel with fifteen rooms at aver-

Eugénie-les-Bains

age rates and a one star Michelin restaurant, very reasonably priced and offering some original dishes. It also has a swimming pool.

About 30 km south of Mont de Marsan by the N124 to Grenade-sur-l'Adour and then by the D11, lies Eugénie-les-Bains. This little spa was made fashionable during the Second Empire by the Empress Eugénie, wife of Napoleon III, and continued to be popular through Edwardian times and until the First World War. Since then it gradually slipped into obscurity and had almost been forgotten when Michel Guérard arrived on the scene in 1974. Guérard is one of the great chefs of France, the man credited – and now sometimes blamed – for the invention of *Nouvelle Cuisine*, which has fallen out of favour in Aquitaine as elsewhere. He took over some of the old spa buildings and has made his hotel one of the three most important destinations for gourmets in France.

Where to stay and eat

Les Prés D'Eugénie et Le Couvent des Herbes, Eugénie-les-Bains, 40320 Géaune, tel. (58) 51 19 01, is not only luxurious but has been decorated throughout with great taste and attention to detail. The restaurant (three Michelin stars) offers a slimming menu for residents only and also a normal menu at higher prices for visitors, while the cellars can produce some memorable wines. There are twenty-eight rooms and seven suites, and if your appetite needs encouragement there are swimming pools and tennis courts.

In 1988 a small extension called Le Couvent des Herbes, a conversion of an eighteenth-century convent, was opened, providing eight further bedrooms. The rooms are slightly less expensive than in the main building.

Monsieur Guérard is not a man whose nerve fails when it comes to charging for his services. The prices here really call for a new set of adjectives in which average, above average and expensive have no place. Exceptionally high gives a feeble idea. Let's say that if a couple stay here and eat lunch and dinner for less than 3,000 fr a day, they will be skimping things rather. On the other hand there are hotels in many world capitals, less well furnished, with less distinguished chefs, no swimming pool, and no great outdoors, which charge as much.

If it is *your* nerve which fails, Eugénie-les-Bains remains a good base for touring and there are several infinitely cheaper and simpler hotels.

Hôtel Relais Des Champs, Moulin de Labat, 40320 Géaune, tel. (58) 51 18 00, is a nicely situated hotel with thirty-two rooms at average prices and a good but inexpensive restaurant.

Dax

This *sous-préfecture* of the Landes department, with a population of 19,600, is the most important spa in France after Aix-les-Bains. It is

Mud baths | famous for its mud baths, the curative properties of which were discovered, according to tradition, by a Roman centurion whose old dog, crippled with rheumatism, took to rolling in the mud at the edge of a warm swamp and was soon completely cured. Another story says that the Roman Emperor Augustus brought his daughter, Julia, to Dax for treatment in 27 BC. Whether or not these stories are true, what is certain is that Dax was the most important Roman city in Aquitaine after Bordeaux – and it is still *the* place to have a mud bath. The mud comes from the banks of the Adour, and is mixed with water from mildly radioactive hot springs. The sticky mixture, prepared by council workmen and delivered to the various thermal establishments, is known as *daxine* or *péloïde*, and is reckoned to be very effective in easing the pain of rheumatic joints.

What to see | The usual spa treatment here includes bathing in hot radioactive water, the main source of which is the famous **Fontaine Chaude** in the middle of Dax. The present fountain was built in the nineteenth century in Tuscan style to replace one on the same site crumbling with age. Said by geologists to well up from 2,000 m below the surface, it is the most abundant hot spring in France, giving 2,400 cubic metres of water per day at a temperature of 64°C (147°F), like a hot bath.

While the popularity of most other spas in France has remained stationary or declined, the number of people taking the cure annually at Dax has doubled in the past twenty years.

Apart from the steaming Fontaine Chaude, which is a surprise to most tourists, there are no other major sights in Dax, though there are some of tolerable interest. The **Borda Museum** is better than those in most small towns and has a particularly fine collection of precious coins, from Greek and Roman times right through to the present day. It includes porcelain money used in Saxony at the time of the disastrous German inflation in 1920.

The **Cathedral of Notre Dame** was started in the seventeenth century after the earlier Gothic building had collapsed, but the work was not rushed and the new church was not completed until 1894, 275 years after it was started. All that remains of the Gothic church is the splendid **Apostles' doorway**, which was originally the west entrance of the building but was placed inside in the nineteenth century to protect it from the weather. Each of its pillars represents one of the apostles, with the figure of Christ in the middle.

Just across the river in **St Paul-les-Dax** there is a Romanesque church which those interested in church architecture will find worth a visit. It has a very fine *chevet*, with some good examples of early Romanesque carving.

The main road through the centre of Dax suggests that it is just a dull, provincial town. However, this is a false impression, for it is a town which bears exploring on foot and reveals a certain amount of charm, with pleasant walks beside the Adour and attractive public parks. There is an extensive pedestrian area with smart shops, and a lively **Saturday market** which has been held in the same square since the year 1356, when the Black Prince licensed the first stallholders. Its long existence has given rise to the Gascon saying, on the transience of things: 'It won't last as long as Dax market.'

Where to stay

Because of its popularity as a spa Dax has about fifty hotels, many of them relatively new and many of them unusual in that they are associated with, or part of, a thermal establishment. A full list of the hotels is available from the *Office de Tourisme*, Place Thiers (tel. [58] 74 82 33). They will tell you which are straightforward hotels and which are spa hotels but they will not recommend particular hotels or make reservations. The following is a short selection of 'normal' hotels.

Hôtel du Parc, Place Thiers, 40100 Dax, tel. (58) 74 86 17, is a member of the reliable Mapotel group, with forty rooms at average prices. The restaurant is also reasonably priced.

Hôtel Vascon, Place Fontaine Chaude, 40100 Dax, tel. (58) 74 12 14, is a centrally situated well-run hotel with thirty bedrooms (showers only), at slightly below-average rates. There is an inexpensive restaurant for residents only.

Auberge Les Pins, 85 Avenue F. Planté (Village des Pins), 40100 Dax, tel. (58) 74 22 46, has fifteen rooms and a good and very favourably priced restaurant.

Where to eat

Hôtel Richelieu, 13 Avenue Victor Hugo, 40100 Dax, tel. (58) 74 81 81, is a simple hotel with twenty rooms at average prices. However, it is much better known for its excellent regional restaurant, with a good choice of menus and a lower price for children.

Magescq

Take the N124 out of Dax, signposted Bayonne, and almost immediately fork right on the D16 for Magescq.

Relais de la Poste, 40140 Soustons, tel. (58) 47 70 25, is a good small hotel in its own grounds with swimming pool and tennis court, and celebrated for its restaurant (two Michelin stars). It is not large but very popular, so it is advisable to book ahead. Prices are not cheap, but fair for the standards offered. There are twelve comfortable bedrooms at above average rates.

Summary of sightseeing inland from the coastal resorts

From resorts north of Lacanau-Océan

Several of the world's most famous wine châteaux, including Château Mouton-Rothschild, Château Lafite and Château Latour, are within easy driving distance of these resorts. From Soulac-sur-Mer, the N215 leads directly to Lesparre-Medoc, and from there the D204 to Pauillac brings you to the area of these châteaux. The D204, which continues all the way to Bordeaux with important wine châteaux on either side, can be reached cross country from any of these resorts.

From Arcachon, Le Moulleau, Pyla-sur-Mer

Château de La Brède, the home of the famous eighteenth-century French author, Montesquieu, is reached from Arcachon by the A63 and then the D211 to Saucats. The Château is on the left of the D108 from Saucats to Labrède. (See p. 165 for a description of the Château.)

About 20 km south-east of Labrède on the D125 between Bazas and Langon, the imposing **Château de Roquetaillade** consists of two buildings, the Château Vieux, a fortress built in the twelfth century, and the Château Neuf, dating from the fourteenth and built by Cardinal Gaillard de la Mothe, a nephew of Pope Clement V. It is a magnificent rectangular construction with a round tower at each corner and two more flanking the entrance, reached by a drawbridge across the now dry moat that surrounds the castle. In the 1860s the then owners employed Viollet le Duc, the most famous Parisian architect of the time, to recreate the interior of the castle according to the nineteenth-century notion of what comfortable medieval apartments would have been. Unfortunately, the phylloxera disease destroyed the vineyards all round Bordeaux, and Viollet le Duc returned to Paris, the work unfinished.

Only 10 km south-west from Roquetaillade, the village of **Villandraut** has a similar castle, though this one is partly ruined and has not been restored. It was built at the beginning of the fourteenth century by Pope Clement V, who came from this region, as a Papal Palace. It is thought that he may have employed an English architect as it has similarities with some English and Welsh castles of the same period. Enough of its massive construction remains for it to be worth a visit, and to make comparisons with Roquetaillade.

A few kilometres north of Villandraut by the D114 is the **Château de Budos**, a massive and splendidly sited castle of the same period, and built by another nephew of Pope Clement V, Raymond Guilhem de Budos. It was lived in by the La Roque de Budos family until the French Revolution, but is now a ruin.

This group of castles is near the Sauternes area and its wine châteaux, including Château de Malle and Château Yquem, and as a contrast to the rugged medieval castles you could visit the delightful eighteenth-century Château de Malle (see p. 166).

From Biscarosse-Plage and Mimizan-Plage

The châteaux mentioned under Arcachon are about the same distance cross country from these resorts. Other possible excursions are to the bigger resorts of Hossegor or Arcachon, or inland to Solferino. Easily reached from Mimizan by the D44, Solferino is a model community, established by Louis Napoleon, who made grants to the settlers, as part of his plan for the regeneration of the Landes.

From Hossegor

The most interesting outings from Hossegor are to Dax (see p. 192), Bayonne (p. 207) and Biarritz (p. 211) and, of course, your choice of the many possible trips into the Pyrenees.

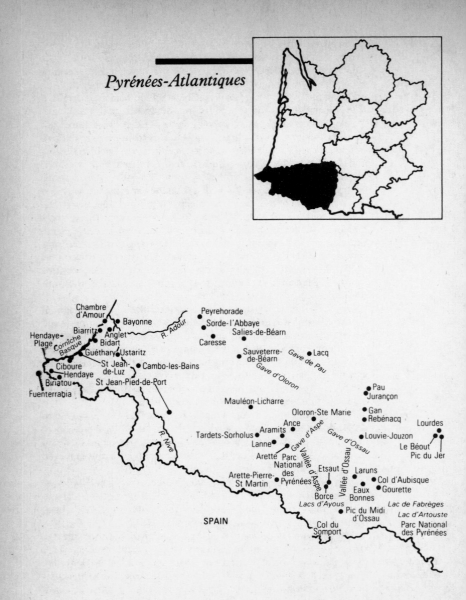

Pyrénées-Atlantiques

Chambre
d'Amour
Bayonne
Biarritz
Anglet
Hendaye-
Plage
Corniche
Basque
Bidart
Guéthary Ustaritz
Ciboure
Hendaye
St Jean-
de-Luz
Cambo-les-Bains
Biriatou
St Jean-Pied-de-Port
Fuenterrabia

Peyrehorade
Sorde-l'Abbaye
Salies-de-Béarn
Caresse
Sauveterre-
de-Béarn
R. Adour
Gave de Pau
Lacq
Gave d'Oloron

Pau
Jurançon
Mauléon-Licharre
Oloron-Ste Marie
Gan
Rebénacq
Ance
Aramits
Lourdes
Tardets-Sorholus
Lanne
Arette
Parc
National
des
Pyrénées
Gave d'Aspe
Gave d'Ossau
Louvie-Jouzon
Le Béout
Pic du Jer

R. Nive

Arette-Pierre-
St Martin
Etsaut
Laruns
Col d'Aubisque
Borce
Eaux
Bonnes
Gourette
Lacs d'Ayous
Lac de Fabrèges

SPAIN

Pic du Midi
d'Ossau
Col du
Somport
Lac d'Artouste
Parc National
des Pyrénées

196

Pyrénées-Atlantiques

Introduction

The department of Pyrénées-Atlantiques offers everything to be found elsewhere in Aquitaine and more besides. Here you can find the wooded hills, green valleys, sparkling streams, orchards and fertile fields, caves and grottoes, and the open sandy beaches, of the other parts of Aquitaine, as well as a rocky coast with cliffs and sandy coves and, visible from all over the department, like an operatic backcloth, the magnificent chain of the Pyrenees.

The Basques   It has, too, the Basques, one of the world's greatest human mysteries, a people of unknown origin who speak a language totally unrelated to any other, a race of great energy and individuality whose life style, even in such basic matters as inheritance and burial, is entirely their own. There are people who believe that the Basques are descended from the last survivors of the lost continent of Atlantis. Could it be possible? There are learned men who do not dismiss this theory.

The territory of the Basques covers approximately one-third of the department – in the south-west against the sea and the mountains – and is continued on the other side of the mountains in Spain. The north-eastern two-thirds is the old province of Béarn, the French part of the former kingdom of Navarre, which included a part of Spain until 1512, when all of Navarre south of the Pyrenees was annexed by Ferdinand of Spain.

Landscape   The wide sandy beaches of the Côte D'Argent continue for a short distance south of the Adour, from Bayonne nearly to Biarritz, where the shore becomes broken by rocky outcrops from the foothills of the Pyrenees. From there south the coast is one of cliffs and coves as well as sandy beaches.

Inland the landscape is shared between the mountain chain itself, rising to the Pic du Midi d'Ossau at 2,884 metres, and the green foothills with their fertile slopes and valleys, watered by the Gave d'Oloron, the Gave de Pau and, further north, the Adour.

Seen from the lower parts of the department, the Pyrenees rise quite suddenly, forming a rugged wall. This is approached in Béarn through the spectacular valleys of Aspe, Ossau and Barétous, which become narrower and more beautiful as they climb towards the passes into Spain. The mountains nearer the coast are gentler and not nearly so high.

This great variety of lovely scenery, coupled with the unfamiliar architecture of Basque houses, villages and churches, makes Pyrénées-Atlantiques one of the most interesting of all the departments of France.

Pau

With a population of nearly 90,000, and probably half as much again with its suburbs, Pau is the largest town of the department, and its *préfecture*. It enjoys a splendid situation and an extremely agreeable climate, the latter having made Pau what it is today.

History

Despite being an ancient settlement, Pau is a place of comparatively recent importance. In the Middle Ages it was insignificant and, unlike the majority of towns in the south-west, it was not on any normal route to St James of Compostella.

Sixteenth century

It was not until the beginning of the sixteenth century that Pau began to acquire an identity. Henri II D'Albret, King of Navarre and a companion in arms with François I of France at the Battle of Pavia, married Marguerite D'Angoulême, sister of the French King, and took her back to his château at Pau. When their daughter, Jeanne D'Albret, married Antoine de Bourbon, she went to live in Nérac, but returned to Pau for the birth of her son. This boy became Henri III of Navarre and, in 1589, Henri IV of France, the first of eight Bourbon rulers of France.

Yet despite this important connection and the fact that it was now the capital of Navarre and the seat of its parliament, Pau remained a small and insignificant place. Even at the end of the sixteenth century its population was only 2,000, and when parliament was convened there was not enough lodging in the town for all its members.

Nineteenth century

As a small market town, Pau lay dormant for hundreds of years, until in the early nineteenth century a few British officers stayed there to recover their health, which had suffered in the campaigns against Napoleon. They liked it, and as the word spread a few more British families went there. It was described in the 1830s as being 'a town where there were a few English families; the Protestant service was held in a wine cellar; few houses were fit to receive strangers; there was not a single carriage to hire; there were no pavements to the streets.' The population then was less than 14,000.

Suddenly the destiny of Pau changed. By 1861 the population had risen to more than 21,000, of which one person in every six was

British. Visitors were spending vast amounts of money, almost all in the winter season. The streets had pavements, new drainage systems had been installed, two Protestant churches had been built and two more were under construction. Pau continued to become more and more fashionable and prosperous.

Healthy climate

This remarkable change in the fortunes of Pau was due to one man and a single book he wrote. He was a Scots doctor named Alexander Taylor, who wrote *The Climate of Pau*. His recommendations as to its suitability for people in need of convalescence after illness, and for those suffering from chest diseases, made it obligatory reading for well-to-do invalids. It was translated into several European languages, with new editions published at regular intervals.

Doctor Taylor distinguished in his book between what he called the 'exciting' climate of south-eastern France, with its excessive dryness of the air and frequent dust-laden winds, which did nothing but irritate lung troubles; the almost windless and mildly humid climate of Pau, which he called 'sedative'; and the warm but heavily humid climate of places like Madeira, which he called 'relaxing'. He argued that the 'sedative' climate was much the best for the invalid, an opinion presumably shared by many doctors, who now began to send their patients to Pau, rather than anywhere else.

Decline

However, the fortunes of Pau changed again in 1889, when Queen Victoria stayed in Biarritz. At once the fashionable world largely abandoned Pau in favour of Biarritz.

Sporting centre

Although the British originally went to Pau to restore their health, they soon created for it a reputation as a sporting centre. In 1842, the racecourse at Pont Long – now one of the most famous steeplechase courses in France – was opened on the outskirts of Pau. Also in the 1840s the British established the first pack of foxhounds in France, which is still in existence today. In 1856 the first golf course on the continent was laid out at Pau. That, too, is still there, with its Victorian club house, and the town has become a popular golfing centre with two other eighteen-hole courses, as well as others in the region. Pau was also one of the first French towns to take up tennis and rugby football. The first flying school in the world was established at Pau in 1909, following flight trials by the Wright brothers, who were attracted by the lack of strong winds.

All this was enough to establish a tradition of sporting activity and leisure in Pau, a reputation which has expanded considerably during the past thirty years, concurrently with a revival of tourism to the town. In the same period, following the discovery and exploitation of natural gas at Lacq, only 25 km away, there has been a steady industrial and commercial growth in the town.

What to see

The **Boulevard des Pyrénées** looks across the valley and the vine-covered and wooded slopes of Jurançon to the great wall of the Pyrenees, only 20 km away. Lamartine called it 'the most wonderful view in the world', and there is no doubt that on a clear, sunny morning or evening, when the shadows define the peaks, it ranks among the finest.

This great terrace, or promenade, runs from the Château Henri IV at one end to the Casino Municipal and the Parc Beaumont at the other. Near the Place Royale, about halfway along, an orientation table enables you to pick out easily the main summits of the western Pyrenees. Behind the casino, the Parc Beaumont with its fine trees and ornamental lake is a pleasant, shady place in the heat of summer.

Château Henri IV is perhaps more interesting for its association with France's most popular king – *'noste Henric'* or 'our Henry' as they call him affectionately in the south-west – than for any intrinsic merits of its own.

It was a simple medieval fortress before its transformation into a livable Renaissance palace by Henri IV's grandmother, Marguerite D'Angoulême. Once Henri became King of France, he held court in Paris, and the château at Pau became more and more neglected. After the French Revolution it was a ruin. Its restoration, together with extensions, was undertaken by Louis-Philippe and completed by Louis Napoleon.

Many sculptures, *objets d'art*, and documents relating to Henri IV are displayed against a background of the royal decor and some superb period furniture in what is now a national museum. Among the finest exhibits are some of the oldest and best preserved Brussels and Gobelin tapestries in France. Some date from 1510; others were made to the order of Henri IV himself by Flemish weavers, whom he had brought to Paris at the end of the sixteenth century. In the south wing there is a subsidiary museum of a different kind, the Musée Béarnais, which is devoted to different aspects of the life of the province, traditional local furniture and craftsmanship, old costumes, and wildlife. The château also has an interesting sixteenth-century kitchen.

The **Musée des Beaux Arts** contains an extensive collection of what, for the most part, are second-rank but by no means second-rate paintings, dating from the seventeenth century to modern times. Among paintings from the Spanish, Italian, Dutch and Flemish schools as well as French, are works by El Greco, Ribera, Jordaens and three paintings by Rubens. The museum also features one of the earliest Impressionist paintings – *The Cotton Merchant's Office, New Orleans* – which was entered in the second Impressionist exhibition in Paris in 1876 by Edgar Degas, who had family in business in New Orleans.

The **Musée Bernadotte** at 8 Rue Tran was the birthplace in 1763 of Bernadotte, one of Napoleon's officers, whose career was equally sensational if on a smaller scale.

In a flat on the second floor, he was born the son of a none too prosperous lawyer. At the age of seventeen he joined the army as a private; nine years later he became a sergeant; three years after that the former

NCO had been promoted to colonel, and in the following year, at the age of thirty, he became a general. He was a companion of Napoleon, and although the two did not always agree, Napoleon nonetheless continued to advance him, making him a Marshal of France and Prince of Ponte Corvo. But as the years passed their disagreements became more frequent and serious, until in 1809 Napoleon sacked him. This would have meant obscurity or worse for anyone else, but not for Bernadotte. In the following year, at the age of forty-seven, he was adopted by Charles XIII of Sweden, whom he succeeded to the throne as King of Sweden and Norway in 1818. His dynasty still reigns in Sweden.

The rooms on the second floor have been refurnished in the style of a home of the late eighteenth century, with a fully equipped kitchen of the time. On the first floor, Bernadotte's career is illustrated by pictures, drawings, books and personal possessions, with souvenirs of his royal relatives and descendants. The whole provides an interesting sidelight on the history of Napoleonic times.

Where to stay
Hôtel Continental and **Restaurant Le Conti**, 2 Rue Maréchal Foch, 64000 Pau, tel. (59) 27 69 31, is the largest hotel in Pau, with 110 soundproofed and comfortable bedrooms at slightly above average prices. The restaurant charges normal rates for this sort of hotel.

Hôtel Bristol, 3 Rue Gambetta, 64000 Pau, tel. (59) 27 72 98, is a comfortable hotel with twenty-five spacious rooms, rather old fashioned in style but soundproofed, at average prices. No restaurant.

Hôtel Commerce, 9 Rue Maréchal Joffre, 64000 Pau, tel. (59) 27 24 40, has fifty-one rooms at average prices. The restaurant is not expensive and offers low-price menus for children.

Le Beau Manoir, Route de Notre Dame de Piétat, Uzos, 64110 Jurançon, tel. (59) 06 17 30, is situated about 6 km outside Pau. A newish hotel in its own wooded grounds with a swimming pool and a view of the mountains, it has thirty-two rooms at average prices, with continental breakfast included, and a moderately priced restaurant.

Where to eat
Restaurant La Gousse d'Ail, 12 Rue du Hédas, 64000 Pau, tel. (59) 27 31 55, offers good regional cooking at moderate prices. Situated in the old quarter of Pau, it features an appropriate decor of beams and stone walls. The proprietor, Christian Marcou, was once chef to the French underwater explorer, Commandant Jacques Cousteau, aboard the *Calypso*.

Restaurant Pierre, 16 Rue Louis Barthou, 64000 Pau, tel. (59) 27 76 86, is Pau's 'smart' restaurant, with an informal and relaxed atmosphere and a high standard of regional cooking at above average prices.

La Table d'Hôte, 1 Rue du Hédas, 64000 Pau, tel. (59) 27 56 06, charges below average prices at lunch time, but is more expensive in the evening.

Restaurant Le Chat Luné, Rue du Hédas, 64000 Pau, tel. (59) 27 09 07, is another restaurant in the old quarter, offering very good and original cuisine, with menus starting at an average price for lunch. The walls are built with pebbles from the Gave de Pau, and there is a huge fireplace.

Discos

Le Paradis, 11 Place du Forail, 64000 Pau, tel. (59) 84 06 73.

Le Windsor, 17 Rue Valérie Meunier, 64000 Pau, tel. (59) 27 44 73.

Le Royale, which is the discotheque of the Casino, in the Parc Beaumont, tel. (59) 27 56 27.

Lourdes

Although not strictly speaking within the limits covered by this book, Lourdes is very easily reached from Pau, being 37 km away by the D937.

St Bernadette

On 11 February 1858, a fourteen-year-old peasant girl called Bernadette Soubirous was gathering sticks beside the Gave de Pau, opposite a cave in a rock face called Massebielle, when, looking into the cave, she had a vision of the Virgin Mary. It was the first of eighteen appearances of the Virgin to the girl. On the ninth occasion, by which time she was being followed to the grotto by crowds of the curious and the faithful, she scratched the ground with her fingers in the presence of numerous spectators, who saw a previously unknown spring burst forth.

In 1862 a sanctuary was built above the grotto, and the first procession took place in 1864, when the statue of Notre Dame de Lourdes was placed there. Two years later Bernadette entered the order of the Sisters of Charity, and was sent to their main convent near Nevers. She died on 16 April 1879, and was made a saint in 1933.

The first organised pilgrimage to Lourdes took place in 1873, and in 1874 it included fourteen invalids. Since then there has been a steady increase in the numbers of the sick in the pilgrimages, which take place in the summer.

What to see

Apart from its significance as the most visited place of pilgrimage in the modern Christian world, Lourdes is a town of rather limited interest. It is pleasantly situated beside the Gave de Pau, immediately below the mountains and dwarfed by them. It really consists of two towns. In the original Lourdes stands a hilltop feudal castle, in which the Black Prince once stayed. Together with all the surrounding territory, it was ceded to the English as part of the ransom for the French King Jean, who had been captured at the Battle of Poitiers. The castle has been restored and now houses a Pyrenean museum, which illustrates many aspects of life in the Pyrenees – costumes, pottery, musical instruments, furniture and crafts. As the importance of Lourdes as a religious centre increased, a new town grew up and steadily expanded around the old part.

You can obtain a fine view over Lourdes from the top of the nearby hill called Le Béout, which is reached by cable car that starts about 1 km from the town centre on the right-hand side of the Avenue Maréchal Foch. It operates from Palm Sunday to mid-October. There is an even better view from the Pic du Jer, 150 m higher at 948 m. It is reached by funicular that starts 0.5 km down the same road at the junction with the N21 and the road to Argelés-Gazost.

Some visitors may find the feverish commercialism of Lourdes somewhat excessive, although it is better now than it used to be.

Where to stay

Although there are plenty of hotels in Lourdes, it can still be difficult to find a room in the summer if you have not booked in advance, and if you want peace and quiet Lourdes is really not the place to stay.

Grand Hôtel de la Grotte, 66 Rue de la Grotte, 65100 Lourdes, tel. (62) 94 58 67, is a comfortable hotel in the Mapotel group, situated below the castle. Rooms on the upper floors have a good view over the city and the mountains. There are eighty-four rooms at slightly above average prices, and a restaurant with cheap menus for children.

Hôtel d'Espagne, 9 Avenue Paradis, 65100 Lourdes, tel. (62) 94 06 30, is a well-run hotel with ninety-two comfortable rooms at slightly above average rates, but with continental breakfast included. It has a garden and a restaurant, which charges average prices with a cheap menu for children.

Hôtel Notre Dame de France, 8 Avenue Peyramale, 65100 Lourdes, tel. (62) 94 91 45, is a functional hotel with seventy-five rooms at average rates, and an inexpensive restaurant.

Hôtel Lutétia, 19 Avenue Gare, 65100 Lourdes, tel. (62) 94 22 85, is a reasonably comfortable hotel, with forty-seven rooms, at average prices, some offering views of the mountains. There is an inexpensive restaurant with cheaper menus for children.

Where to eat

Restaurant l'Hermitage, Place Monseigneur Laurence, 65100 Lourdes, tel. (62) 94 08 42, is a sound restaurant, where the cooking often has a touch of originality. Moderate prices.

Le Relais de Saux, Saux, 65100 Lourdes, tel. (62) 94 29 61, 3 km from Lourdes by the D914 and N21, in a peaceful situation far from the crowds. In an old house with its own vegetable garden, this is a restaurant where you will find first-class regional cuisine based on local produce. Madame Hérès keeps everything up to scratch and also offers eight spotless rooms at rates which vary from average to above average. During the season *demi-pension* is obligatory.

Vallée d'Ossau

This is an excursion for those who would enjoy a good look at the High Pyrenees but without mountaineering and where even walking is optional. Although it involves a drive of only about 65 km in each direction, it also includes a journey of ten rather slow kilometres on the highest tourist train in Europe, so some planning is necessary. It is advisable to check the timing with the Régie Départmentale des Stations d'Altitude, 47 Avenue Norman Prince, 64000 Pau, tel. (59) 80 17 28 (before 14 June) or (59) 05 36 99 (after 14 June). You should also check the weather forecast, so that you can choose a suitable day to enjoy the wonderful views at altitude.

Laruns and Eaux Bonnes

Leave Pau by the N134 to Jurançon, continue to Gan and keep left on the D934 for Rebénacq, Louvie-Jouzon and Laruns. Just beyond the old village of Laruns, turn left on to the D918 for Eaux Bonnes. This is a route where the scenery varies from pleasant to splendid. Almost a thousand years ago, more than a hundred families made a living in Laruns from flocks of sheep, which they kept in the mountains in summer, making cheese from the milk, bringing the flocks down to the foothills of Béarn to pass the winter. This is still their way of life today, although the village is now somewhat larger.

Eaux Bonnes, an attractive mountain spa tucked away in a wooded valley, was made fashionable at the end of the nineteenth century by the Empress Eugénie.

Where to eat

Unless you start very early in the morning, you will probably find it convenient to have an early lunch before taking the tourist train. There are two sound and inexpensive restaurants in Laruns.

Auberge Bellevue, Ancienne Route de Pau, 64440 Laruns, tel. (59) 05 31 58.

Hôtel Le Lorry, Route des Eaux Bonnes, 64440 Laruns, tel. (59) 05 31 22.

There are also two inexpensive restaurants in Eaux Bonnes.

Hôtel des Pyrénées, Rue Louis Barthou, Eaux Bonnes, 64440 Laruns, tel. (59) 05 38 60.

Hôtel de la Poste, Rue Louis Barthou, Eaux Bonnes, 64440 Laruns, tel. (58) 05 33 06.

From Eaux Bonnes return to the D934 and continue south towards the frontier, passing the side of the Lac de Fabrèges. Turn left off the main road to follow round the opposite bank of the lake to the point from which the cable car leaves to take you up to the train. A new winter sports resort, Fabrèges-Village, is being built on the slopes above the lake.

Tourist train

The little train, which runs from June to September only, covers 10 km at an altitude of over 2,000 m, with a compulsory stop of an hour and a quarter at the terminus. A footpath leads to the beautiful mountain lake of Artouste, about forty minutes' walk there and back (wear sensible shoes and take a pullover), but if you are not feeling energetic, there is a bar restaurant at each end of the railway.

Col d'Aubisque

If the train ride does not appeal, you could instead continue about 10 km from Eaux Bonnes along the D918 to the Col d'Aubisque via

Gourette, which in winter is a popular ski resort. The Col is at an altitude of 1,709 m, affording panoramic views.

Vallée d'Aspe

Oloron-Ste Marie

The Vallée d'Aspe is reached via Oloron-Ste Marie (33 km from Pau by the N134), a town of about 12,000 inhabitants at the confluence of the Gave d'Ossau and the Gave d'Aspe. Oloron is not especially interesting, but does contain a Romanesque portal in the **Église Ste Marie**, which those interested in church architecture will find worth a visit. This beautifully carved doorway was erected early in the twelfth century by Gaston IV, Viscount of Béarn, on his return from the First Crusade, to mark the capture of Jerusalem in which he played a leading part. It has survived undamaged through religious wars, invasions and the passage of the centuries. Its carvings are almost as clearly defined now as when they were made nearly a thousand years ago. This is due to the purity of the air, as well as the material – hard grey and gold Pyrenean marble, which over the years has taken on the patina of old ivory.

Where to eat

Relais Aspois, 17 Route de Somport, Gurmençon, 64400 Oloron-Ste Marie, tel. (59) 39 09 50, lies about 4 km outside Oloron-Ste Marie on the N134. It is a pleasant restaurant with a rustic interior, where you get a generous regional meal at a very moderate price. It also has eighteen rooms, a few with private bath, at inexpensive rates.

The Valley

From Oloron, the N134 follows the Valley of the Aspe, beside the river, the whole way to the Spanish frontier at the **Col du Somport**. At 1,632 m, this pass is one of the major routes into Spain across the mountains, and is kept open all year round.

The narrow, steep-sided glacial Valley of the Aspe offers one display of scenic grandeur after another. In winter several of its villages are popular centres for cross-country skiing, and in summer the valley is a base for pony trekking, rock climbing and mountain walking. One of the national footpaths, the GR10, crosses the head of the valley near the Col du Somport. Its route lies through the Parc Nationale des Pyrénées to the **Lacs d'Ayous**, just below the **Pic du Midi d'Ossau**, whose rugged cone mirrored in the still lake is one of the finest sights in all this splendour.

Pyrenean bears

In the remoter side valleys of the Vallée d'Aspe live the few remaining Pyrenean bears, at long last, and almost certainly too late, a protected species. A study is being made of how best to preserve the dozen or so left, and of the possibility of reintroducing bears brought from other mountains. You can see one in captivity in an enclosure in the village of **Borce**, about 20 km on the French side of the Col du Somport, just off the N134. On the opposite side of the road, in the village of Etsaut, the Parc Nationale des Pyrénées maintains a permanent exhibition, showing the life of the bears in the mountains, their food, movements, relations with hunters and shepherds and their future.

Vallée du Barétous

This valley is also reached from Oloron-Ste Marie, by the D919 to Ance, Aramits, and Arette. More open than the Vallée d'Aspe, its scenery is softer and less grandiose, though equally beautiful, with hills and maize fields, green pastures and small oak woods, all backed by the majestic peaks.

Aramits

Its chief village, Aramits, is by tradition associated with one of Dumas' musketeers, Aramis, whose family were nobles benefiting from the tithes of the local abbey. Of this building all that remains is a seventeenth-century church.

Arette

Further up the valley, the village of Arette was largely destroyed by an earthquake on 13 August 1967, but has since been rebuilt in the same style. A few kilometres to the north-west of Arette is **Lanne**, a village which has an attractive church, restored in the eighteenth century, and a seventeenth-century fortified manor, which another tenacious tradition claims as the home of Isaac de Porthau, the original of another musketeer, Porthos.

Caves

From Arette the D132 winds up through 20 km of lovely scenery to Arette-Pierre-St Martin, a winter sports resort at 1,640 m. Beneath your feet here lies one of the largest systems of caves and underground rivers anywhere in the world. It was discovered in 1950, when a Belgian doctor and an experienced caver measured the depth of a hole in the ground not far from the Col de la Pierre St Martin. They found that it went straight down for 346 m. Since then an underground river 450 m below the surface has been found, as well as a series of large caves, one of which, the Salle de la Verna, is 230 m long, 180 m wide and 150 m high. Further explorations have shown the system, which is not open to visitors, to be more than 30 km long and to reach a depth of more than 1,300 m.

Mauléon-Licharre

From Aramits a very picturesque route, the D918, leads via Lanne and Tardets-Sorholus to Mauléon-Licharre. To look at it you would not think that Mauléon-Licharre is in fierce competition with China, but it is. Most espadrilles these days seem to come from China or some other part of the Far East, but these rope-soled sandals originally came from this pretty, apparently sleepy little town, where 70 per cent of all the genuine French espadrilles are still made. From this village take the D11 and D231 to Sauveterre-de-Béarn.

Where to stay

Hostellerie du Château, 25 Rue de la Navarre, 64130 Mauléon, tel. (59) 28 19 06, is a pleasant hotel with thirty rooms at below average prices, and an inexpensive restaurant.

Sauveterre-de-Béarn

A picturesque old town built on a promontory overlooking the Gave d'Oloron, Sauveterre-de-Béarn has an early Gothic church, from the terrace of which you can enjoy an excellent view of the Gave and an old, ruined bridge. A section of the ancient fortifications remain, including an old tower, but apart from its photogenic qualities the interest of Sauveterre is fairly quickly exhausted.

Salies-de-Béarn

North of Sauveterre-de-Béarn by the D933, lies the equally charming Salies-de-Béarn, an old town which grew up around an abundant salt spring, the waters of which are used not only for the production of high-quality salt, but also in a thermal establishment for the treatment of rheumatism and allied conditions. Salies-de-Béarn still has the character of an old-fashioned spa, although the actual medical installations have been completely modernised. As with Sauveterre-de-Béarn, its chief attraction is in its overall picturesque qualities.

Where to stay and eat

Hôtel du Golf, 64720 Salies-de-Béarn, tel. (59) 65 02 10, is a newish three-storey building of unusual and appealing design. It has thirty-three spacious bedrooms, a swimming pool on an open terrace overlooking its nine-hole golf course, and tennis courts. The restaurant was closed in 1988 for want of a good chef, but is expected to reopen in 1989. (This hotel is not to be confused with the adjacent and rather less comfortable Golf Helios Hôtel, about 100 m away, which is an older and simpler building, with restaurant.)

Restaurant Terrasse, Rue Lume, 64720 Salies-de-Béarn, tel. (59) 38 09 83, is an appealing little restaurant with inexpensive menus, pleasantly situated by the riverside.

Sorde-l'Abbaye

From Salies-de-Béarn take the D17 via Caresse and Sorde-l'Abbaye to Peyrehorade and from there join the N117 to Bayonne. In Sorde-l'Abbaye stands a partly ruined Benedictine monastery, which was originally built on the site of a Roman villa. Important mosaics of the third and fourth centuries can be seen, together with the remains of the Roman central heating system.

Bayonne

Situated at the confluence of the Rivers Adour and Nive, Bayonne is a likeable place, both unusual and animated. It must once have been Basque, for its name is a corruption of *Ibai-Ona*, which means lovely river in the Basque tongue and refers to the Nive. Today, although it is the *sous-préfecture* responsible for the administration of the French Basque territory, it is an essentially Gascon town.

History

Like most of the other large towns of the south-west, Bayonne was founded by the Romans, who called it Laburdum, a word which survives in the name of the Basque province, Labourd, in which Bayonne is situated. Very little is known of Bayonne between Roman times and the late Middle Ages. Then, as part of the lands inherited by Eleanor of Aquitaine, it became English in the twelfth century when she married Henry Plantagenet, and it remained English for 300 years.

Bayonne's activities as a port suffered because of the vagaries of the Adour (see p. 187). Because of the strategic importance of its proximity to Spain, Charles IX of France sent the engineer, Louis de Foix, to Bayonne with instructions to bring the Adour back to Bayonne, in case it should be needed as a naval base against Spain. Louis de Foix diverted the Adour back into its old bed by blocking the new one, a project that took six years to complete. Finally in 1578, storm waters came flooding down the Adour, the dykes held, and the river poured back to Bayonne.

From this time on, the prosperity of Bayonne increased, reaching a peak in the eighteenth century, when the town was famous for its corsairs, who won an enormous amount of wealth from raids on foreign shipping, mostly British.

Napoleonic | Bayonne played a small but significant part in the Napoleonic
Wars | Wars; its capture in April 1814 by the Duke of Wellington's army was the last important event of the Peninsular War, and was achieved by one of the most ingenious and daring exploits in the history of war.

In order to surround the city to besiege it, Wellington had to get his army across the Adour from south to north. He chose a point about 5 km below Bayonne and 2 km above the sandbanks which partially blocked the estuary. In bad weather the passage into the Adour past the sandbanks was extremely dangerous, but Wellington realised that he could not bring up bridging materials by land without making his intentions obvious to the enemy. What he did was so unlikely that the capable French commander, Marshal Soult, thought it impossible and disregarded it.

Against all advice Wellington decided to bridge the Adour, 250 m wide at that point and with a tidal rise and fall of 4 m, by bringing his materials from Spain by sea. On 23 February 1814, Sir John Hope, to whom Wellington had given command of the operation, sent one man to swim across with a line. Despite the rough weather, the man succeeded and was followed by others, until there were enough of them to pull across a hawser tied to the line. Using this hawser to drag themselves across, 600 men of the Guards followed on roughly made rafts. The French, who should have prevented this initial landing, were driven back by rocket fire.

The next day, in even wilder weather, Wellington's small ships, with men-of-war cutters being rowed through the surf to guide them, battered their way into the Adour. Several of them ran aground, but twenty-six got through. Moored head-to-stern across the river and joined by planks and cables they had carried with them, they formed a bridge which rose and fell with the tide. While the Guards held the bridge head, Wellington's troops and artillery crossed this makeshift bridge and set siege to the town. On 14 April the beleaguered garrison tried to break out and a fierce battle ensued, but the sortie was unsuccessful and a few days later Bayonne surrendered.

Bayonne today

Today Bayonne is a crowded, lively and prosperous city. Its port activities have decreased in recent years, although it still exports maize and the chemical by-products of the petroleum industry at Lacq, near Pau. Its prosperity now is due to the diversity of its industry and commerce and the fact that, although it has a population of only 42,000 itself, it is the administrative and business centre of an agglomeration of about 160,000.

The two rivers divide the town into three parts: the St Esprit quarter lies north of the Adour, while south of the Adour the Nive divides the town into Grand Bayonne and Petit Bayonne. Several factors combine to give Bayonne its individuality, colour and interest. The old town, on both sides of the Nive, is still encircled by its old fortifications, while in Grand Bayonne there is a massive old fortress, the Château Vieux, which was originally built in the thirteenth century, but was rebuilt in the sixteenth. An even bigger fortress, the Château Neuf, stands against the ramparts in Petit Bayonne, and is in fact older than the present Château Vieux, having been built in the late fifteenth century. Across the river in the St Esprit quarter stands a seventeenth-century citadel built by Vauban, on the orders of Louis XIV. There is a splendid Gothic cathedral, as well as five bridges linking Grand and Petit Bayonne across the Nive, and the Pont St Esprit across the Adour. Also to be seen are fascinating old pedestrianised streets and attractive gardens, particularly the Parc de Mousserolles, which has a lake, an open air theatre, and games areas.

What to see

The **Cathedral Ste Marie**, which is in the centre of Grand Bayonne, is built on the site of an earlier Romanesque cathedral. Most of the existing building was erected in the fourteenth century in the early Gothic style, the flamboyant Gothic sacristy and chapter house being added in the sixteenth century. It is a building of harmonious proportions, although it did not escape the nineteenth-century passion for adding twin spires to old cathedrals. There is some fine Renaissance stained glass in the nave and side chapels, while the window in the St Jerome chapel dates from 1531. Three sides of the beautiful fourteenth-century cloister remain, though very much restored, especially during the nineteenth century.

The **Rue Port Neuf** is a delightful little pedestrian street with old arcades, under which there are cafés and *pâtisseries* where you can taste the famous Bayonne chocolate. When Cortez was introduced to chocolate during his conquest of Mexico, he tasted a rather uninviting mixture made with ground maize, ground cocoa beans, peppers and other spices. The secret of making chocolate more or less as it is today was discovered by the Spanish Jews, who brought their skills with them to Bayonne when they were driven out of Spain in the seventeenth century. Chocolate thus became an important item in Bayonne's trade, and although less is made nowadays, superb chocolate can still be obtained. Cazenave, the chocolate shop at 19 Arceaux de Port Neuf, has been established more than a hundred years, and is known all over the south-west.

Much of the collection in the **Musée Bonnat** in Rue Jaques Lafitte in Petit Bayonne was bequeathed by Léon Bonnat, a fashionable portrait painter at the end of the nineteenth century. He used his wealth to accumulate a remarkable collection of art and antiquities, which he left to the state on condition that it should remain in his birthplace, Bayonne. It has since been added to, and now has a room devoted to Rubens, five Van Dycks, paintings by El Greco, Ribera, Murillo, Goya, David, William Etty, Joshua Reynolds and Sir Thomas Lawrence, as well as ten paintings and ninety-five drawings by Ingres, among many other works. Bonnat's own collection included 1,800 drawings from the fifteenth to the nineteenth centuries, which can be seen by appointment – telephone (59) 59 08 52.

Also in Petit Bayonne, in Rue Marengo, the **Musée Basque** is a must for all who are interested in the mystery of the Basques. It covers every aspect of the known history and traditions of the Basque race: their sacred art, costumes, houses and furniture, dances and games. It is a fine exposition of a complete society brimming with originality.

Where to stay

Hôtel Agora, Avenue Jean Rostand, 64100 Bayonne, tel. (59) 63 30 90, has 104 rooms at a little above average prices. One of a modern chain of hotels, it is large and well designed, featuring a bar with a terrace overlooking the Nive, and an inexpensive restaurant which offers simple meals and special menus for children.

Hôtel Aux Deux Rivières, 21 Rue Thiers, 64100 Bayonne, tel. (59) 59 14 61, is a rather old-fashioned hotel with eighty-six spacious, well-kept rooms at average rates. It is well placed in a quiet part of Grand Bayonne, but has no restaurant.

Where to eat

Restaurant Cheval Blanc, 68 Rue Bourgneuf, 64100 Bayonne, tel. (59) 59 01 33, is a pleasant restaurant with a high standard of cooking and good service. Prices are above average but it offers good value for money.

Restaurant de la Tour, 5 Rue des Faures, 64100 Bayonne, tel. (59) 59 05 67, is a traditional Basque restaurant in which the chef/proprietor offers generous portions of regional food at moderate prices.

Outside Bayonne

Restaurant La Patoula, 64480 Ustaritz, tel. (59) 93 00 56, is situated about 12 km from Bayonne on the D932 to Cambo-les-Bains. An attractive country-house restaurant on the banks of the River Nive, it offers excellent regional dishes and pleasant, efficient service, at above average prices. It has a summer dining room with picture windows, and a winter dining room with a huge log-burning fireplace. There are also nine very well-furnished bedrooms, with bath or shower, at a little above average rates.

The Côte Basque

The best route from Bayonne to Biarritz is by the road which follows the south bank of the Adour towards the sea. Do not turn left until you reach the end, where the road bears round left and becomes the Blvd des Plages, leading to Biarritz, with the Chiberta golf course on the left and the seashore on the right.

Every few hundred metres on the right of this road there is a signpost indicating a beach, all of which are within easy driving distance of any part of Bayonne, Biarritz or Anglet (pronounced Onglette), the resort which joins them, the whole complex often being referred to as BAB. Except that there are occasional large rocks and no real sand dunes, the beaches here resemble those of the Côte D'Argent – wide, flat sands. The **Plage de Madrague** has excellent parking arrangements just behind the beach, a pleasant little snack bar, clean public toilets, neat footpaths covering the short distance to the beach, and supervised bathing. Another recommended beach, slightly nearer Biarritz, is the **Plage des Corsairs**. Rather more rough and ready is the **Plage de Marinella**, whose parking area is a favourite for mobile homes and caravans. There are at least half a dozen of these beaches, all slightly different. Some allow dogs, for example, some do not. It is simply a matter of sorting them out systematically and deciding which you prefer. They all have the advantage over many ocean beaches that the absence of sand dunes enables parking to be much closer to the beach.

As you approach Biarritz you come to the beach known as the **Chambre d'Amour**. It gets its name from a legend, which tells of two lovers long ago dallying in a cave by the beach, who were caught by the rising tide and drowned. It is actually a less intimate place than it sounds, more suited to surfing than amorous dalliance.

Biarritz

History
Whaling

In the fourteenth century, Biarritz was a tiny fishing port, specialising in the hunting of whales. A watchman, keeping a lookout in a tower called an *atalaye* on a headland which today bears this name, would light a fire when he saw a whale. The smoke was a signal to the men to go to their boats in the port below. By the end of the seventeenth century the whales had deserted Biscay, and no more fires were lit in the watch tower.

Sea bathing

It remained an obscure little place for hundreds of years, until the nineteenth century, when people from Bayonne began to visit the

211

sheltered beach of Le Vieux Port at Biarritz, to indulge the new fad of sea bathing. They made the journey on horseback or by donkey. In 1843 Victor Hugo wrote: 'Biarritz is a lovely place. I have only one fear, that it may become fashionable. Already people come from Madrid. Soon they will be coming from Paris.' His fears were well founded. Among the distinguished visitors from Spain was Eugénia de Montijo, Countess of Teba, who was to become the wife of Napoleon III and Empress Eugénie of France. Having loved Biarritz since she visited it with her mother from childhood, she took the Emperor there and persuaded him to build a 'villa'. I put villa in quotes because the house he had built, the Villa Eugénie, was much closer to a palace than a villa. It is today the Hôtel du Palais.

From that time on Biarritz has been a fashionable resort. Queen Victoria, who was very fond of the lively Eugénie, visited her there, and other royalty followed, including Leopold I of Belgium, Edward VII of England, Alphonso XIII of Spain, and enough Russian Grand Dukes to require a Russian Orthodox church to be built. In those days Biarritz was known as 'the beach of kings'.

Smart people need smart shops. Coco Chanel was the first of the great designers to have a salon in Biarritz, followed, among others, by Molyneux, Lelong, Lanvin and Hermes. It was typical of the style of Biarritz then that the designer, Jean Patou, used a white limousine driven by a black chauffeur on sunny days, and a black limousine driven by a white chauffeur when skies were grey.

Biarritz today

The popularity of Biarritz has waxed and waned without ever dying, and today it is once again very much in fashion, in a more discreet way, with the super-rich and famous.

Biarritz is set on a coastline of almost orchestrated beauty. The first note is struck by the Pointe St Martin with its white lighthouse. Beyond that is the Plage Miramar, which runs on into the wider Grand Plage, closed by the headland of the Pointe Atalaye. Beyond that lies the sheltered sandy beach of Le Vieux Port, followed by more rocks and the long, exposed beach of the Côte des Basques, leading to the smaller Plage Marbella and the Plage Milady. Around the Pointe Atalaye are coves which might have been imported direct from Cornwall or Brittany. Everywhere large rocks lie scattered here and there offshore, as if set there expressly for great Biscay waves to smash themselves thunderously in great clouds of spray. The little fishing port, built in the nineteenth century to replace the unserviceable old port, is of tiny, almost toy dimensions.

Promenades lined with tamarisks and gardens bursting with mammoth hydrangeas have been added to this lovely setting, the whole making Biarritz one of the most pleasant resorts anywhere for taking a stroll. There is plenty to look at, even when you turn away from the sea, though very little in the way of conventional sights. Biarritz must be an architectural student's delight with its confident mixture of nineteenth-century grotesque, art deco, and twentieth-century luxury matchbox styles. This strange blend gives the whole town a bizarre charm, particularly since each style has been carried out with the assertion allowed by unlimited wealth.

What to see

The **Musée de la Mer**, situated on the flat part of the Atalaye headland, is a must for all naturalists. It has a fine collection of the sea birds of Biscay, and a comprehensive aquarium, as well as an unusual exhibition devoted to the techniques of fishing. Visitors are greeted by a statuesque but taciturn polar bear (stuffed), and a friendly seal (unstuffed). The visit can be combined with a stroll around the headland which gives panoramic coastal views.

Rocher de la Vierge

Rocher de la Vierge is a small, finger-like island just off the shore, linked to it by a frail-looking footbridge. A height in the centre of the island-rock is surmounted by a statue of the Virgin Mary, from which its name derives. Napoleon III envisaged building a new port at this point, but it was never completed, and most of what was constructed at the sea end of the island has been washed away by rough seas. A tunnel through the rock takes you to the extreme end of the island, and a path leads up to the holy statue. The walk out here is a pleasant, breezy outing in summer, a bracing struggle on windy days, and in the roughest weather the bridge is closed because heavy seas break right over it.

Rocher du Basta

Near the southern end of the Grand Plage another picturesque rock, the Rocher du Basta, is linked to the shore by an elegant stone footbridge. A balustraded footpath around the island-rock offers another enjoyable walk.

Where to stay

Biarritz has always been an expensive resort, so that at all levels its fifty-odd hotels tend to be more expensive than something similar elsewhere. The following is a brief selection in descending order of cost.

Hôtel du Palais, 1 Avenue Impératrice, 64200 Biarritz, tel. (59) 24 09 40, has 116 bedrooms and twenty-four suites at celestial prices. The former Imperial home is a palace hotel in the grand tradition, its luxury meticulously maintained. It has a sumptuous swimming pool with its own grill-restaurant. The hotel belongs to the municipality of Biarritz, who have recently given it a face lift – notably the magnificent mirrored dining room in a rotunda overlooking the ocean. Both this and the pool restaurant are very expensive, but offer very high standards.

Hôtel Miramar, Avenue Impératrice, 64200 Biarritz, tel. (59) 24 85 20, is a modern version of the grand palace hotel, with large, superbly comfortable rooms and impeccable service. It has 109 rooms and seventeen suites at prices similar to the Hôtel du Palais, as well as indoor and outdoor pools, a sea-water health clinic and gymnasium of the highest standards, with controlled 'cures' and exercise. The restaurant **Relais Miramar** is superb (one Michelin star) and correspondingly expensive.

Hôtel Windsor, Grande Plage, 64200 Biarritz, tel. (59) 24 08 52, offers thirty-seven comfortable rooms, overlooking the sea. Prices are somewhat above average, although the restaurant is moderately priced, with a cheaper menu for children.

Hôtel Atalaye, 6 Rue Goelands, 64200 Biarritz, tel. (59) 24 06 76, has twenty-five rooms at average prices. No restaurant.

Hôtel Marbella, 11 Rue du Port Vieux, 64200 Biarritz, tel. (59) 24 04 06, has twenty-eight rooms and a modestly priced restaurant. It is situated not far from the best swimming beach.

Hôtel Palacito, 1 Square Gambetta, 64200 Biarritz, tel. (59) 24 04 89, is a well-run middle-of-the-range hotel, with twenty-six rooms at average prices, and no restaurant.

Hôtel de la Côte des Basques, 62 Rue Gambetta, 64200 Biarritz, tel. (59) 24 10 03, is a small, neat, simple hotel facing the beach, with twelve rooms at below average prices and a restaurant which offers very good value.

Where to eat

Auberge du Relais, 44 Avenue de la Marne, 64200 Biarritz, tel. (58) 24 85 90, has appealing decor and sound cuisine at value-for-money prices. The Auberge also has a dozen rooms at below average prices.

Auberge de la Negresse, Blvd Aérodrome, 64200 Biarritz, tel. (59) 23 15 83, is a lively, friendly restaurant, charging reasonable prices.

La Baleine Bleue, 10 Place Ste Eugénie, 64200 Biarritz, tel. (59) 22 03 89, is a straightforward no-frills restaurant specialising in sea food at moderate prices. It enjoys a view over the busy square and the ocean.

Night life

Le Tentation, at the Bellevue Casino, tel. (59) 24 11 22, is a straightforward standard disco.

Le Caveau, 4 Rue Gambetta, 64200 Biarritz, tel. (59) 24 16 17, has two sections – one room for men and one for women.

Le Port Vieux, Place du Port Vieux, 64200 Biarritz, tel. (59) 22 03 15, features period songs and music.

Bidart

Perched on the cliffs halfway between Biarritz and St Jean-de-Luz, Bidart is a small resort for which I have a particular affection, having spent part of my honeymoon there. In those days it was a simple Basque village with only one small hotel. In season it is now a busy little resort with at least a dozen hotels – an ideal place for a family holiday, with an excellent sandy beach below the cliffs. There are three days of energetic Basque festivities around 15 August.

Where to stay

Hôtel Ypua, Route de la Chapelle, 64210 Bidart, tel. (59) 54 93 11, offers twelve rooms, some with shower *en suite*, at below average prices. The restaurant offers cheap menus for children.

Hôtel Bidartea, RN 10, 64210 Bidart, tel. (59) 54 94 68, lies about 3 km outside the village on the RN 10 towards Biarritz. One of the Mapotel group, it has thirty-six rooms at average prices, and a sound restaurant, also moderately priced.

Restaurant La Chistera, RN 10, 64210 Bidart, tel. (59) 26 51 07, is entirely Basque in atmosphere and run by a former champion pelota player. It is particularly good for fish dishes, but rather expensive.

Surprisingly Bidart has an active night life, with discos which attract clients both from St Jean-de-Luz and Biarritz.

La Licorne, 64210 Bidart, tel. (59) 54 94 77, is a very popular disco.

Le Dandy, 64210 Bidart, tel. (59) 23 00 24, is another animated disco.

About 3 km south of Bidart, Guéthary is another little resort of the kind you might find in Cornwall or Brittany, sited on a rise which slopes gracefully down to curving sandy beaches. When I first knew it, there were no hotels, but it now has four and is still growing. It is a good place for a family holiday, though crowded in August.

St Jean-de-Luz

Like Biarritz, St Jean-de-Luz was known as long ago as the fourteenth century as a whaling station. When the whales became scarce, the fishermen sailed to the waters of Iceland and Newfoundland in search of cod, until the terms of the Treaty of Utrecht in 1713 banned them

from these waters. Looking for something else to do, they turned to piracy, and became very good at it. Some of the best captains amassed large fortunes and were honoured or ennobled by the French king.

The greatest day in the history of St Jean-de-Luz was 9 June 1660, when the young Louis XIV married the Infanta Marie-Thérèse, daughter of Philip IV of Spain. The marriage was intended as a guarantee for the observance of the Treaty of the Pyrenees, signed the previous year in the hope of settling differences between France and Spain. The final negotiations for the marriage were carried out on the Ile des Faisans, in the River Bidassoa, through which the boundary between the two countries passes. The pavilion specially erected for these discussions was decorated by the Spanish painter, Velazquez, who, during the course of the works in winter, caught a chill from which he died.

At twenty-two, Louis XIV had already been on the throne for seventeen years, and was to reign for another fifty-five. He went reluctantly to the altar, being in the throes of a youthful passion for another Marie – the lovely Marie Mancini, niece of Louis' Prime Minister, Cardinal Mazarin. However, Mazarin settled that situation by exiling his niece and persuading Louis that he must go ahead with the Spanish marriage in the interests of state.

The wedding was of a lavishness and luxury fit for an eastern fable. Swiss Guards lined the route to the church. The procession was headed by twenty splendidly dressed courtiers flanking Cardinal

Mazarin in even more magnificent costume, followed by Louis XIV in black decorated with white and gold lace. A few steps behind him came Marie-Thérèse, wearing a dress of sparkling silver fabric, a purple velvet cloak and a golden crown supported by a lady-in-waiting. Next were Monsieur, the King's brother, and Anne of Austria, Louis' mother, and finally the whole court, all in their finest clothes.

The wedding presents could have come straight out of Ali Baba's cave: six superb necklaces of diamonds and pearls from Louis to his bride; twelve thousand *livres d'or* worth of diamonds and pearls to the bride from Mazarin, together with a ceremonial dinner service in solid gold, and two coaches, one drawn by six Russian horses and the other by six Indian horses, all caparisoned to match the colours of the coaches. Monsieur gave the bride a dozen sets of dress ornaments, all studded with diamonds, rubies and other precious stones. There was much more besides, from ambitious courtiers.

Marie-Thérèse made the king a gentle and dignified wife; when she died, Louis said that 'It was the only pain she ever caused me'.

St Jean-de-Luz today

St Jean-de-Luz is really a twin town with Ciboure, separated only by the narrow River Nivelle, the mouth of which forms the port. It is an interesting town, being both an active deep-sea fishing port, and a resort situated around a lovely bay with a fine sandy beach. The bay is protected from the open sea by incurving headlands, which have been prolonged by jetties, built after part of the town had been washed away by violent storms.

The old town is largely one of tall seventeenth- and eighteenth-century houses lining narrow streets, which are almost impassable for motor traffic, though in constant use. For the British motorist, used to driving on the left, the crossing of the old centre of St Jean-de-Luz towards the beach in August ranks as an experience with the Paris Périphérique or Place de la Concorde in the rush hour.

On the hills behind the old town, lies a completely different new town of pretty Basque villas with sub-tropical gardens, in a maze of winding avenues.

What to see

The most important tunny fishing fleet in France is based here, and the boats go as far as the West African coast of Senegal in search of their catch. They also make big catches of sardines and anchovies closer to home. The colourful harbour and picturesque houses lining the quays of Ciboure attract many artists and photographers. In the early part of July there is a lively Tunny Fair, with games, fireworks and dancing.

It is worth walking over the bridge to Ciboure, which has a number of interesting old houses, particularly along the Quay Ravel, named after the composer, who was born at No. 27.

Maison Louis XIV, in which the king stayed during the weeks immediately preceding his wedding to Marie-Thérèse, is in the corner of the square now called Place Louis XIV. Built in 1643 by a shipowner named Lohobiague, it is still in good condition and can be visited from 1 January to the end of September, mornings and afternoons; it is closed on Sunday mornings and on public holidays. While Louis was staying here the Spanish princess lodged in another house nearby, overlooking the port and now called the Maison de l'Infante. It is not open to the public.

The **Église St Jean Baptiste** is a church unlike any other. Originally thirteenth-century Gothic, it was burned down and rebuilt in 1558, and has been repeatedly altered and restored. The entrance now is by the fifteenth-century side door, because the main door was bricked up after the wedding of Louis XIV and the Infanta Marie-Thérèse, so that lesser mortals should not be able to follow in the royal footsteps. The interior is both sumptuous and astonishing, its ceiling vaulted with great painted and gilded wooden beams, in shape like the ribs of a wooden ship turned upside down. On both sides of the nave are two tiers of wooden galleries, usual in Basque churches and traditionally reserved for men. Most impressive of all is the magnificent reredos, with carved and gilded life-size wooden figures of saints, about twenty in all, on three levels. So do not be put off by the sober, plain exterior of this church; it really is worth having a look inside.

Where to stay

Before listing one or two hotels, it is worth saying a word on *when* to stay. Except for those who actually like a good bustle and rubbing shoulders with hordes of other visitors, St Jean-de-Luz is best avoided in August, when it becomes impossibly crowded. On the other hand, the whole Basque coast from Biarritz to Hendaye enjoys a warm late summer which drifts on through autumn, so that any time from the beginning of September to the end of October is good for a holiday in St Jean-de-Luz. The crowds have gone, the sea is at its warmest, there is room in the restaurants and the whole place is more relaxed. The beach, which the protective jetty makes one of the safest on the Aquitaine coast, can be fully enjoyed.

Hôtel Madison, 25 Blvd Thiers, 64500 St Jean de-Luz, tel. (59) 26 35 02, is situated near the beach, with comfortable well sound-proofed rooms at average prices. No restaurant.

Villa Bel Air, Promenade Jacques Thibaut, 64500 St Jean-de-Luz, tel. (59) 26 04 86, is a comfortable though rather old-fashioned hotel, with the advantage of off-street parking just behind the beach. It has twenty-three rooms at average prices but no restaurant, although there is a snack bar during the June–September season.

Hôtel/Motel Basque, Rond-Point St Barbe, 64500 St Jean-de-Luz, tel. (59) 26 04 24, lies 2 km north of St Jean-de-Luz, overlooking the golf course and the sea. It is a hotel and motel complex with fifty-two rooms about equally divided between them, at slightly above average prices. The restaurant, **La Réserve**, merits a visit in its own right, offering good value at a little above average price.

Hôtel La Devinière, 5 Rue Loquin, 64500 St Jean-de-Luz, tel.

(59) 26 05 51, is a little haven of comfort and good taste, in the heart of town with just eight bedrooms and no restaurant. Prices are above average.

Hôtel Chantaco, Golf du Chantaco, 64500 St Jean-de-Luz, tel. (59) 26 14 76, is a luxurious Basque-style mansion, with excellent rooms overlooking the garden and grounds adjoining the golf course. Prices are well above average, and the restaurant is also quite expensive, less so for children.

**Where to
eat**

Restaurant Maria Christina, 13 Rue Paul Gelos, 64500 St Jean-de-Luz, tel. (59) 26 81 70, is one of the very best fish restaurants on the coast south of Bordeaux, charging above average prices. There are also thirteen bedrooms, some of which have bath or showers *en suite*, at average prices.

La Vieille Auberge, 22 Rue Tourasse, 64500 St Jean-de-Luz, tel. (59) 26 19 61, offers a choice of three menus at moderate prices, cheaper for children. This is one place where they serve the excellent Basque cider – it is said the Basques taught the Normans how to make cider.

Restaurant Le Tourasse, 25 Rue Tourasse, 64500 St Jean-de-Luz, tel. (59) 51 14 25, is a pleasant, air-conditioned restaurant with a clever and enthusiastic young chef. Menus at average prices are very good value for money.

Auberge de la Corniche, Route de la Corniche, 64122 Urrugne, tel. (59) 47 30 23, lies 3 km from Ciboure on the Corniche Basque. It is a moderately priced restaurant, where meals can be taken alfresco, with a pleasant view of the Pyrenees.

Hendaye

The last of the resorts on the Basque coast before the Spanish frontier, Hendaye Plage is characterised by its enormous beach, which is 3 km long, very wide, absolutely flat and with safe bathing for the whole family, including small children and non-swimmers. This lovely beach has made it a popular and fast-developing resort. Another characteristic of Hendaye is its lush vegetation of palm trees, mimosas, magnolias, tamarisks, oleanders and eucalyptus, which line the avenues and overflow the gardens.

Hendaye is in three parts – Hendaye Plage which is the resort, Hendaye Ville, the old town at the mouth of the Bidassoa, separated from Hendaye Gare by the railway line to the frontier, which is crossed by a double railway bridge and two road bridges.

**What to
see**

Except for those fascinated by trains and the paraphernalia of frontier crossing, there is nothing of special interest in Hendaye Gare.

In Hendaye Ville it is worth visiting the old fort, which has its own parking area. The site offers a fine view across the Bidassoa to Fuentarrabia and its castle on the Spanish side. In a street by the riverside near the fort, the Rue des Pêcheurs, stands a white house with green timbers and shutters. It was here that the brilliant but eccentric French writer, Pierre Loti, died in 1923. A professional naval officer who liked to wear make-up, smoke opium, and wear Eastern dress or an evening gown for a change, he had been in command of the naval station on the Bidassoa.

The **Église St Vincent**, which has been burned down at least twice in its long history, was completely restored in 1874. It is a church in the Basque style, with wooden galleries on either side of the nave, and a magnificent large thirteenth-century Christ in the right-hand side chapel.

Also called Ile de la Conférence, **Ile des Faisans** (Pheasant Island) has played an important part in Franco-Spanish history, providing a neutral meeting ground for argument and discussion between the rulers of the two countries or their representatives. Having been steadily eroded over the centuries by the sea and river currents, it is today a fairly insignificant strip of land with a few trees and bushes.

Hendaye Plage

Hendaye Plage is for the most part fairly new, although some old villas have escaped replacement by modern blocks. It also has a fanciful Moorish-style casino, built at the turn of the century when there was a vogue for this kind of style. This is a particularly ugly example of the style, although some visitors find that it has a kind of crazy charm; a more graceful example stood at Arcachon before it was burned down in 1977.

Where to stay

Hôtel Liliac, Rond-Point, 64700 Hendaye, tel. (59) 20 02 45, has twenty-four comfortable bedrooms at average prices. No restaurant.

Hôtel Santiago, 29 Rue de Santiago, 64700 Hendaye, tel. (59) 20 00 94, is a small modern hotel with nineteen rooms at rather below average prices.

Hôtel Pohoténia, Route Corniche, 64700 Hendaye, tel. (59) 20 04 76, has fifty-two bedrooms at average prices, a swimming pool and a rather good restaurant at slightly above average rates.

Where to eat

Restaurant Gitanilla, 52 Blvd Leclerc, 64700 Hendaye, tel. (59) 20 04 65, is a pleasant restaurant with menus at moderate prices. It also has a few bedrooms at reasonable rates.

Chez Antoinette, Place Pellot, 64700 Hendaye, tel. (59) 20 08 47, is a typically Basque restaurant in both decor and cuisine, with prices a shade above average. There are also twenty-four inexpensive bedrooms.

Biriatou

Restaurant Bakéa, Biriatou, 64700 Hendaye, tel. (59) 20 76 36, is situated in a delightful Basque village, 4 km from Hendaye by the D258 through Béhobie. Biriatou merits a visit whether or not you decide to eat in the restaurant. It consists of an inn, a church, a few houses and has lovely views over the wooded mountain-sides and across the river to Spain. The restaurant is first class (one Michelin star), with a shady terrace overlooking the valley. Prices a little above the norm. The inn has fifteen rooms, some with bath *en suite*, also at slightly above average prices.

St Jean-Pied-de-Port

This ancient town, whose name means St John at the Foot of the Pass, lies in a bowl surrounded by green mountain slopes and watered by the Nive and Petite Nive. It is situated on the D918, 62 km from St Jean-de-Luz. From Bayonne, take the D932 to Cambo-les-Bains (20 km), and then the D918. It was built in the thirteenth century by the kings of Navarre to replace their old capital, St Jean-le-Vieux, which had been destroyed by Richard the Lionheart in 1177. The town was surrounded by ramparts, sections of which still exist, with a citadel, restored by Vauban in the seventeenth century.

St James of Compostella   The town was the last halt for pilgrims on the road to St James of Compostella, before they climbed up to the pass of Roncesvalles to make their way across Spain. It is difficult nowadays to imagine the importance in the Middle Ages of the pilgrimage to Compostella, which ranks with the Crusades and the building of the Cathedrals as one of the most complete expressions of Christian faith at that time. The pilgrims came from all over Europe – in their thousands during the most popular period. In one year as many as 6,000 would leave England alone, half by ship and half tramping all the way through France. The pilgrimage became an industry.

Legend   Why? As with so many other aspects of early Christianity the facts are somewhat blurred. The legend seems to be that James the Apostle, the brother of John, was shipwrecked on the Galician coast of northern Spain. He stayed in the country seven years, converting it to Christianity, before returning to the Holy Land, where he died a martyr's death in AD 44. According to the legend, his disciples placed his body in a boat, which was divinely steered to that point on the shores of Galicia where he had first been shipwrecked. There he was buried and his tomb venerated for 300 years. It was gradually forgotten until 600 years later, when holy men set out to find it again, guided by a moving star. Hence the name of the place – *Campus Stellae* – the field of the star.

Pilgrimage   There was clearly a good deal of elasticity and expediency in the attitudes of the early Christian church towards anything touching upon the miraculous or saintly. It is also clear that the tremendous fervour of Christian faith at that time required a pilgrimage of some kind. Jerusalem was far away and difficult to reach, but St James of Compostella was accessible yet far enough away and hard enough to reach to make a pilgrimage there a serious holy undertaking.

Compromise

Even here, though, the Church showed a degree of elasticity. It is said that many pilgrims lost heart when they saw the bleakness of the mountains on the Spanish side, and thought of the distance still to go. So the Church conveniently 'reburied' some relics of St James at St Sernin in Toulouse, so that faint-hearted pilgrims could divert there.

Benefits

In St Jean-Pied-de-Port the pilgrims were welcomed. As Christians they were obliged to give alms, and some of them were rich, so that the hospices and monasteries *en route* benefited from them, just as hotels benefit from tourists today. The pilgrims were also accompanied by beggars who knew that the Christian pilgrims dared not ignore them. St Jean-Pied-de-Port had its own beggars, too, and these rival gangs of the maimed and diseased would frequently set about each other in the streets.

Throughout the summer months, each time a new caravan of pilgrims was sighted, bells were rung, the priests began to say prayers and the inhabitants came out of their houses to welcome them.

St Jean-Pied-de-Port today

Today, I suppose, the town comes to life in a similar way when the first tourist coaches arrive at the beginning of the summer season. In itself St Jean-Pied-de-Port is still a lovely place, but at the height of the season it becomes one enormous souvenir shop. The visitor who prefers to avoid the commercialism, and to appreciate the true significance of this old town, should perhaps visit either side of the season, in June or September. It is easier then to walk down from the Port St Jacques, where the pilgrims entered the town, and to follow their route across the bridge over the pretty River Nive, and up the Rue d'Espagne to the Porte d'Espagne, trying to imagine the feelings of the pilgrim with twenty miles and several thousand feet to climb to the pass of Roncesvalles, and with his destination still so far away.

Where to stay

Hôtel des Pyrénées, 19 Place du General de Gaulle, 64220 St Jean-Pied-de-Port, tel. (59) 37 01 01, has twenty-five rooms, which are for the most part on the small side but comfortably and charmingly furnished, at above average prices. The restaurant is one of the very best in the Basque country (two Michelin stars) and is accordingly quite expensive.

Hôtel Continental, 3 Avenue Renaud, 64220 St Jean-Pied-de-Port, tel. (59) 37 00 25, offers twenty-two comfortable rooms at slightly above average rates. No restaurant.

Hôtel Ramuntcho, 1 Rue de France, 64220 St Jean-Pied-de-Port, tel. (59) 37 03 91, has fifteen rooms, some with bath *en suite*, at very moderate prices. Its sound restaurant offers a choice of menus at below average prices.

Where to eat

Restaurant Ipoutchaïnia, Ascarat, 64220 St Jean-Pied-de-Port, tel. (59) 37 02 24, 1.5 km outside town by the D15 Irouléguy road, is an attractive little restaurant with inexpensive menus. It also has twelve rooms at below average rates, some with bath.

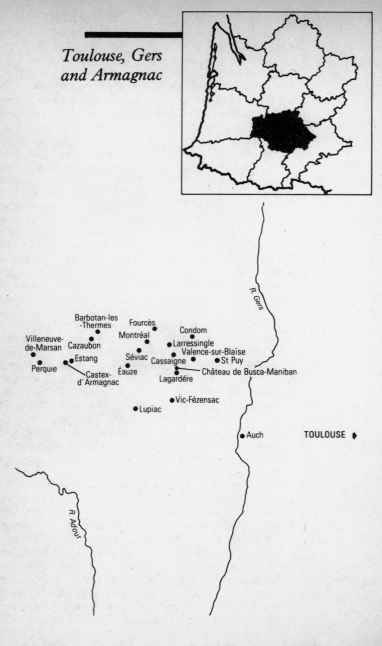

Toulouse, Gers and Armagnac

Barbotan-les-Thermes
Fourcès
Montréal
Condom
Villeneuve-de-Marsan
Cazaubon
Larressingle
Valence-sur-Blaïse
Estang
Séviac
Cassaigne
St Puy
Perquie
Éauze
Château de Busca-Maniban
Castex-d'Armagnac
Lagardére
Vic-Fézensac
Lupiac
Auch
TOULOUSE

R. Gers

R. Adour

Toulouse, Gers and Armagnac

Introduction

This chapter deals with one of the most peaceful stretches of country-side in the whole of France, the department of Gers, and also with the noisy, aggressive and colourful city of Toulouse, just across the boundary in Haute Garonne.

The direct routes to Spain and the Mediterranean coast of France by-pass Gers (pronounced 'zhairs') and it has few main roads of its own. It is farming country that depends chiefly on the production of maize, good local wines, and the excellent brandy of the Armagnac region. In this little-known department the adventurous motorist can make his own discoveries. The village inn, with only a few bedrooms but good food and a warm welcome, is more usual here than the modern tourist hotel. Near the inn is bound to be a farm or a château making its own Armagnac, where there will be someone pleased to show you round. For those who like something different, often inexpensive, and sometimes very good, Gers can be rewarding.

I begin with Toulouse because many tourists will arrive there first, by air, rail, or road, on their way to Gers or the Pyrenees, and may wish to see something of this unusual city.

Toulouse

Toulouse lies on a natural main route – the N20, from northern France to the Pyrenees via Limoges, Brive, Cahors and Montauban – as well as the A61–A62 autoroute, which links Bordeaux with the Mediterranean coast. Although Toulouse is in the Midi-Pyrénées region and not in Aquitaine, it is included in this book because its flourishing economy has an important influence throughout the south-west.

A city of the south, of the Midi, it is a vibrant, schizophrenic place, both ugly and beautiful, indolent and energetic. Its split personality is most apparent in the two very different environments of which it is composed. At its heart lies an extensive old quarter built in rose-red brick, enclosed by a brash modern city whose development has little to recommend it.

For many years the aviation capital of France, Toulouse is now the aviation capital of Europe. It was here in the 1920s that the first passenger group-carrying aircraft were built. The steady development, with military as well as civil aircraft, was accelerated with Concorde and continues with Airbus Industries, the European Space Agency and Aerospatiale, of which the aircraft division alone employs 8,000 people. Toulouse is also the home of the National Centre for Space Studies. All this, together with electronic and other subsidiary and service industries, has made Toulouse one of the most active business and industrial centres in France.

However, there is another side to this thriving industry. The rate of development has consistently outpaced the local authority's ability to control it, so that, away from its historic centre, much of Toulouse is a sprawl of hoarding-ridden industrial estates, swamping those few gems of modern architecture which the new city does contain. There can be few uglier approaches to a large town than that along the N20 from the north.

Undeniably, Toulouse is commercially prosperous, but there is more to it than materialism. It is also an important arts centre, with five museums of art and architecture, as well as a famous museum and gallery of photography plus a gallery of graphic art, posters and post-cards. After Paris it has the largest university facilities in France, with more than 70,000 students.

History

The city the visitor sees today had its origins more than 2,000 years ago, when a settlement grew up on the banks of the Garonne at a point where the river could be forded. This rocky crossing, called the Chaussée de Bazacle, can still be seen between the modern Pont des Catalans, and the Pont St Pierre.

The Romans

As with so many other towns in the south-west, it was the Romans who formalised the town, which they called Tolosa, giving it proper roads and putting a 3 km wall around the centre. The importance of Toulouse in its early history was recently confirmed when, during periods of low water in the Garonne between 1971 and 1973, archaeological searches below the Chaussée de Bazacle brought to light 46,000 small articles from the past. Ancient coins, rings, buckles and medals were among items found on the river bed, as were medieval pilgrim badges, some of them probably thrown in as a symbolic thanks offering for having successfully reached and crossed the Garonne.

After the Romans, it was the Visigoths who made Toulouse their capital in this area in the fifth century AD.

Counts of Toulouse

The Emperor Charlemagne created the first Counts of Toulouse, who steadily extended their power, until by the beginning of the thirteenth century, under Raymond VI, they controlled all the territory from the Pyrenees to the Rhône, and to the north as far as the southern part of the Massif Central.

Albigensian Crusade

As did most other nobles in the area, the Counts of Toulouse tolerated the Cathari (Albigensians), a strict Christian sect who refused to accept all the sacraments of the Catholic church, rejected the authority of the Pope and were naturally regarded by him as heretics. In the early thirteenth century the Albigensian Crusade was launched against them, centred on the towns which were their chief strongholds – Toulouse, Albi and Agen. It was joined by many nobles from the north, who were hoping both to earn forgiveness for their sins – which was part of the deal – and to gain land and spoils from the defeated nobles of the south. It was the first of many bloody religious struggles in France, and on this occasion the nobles of the north who survived did well out of it, while those of the south lost, the lands of the Counts of Toulouse being annexed in 1271 to the kingdom of France.

Prosperity

From the mid-fifteenth century, after the end of the Hundred Years War, Toulouse was a rich city. Its prosperity was based on the sale of a blue dye – *pastel* in French, woad in English – which the ancient Britons are said to have used as war paint. The dye, suitable for use with any good cloth, was exported all over Europe from the warehouses the Toulouse merchants established in London, Flanders and Italy.

In 1464 Toulouse was almost completely destroyed by a terrible fire, which spread rapidly through its narrow streets and wooden-framed houses. After this fire, laws were passed obliging people to rebuild without using wood. Many defied the law, but the rich dye merchants, who could afford to build in brick, put up splendid mansions, many of which have been beautifully restored.

Following the successful Crusade against the Cathari, the Catholic church reinforced its position in the area, continuing this policy for hundreds of years, so that by the time of the French Revolution in 1789, there were a hundred churches and sixty convents and monasteries in and around Toulouse, where they owned one-quarter of all the land. As it did throughout France, the Revolution turned the priests out and put the religious buildings to other uses.

Decline

When the dye, indigo, began to be brought from India in the 1560s, the one-product economy of Toulouse suffered very badly, so that the city entered a long period of depression and poverty. In 1652–53 an epidemic of the plague wiped out one-tenth of the population of 40,000, and in the later part of the seventeenth century the poverty and malnutrition were such that the infant mortality rate was 50 per cent.

During the eighteenth century, some improvement in the economy enabled the people of Toulouse to rebuild their Town Hall, the Capitole, but Toulouse had now become little more than a provincial market town, and in the nineteenth century the Industrial Revolution passed it by.

225

Revival

Even the arrival of the railway from Bordeaux in 1856, and a new line from Paris via Cahors in 1884, failed to rouse Toulouse from its rustic doze. Yet despite its feeble economy, the town grew slowly, and at the end of the nineteenth century its population, at 150,000, was double that of a hundred years earlier. New streets and squares had been built, but with a total disregard for the past. Many beautiful things, including the cloisters of the Cathedral of St Etienne, disappeared to make way for functional buildings.

It was the First World War which revived the economy of Toulouse, with the manufacture of explosives, cartridges and arms, as well as uniforms and boots for the soldiers. A Monsieur Latécoère moved his aircraft factory from Lille, where it was threatened by the war, to Toulouse. By the mid-1920s this factory was producing many aircraft every month and the city had already become a pioneer centre of aviation. From here France was first linked by air to Morocco, then to West Africa and finally to South America. This was the base of the first long-distance commercial pilots, legendary fliers like Mermoz and St Exupéry, who took the first air mails across the south Atlantic.

Since those days the importance of aviation in Toulouse has never ceased to grow.

What to see

Despite the demolition carried out in the nineteenth and twentieth centuries, the old heart of Toulouse remains extensive. More than 230 buildings, including churches, are classified as historical monuments. In addition, there are whole streets of Renaissance buildings and, despite the old law banning the construction of timber-framed houses, there are still more than 200 houses with *colombages* – bricks or plaster between visible beams in the façade.

For centuries the old quarter was allowed simply to decay, when it was not being knocked about or destroyed altogether. In recent times, however, the authorities have come to appreciate that their city has one of the largest and most interesting old quarters in France. This realisation, which happened to coincide with the growth of tourism, led to an official programme of restoration of old buildings, beginning with the old churches and monasteries, and following with the most important of the private mansions. Much has already been achieved.

A number of interesting sights in Toulouse are hidden beyond archways which most tourists would take for private entrances, or down unpromising-looking alleys. For this reason Toulouse is a city where you will see far more with a guided tour on foot than you might exploring on your own. These tours start from the Tourist Office, which is in the building called the Donjon (Keep) of the Capitole. (Donjon du Capitole, 31000 Toulouse, tel. [61] 23 32 00.)

However, if you want to go it alone, here are some of the more important places of interest.

St Sernin

St Saturnin (to use his Roman name – the French form is St Sernin) was Bishop of Toulouse and became one of the early Christian martyrs in AD 250. When he refused to take part in the sacrifice of a bull, the Romans attached him by ropes to its horns and drove it out of town, dragging St Saturnin along the ground until he died. The route which the bull took is still called the Rue du Taur (the road of the bull); *taur* is the old Languedoc word for the French *taureau* (bull). The road starts from the north-west corner of the Place de la Capitole.

The **Basilica of St Sernin** stands over the tomb of the saint, on the spot where the first church was built in the fourth century. As well as being the largest and most splendid of all the Romanesque churches of western Europe, it is the richest in relics, including a reliquary of St James of Compostella and a gilded one of St Sernin, depicting him being dragged along by the bull. Built at the end of the eleventh and the beginning of the twelfth centuries, it was the last 'port of call' in France for the thousands of pilgrims who made their way every year to St James of Compostella. It was built on a scale to accommodate these large congregations, with a vast transept, double aisles on either side of the spacious nave, and an apse with radiating chapels and a wide deambulatory. St Sernin also has a particularly fine organ, which is often used for recording classical organ music.

The church is full of superb Romanesque sculpture, which served as a model for churches throughout the south, and is seen at its best in the Porte Miègeville on the south side, which was completed in 1100. There are Spanish elements in the sculpture, and the figures of St James and King David are repeated on the Goldsmith's Portal of the Church of St James of Compostella. Most of the sculpture at St Sernin came from the workshop of Bernard Guildin, including the original marble altar table, which was consecrated by Pope Urban II in 1086, and now stands under the dome of the transept crossing.

The cloisters were demolished during the nineteenth century.

Almost in the shadow of the church stands a building which today bears the name Lycée St Sernin on its façade. It was the home of Madame du Barry and her husband, before she went off to serve the court as mistress of Louis XV.

Completed in 1340 as the headquarters of the Dominicans in France, **Les Jacobins** is a masterpiece of southern Gothic architecture, and a classic example of the scale and energy with which the Catholic church set about ensuring its influence in this 'heretical' part of France. The main body of the church consists of a double nave with seven great pillars down the centre, supporting a vaulted roof 28 m above the floor. The first pillar, in the apse, carries the best example of palm vaulting to be found anywhere. This beautifully proportioned building contains a reliquary of St Thomas Aquinas, placed there in 1974 on the 700th anniversary of his death.

With the exception of the two rose windows in the façade, which date from the fourteenth century, the rest of the stained glass was made and installed in the 1920s as part of the restoration of the building, which was used as a cavalry barracks during Napoleonic times. The restoration, started towards the end of the nineteenth century, was completed about fifteen years ago. Most of the fine cloister had been destroyed, but parts of it were found and used as models, enabling it to be rebuilt as it was.

Just around the corner from Les Jacobins, at 1 Rue Gambetta, is the **Hôtel de Bernuy**. (*Hôtel* originally meant only a private mansion, and is still used in this sense in towns.) Now restored and used as a school, it is one of the most impressive of the mansions built by the rich dye merchants in the early sixteenth century. The second of its two courtyards is a fine example of the Renaissance charm of old Toulouse, while its staircase tower is the highest of these status symbols, which were built by the *capitouls* or aldermen of Toulouse to show, rather naïvely, how important they had become.

Jean de Bernuy was said to have been literally worth a king's ransom. When Francis I of France was captured at the Battle of Pavia in 1524, it was Jean de Bernuy who paid the ransom of 1,200,000 gold crowns demanded by the Emperor Charles V (ruler of Spain, Germany, the Netherlands, most of Italy, Mexico and Peru). To be precise, the money was paid for two of the sons of Francis I, boys of ten and eight, whom the king had exchanged for himself and left behind as hostages. So many false and underweight coins were included in this amount that it took the Spaniards two months to count and check it, and have the bad ones replaced.

Jean de Bernuy's was the first of the truly palatial mansions of Toulouse, but other rich dye merchants soon followed his example. One who was not outdone was Pierre d'Assézat.

The magnificent **Hôtel d'Assézat**, designed by Nicholas Bachelier and built between 1555 and 1557, combines richness, splendour and elegance. The finest of many examples of Renaissance architecture in Toulouse, it is more a palace than a house. It was not quite finished when Pierre d'Assézat, who had been converted to Protestantism, was driven into exile and ruined. But other rich Toulousains continued, on a more modest but still splendid scale, in a kind of competition to build the most beautiful houses. Some of them in the Rue St Rome and the Rue des Changes can be picked out by their staircase towers rising above the skyline. Almost all the houses in the Rue St Rome, now a pedestrian precinct with many smart shops, date from this period. No. 39 was the house of Catherine de Médici's doctor, Augier Ferrier.

From the top of the staircase tower of the Hôtel d'Assézat there is a fine view over the roofs of old Toulouse, including some of the other staircase towers, and in clear weather the Pyrenees can easily be seen.

The extraordinary **Cathedral of St Etienne** has a kind of bizarre charm. It was built between the eleventh and seventeenth centuries, the long time-span being due to the fact that there was never enough money available to finish what had been started. For example, the nave and the choir, built separately and not in line, seem to have little to do with each other. In the thirteenth century a huge rose window was put into the eleventh-century façade, to which an entrance was added in the fifteenth century. In the sixteenth century a rectangular bell tower was built, quite unlike any other in the region, and at some time, probably during the nineteenth century, a round clock face, which appears to have been purloined from a railway terminus, was added.

The interior walls of the church are hung with sixteenth- and seventeenth-century tapestries showing scenes from the life of St Etienne; the five large stained glass windows in the apse date from the seventeenth century, and there is a fifteenth-century stained glass window of Charles V wearing his crown (he came to the throne in 1422) and his son, the future Louis XI, kneeling.

If you like museums, the **Musée des Augustins** is well worth a visit. Not only does it have a first-class collection of Romanesque, Gothic and Renaissance sculpture, but it is housed in the buildings of a former Augustinian monastery, which has been beautifully rebuilt and has an elegant fourteenth-century cloister, restored with total authenticity. The museum also has a collection of religious and other paintings from the sixteenth century to the present day.

From the very earliest times the affairs of the town were conducted by an assembly of *capitouls*, the early councillors of Toulouse. Even in the great days of the Counts of Toulouse from the ninth to the twelfth centuries, the Counts consulted with the *capitouls*, but left to them the day-to-day running of the town. The Town Hall, called **Le Capitole**, is a most impressive building, the façade of which as it is today dates from about 1750. Some of the official reception rooms are open to the public and are worth looking at. The Salle des Illustrés (the Hall of Fame) is decorated with nineteenth-century elaboration and pomp, which, in conception, if not in execution, would make Michelangelo green with envy, or perhaps some other strong emotion. Another room, named after the Toulouse painter, Henri Martin, contains ten of his very large paintings. Four are devoted to the seasons, and some to the banks of the Garonne, where famous people of the time, himself among them, are depicted strolling.

The above is only a selection of what there is to see in Toulouse. There are, for example, twenty beautiful public fountains, modern as well as ancient.

Where to stay

There are more than a hundred hotels in Toulouse, and others on the outskirts. Many of them, as is often the case with towns in the south of France, do not have restaurants. The following is a short selection of hotels within easy reach of the old quarter and which have parking in or next to the hotel.

Hôtel Altea Wilson, 7 Rue Labéda (Place Wilson), 31000

Toulouse, tel. (61) 21 21 75, is a modern hotel with ninety-one rooms at above average rates. There is no restaurant.

Hôtel Raymond IV, 16 Rue Raymond IV, 31000 Toulouse, tel. (61) 62 89 41, is near Place Jeanne d'Arc. It has forty rooms at average prices and no restaurant.

Hôtel Le Président, 43–45 Rue Raymond IV, 31000 Toulouse, tel. (61) 63 46 46, is a new hotel with thirty-one soundproofed rooms and modern decor. A pleasant, well-run hotel charging average prices, it has no restaurant.

Hôtel Le Progrès, 10 Rue Rivals, 31000 Toulouse, tel. (61) 23 21 28, is situated not far from Place du Capitole. It is a comfortable small hotel, with thirty-three rooms at average prices and no restaurant.

Hôtel Taur, 2 Rue du Taur, 31000 Toulouse, tel. (61) 21 17 54, is situated on the corner of Place du Capitole. An old-established hotel with adequate comfort at a little below average prices, it has forty-one rooms and no restaurant.

Novotel, Ibis, Climat and Campanile groups all have at least one hotel in Toulouse, some quite close to the centre, though further from the old quarter than those mentioned. (See p. 96 for central booking numbers.) There is an enormous multi-level underground car park below the Place du Capitole which always seems to have space.

Where to eat

Restaurants are as plentiful as hotels, with more than a hundred 'serious' establishments, some among the best in France. Most of them offer classical French and/or regional cuisine, but Toulouse has more variety than most towns in the south, with Moroccan, Italian, Greek, Chinese, Brazilian, Middle Eastern and Spanish restaurants as well as French. There is a touch of Spain about Toulouse in that it is a city which comes to life late in the evening, the animation continuing into the small hours.

Expensive

Restaurant Vanel, Rue Maurice Fonvielle, 31000 Toulouse, tel. (61) 21 51 82, is situated just off Place Wilson. It is one of the greats, with two Michelin stars, all *à la carte* except for children's menus. Expensive but fair for the standard, it is closed on Sundays and the whole of August.

Jardins de l'Opéra, 1 Place Capitole, 31000 Toulouse, tel. (61) 23 07 76, is the restaurant of the Grand Hôtel de l'Opéra, and also has two Michelin stars. It offers luxury, high standards and high prices, and is closed from 11 to 21 August and on Sundays.

Restaurant Darroze, 19 Rue Castellane, 31000 Toulouse, tel. (61) 62 34 70, is a good but quite expensive restaurant, specialising in sea food and with one Michelin star. It is closed on Saturday mornings, Sundays and from 15 July to 15 August.

Pujol, 21 Avenue General Compans, 31700 Blagnac, tel. (61) 71 13 58, is a little way out of town, near the airport, but is worth finding. Well-known for its regional dishes (*à la carte* only) and remarkable

Armagnacs, it is expensive but fair, and offers easy parking in its own grounds.

Moderate   Those are some of the big boys. Now for some places that are good, but rather less exotic and costly.

Au Chat Dingue, 40 bis Rue Peyrollières (near La Daurade Church), 31000 Toulouse, tel. (61) 21 23 11, features turn-of-the-century decor and subdued lighting. It is a good and reasonably priced restaurant, with a cheap menu at lunch and special low prices for children. It is advisable to book in high season.

La Frégate, 15 Place Wilson (1 Rue Austerlitz), 31000 Toulouse, tel. (61) 21 62 45, is comfortable and centrally situated. Prices are reasonable, and good house wines are offered.

Grand Café de l'Opéra, 1 Place du Capitole, 31000 Toulouse, tel. (61) 23 37 02, is the brasserie of the Grand Hôtel de l'Opéra. Especially good for fish and sea food, the menu is of average price.

Restaurant La Bohème, 3 Rue Lafayette (off Place Wilson), 31000 Toulouse, tel. (61) 23 24 18, is centrally placed and charges average prices.

If none of these appeals, there are several restaurants of all kinds, pizzerias upwards, in the Boulevard Strasbourg, adjacent to Place Wilson.

Gers

From Toulouse, the N124 leads due west into the department of Gers, the heart of Gascony, and to its capital, Auch (pronounced Oh-sh), whence it is a short drive to the most famous part of Gers, the Armagnac region.

The chief characteristic of the department of Gers (the final 's' is always pronounced) is its rustic charm. Unspoilt and untouched by industry, this is the country as it used to be in pre-war Devon and Dordogne. Although it contains no spectacular elements – there are no mountains, gorges or great lakes – the landscape is nonetheless full of scenic attraction, with rolling hills which here and there offer vast panoramas, wooded slopes, large cultivated fields, sparkling streams, meadows and great farmhouses which often look like castles. Because the soil of Gers is on the whole less fertile than that of the Lot and Garonne Valleys, the farms have to be big to be economically viable. In the days before mechanisation, large numbers of men and horses were needed to work the farms, so that each farm was a community, with its stables, barns, outhouses and cottages, which from a distance can still be mistaken for a village. The overall effect is one of self-sufficiency and independence.

There are few towns, and the villages are old and often very picturesque. Gers is too far off-the-beaten track for there to be any stock-broker belts.

Auch

The *préfecture* of Gers, Auch is not a large town, its population being just 25,000. It is immediately pleasing to the eye as it is approached with red-roofed houses climbing the flanks of a hill, crowned by a cathedral.

Despite its position at the centre of the town, the cathedral is not hemmed in. Its own spacious square in front joins with the main square of the town, Place de la Libération, while at its side is the Place Salinis, with a terrace overlooking the Valley of the Gers. Some attractive buildings are grouped around the cathedral, although set back from it, including the eighteenth-century Town Hall and the eighteenth-century Archbishop's Palace, today the office of the *préfecture*.

An unusual feature of Auch is a monumental staircase, whose 232 steps join the Place Salinis to the riverside below, and which was constructed in the latter part of the nineteenth century, during the reign of Louis Napoleon. The old tower on the left (going down), known as the Tour d'Armagnac, dates from the fourteenth century.

What to see

The building of the **Cathedral of Ste Marie** was started in 1489, but was not completed until 200 years later. It has two remarkable features. The chapels of the deambulatory contain a superb series of eighteen stained glass windows from the early sixteenth century. The work of a Gascon painter, Arnaud de Moles, they constitute one of the masterpieces of French art of this period. There is no better series of Renaissance stained glass windows anywhere in France.

The other great masterpiece of this cathedral is the carving of the 113 oak choir stalls, more than half of which are canopied. These carvings, which consist of more than 1,500 faces and figures, were executed over more than fifty years, from 1500 to 1552. Themes from the Bible are mingled with those of myth and legend, as is the case with the subjects of the stained glass windows.

D'Artagnan

On a spacious landing about halfway down the monumental staircase, stands a statue of D'Artagnan, placed there in 1931. He was a real person as well as being a hero of fiction, although his true name was not D'Artagnan, and he was not much like Alexandre Dumas' hero of *The Three Musketeers*.

D'Artagnan was born Charles de Batz, probably around 1615, at the château of Castelmore, near the village of Lupiac in Gers. The château is still there, though not open to the public. When he went to serve in the French Regiment of Guards, de Batz took the name D'Artagnan from his mother's family, thinking it would sound better at court. Serving all his life as a professional soldier and becoming a captain in the First Company of Musketeers, he was more a tough disciplinarian, in the style of the traditional British army sergeant-major, than the devil-may-care swordsman depicted by Dumas, although as a true Gascon he was probably hot-headed and ready to fight anyone who seemed to question his honour. A brave and loyal soldier, he was killed in 1673 at the siege of Maastricht, during the Thirty Years War. He had been sufficiently well known for someone to put together a book, supposed to be the Memoirs of Monsieur D'Artagnan, which was published in 1700. It was forgotten for more than a hundred years until Alexandre Dumas came across it and used the material as the basis of his novel.

Where to stay and eat
Expensive

Hôtel de France, Place de la Libération, 32000 Auch, Gers, tel. (62) 05 00 44. André Daguin is one of the best-known chefs in France, and although his hotel has twenty-eight comfortable bedrooms at slightly above average prices, its reputation is primarily as a restaurant with two Michelin stars. The spacious main dining room is both well-furnished and attractive, although of course it is the cooking which counts. Not surprisingly it is expensive, with menus from 250 fr to 410 fr, and *à la carte*. It is one of *the* temples of Gascon cuisine, offering wonderful Armagnacs, as well as regional wines at affordable prices. The hotel has two other less expensive restaurants, the Côté Jardin (open from 1 May to 15 October) and Le Neuvième, but they are still rather above average price.

Moderate

Relais de Gascogne, 5 Avenue Marne, 32000 Auch, Gers, tel. (62) 05 26 81, is situated just off Place de Verdun in the lower town. A sound, everyday hotel with thirty-two rooms at a little below average prices, it has a popular restaurant with good regional cooking at average prices.

Condom

A pleasant drive can be made from Auch to Condom and the *bastides* of northern Gers.

Take the N124 westwards from Auch and then fork right on to the D930 for Condom, via Valence-sur-Baïse. Condom is an old town, whose narrow streets near the Cathedral give it a medieval air. The Gothic Cathedral of St Pierre was rebuilt in the sixteenth century in its original style. Although its interior is rather plain, it has some modern stained glass windows on the south side of the nave, which were made in Limoges in 1969. There are also several eighteenth-century mansions in the town, such as those in the Rue Jean Jaurés, on opposite corners of the Rue Roquepin, although none is open to the public. Near the Cathedral, in the Rue J. Ferry, is the Musée d'Armagnac.

Where to stay and eat

Condom has an excellent and unusual restaurant, the **Table des Cordeliers**, Rue des Cordeliers, 32100 Condom, Tel. (62) 28 03 68, in a restored Gothic chapel. It has a high standard of service, presentation and cuisine at reasonable prices, as well as twenty-one hotel bedrooms at average prices, in a modern building, set in a pleasant garden with a swimming pool.

Larressingle

From Condom take the D15 west, signposted to Montréal. This is rather easier said than done: from the main part of the town, cross the bridge over the river and avoid the D931 to Eauze, taking the right

233

side of the fork to Montréal and not the right turn to Nérac (D930). About 5 km along the D15 at a point where the road bears right, you will see a signpost on the left pointing uphill to Larressingle. Turning up here you quickly arrive at a fortified village too small to be called a *bastide*, If the word *bastidette* existed, it would perfectly describe Larressingle.

Built by the English in the thirteenth century, the village is surrounded by ramparts and a deep, dry moat. Crossing this by a bridge, you pass through a fortified gateway into what remains of the old village – a ruined keep, a partly fortified Romanesque church, a number of very old houses which have been restored and put to use as craftsmen's workshops, a café-restaurant where you can obtain an inexpensive light meal, and a souvenir shop. With its banks of flowers and the palm trees flourishing in the sunny corners of ruined courtyards, it could appear to be a highly stylised film set, but the solidity of the old stones, the cobbles beneath your feet and the ruggedness of Larressingle banish this idea almost before it is formed, leaving instead a memory of a unique and charming place which, incidentally, has an acceptable brand of Armagnac named after it.

Montréal Return down the hill to the D15 and continue on to Montréal. Built by the French in the late thirteenth century, this picturesque village is one of the oldest *bastides* in the south-west. Although much of it was destroyed at the time of the French Revolution, it retains a part of its ramparts, a fortified gate and the ruins of a Romanesque church, with a monogram of Christ dating back to the seventh or eighth century over the doorway. *Bastides* were sometimes built around an existing church or settlement.

Séviac There are two other interesting sights within easy reach of Montréal. Only a couple of kilometres to the south-west, at Séviac (signposted), archaeologists have uncovered the remains of a luxurious **Roman villa** with fine mosaics, marble columns and important Roman baths. An interesting collection of coins from the first to seventh centuries AD was also found, together with bone and ivory objects.

Fourcès Five km north of Montréal by the D29 lies Fourcès, built by the English in the thirteenth century and one of the prettiest and most unusual of all the *bastides* in the south-west. Reached by a small bridge across the River Auzoue, it is circular in plan, its houses grouped around a large central space with shady trees. Most of the circular stone arcade beneath the houses remains, several of the ground floors now turned into workshops, including that of a weaver who produces a large range of hand-woven articles of a high standard, and a painter's studio. It is a good place for a photographic stop.

To return to Auch, take the D29 back through Montréal to Éauze then the D626 (or D931, D20 and N124) to Vic-Fézensac, where you can join or continue on the N124 to Auch.

Armagnac

The region has three sub-divisions, Tenarèze (around Condom), Haute Armagnac (around Auch) and Bas Armagnac (around Éauze pronounced Ay-oze), which is reckoned to produce the best Armagnac. Each of these areas contain numerous properties producing Armagnac brandy, whose proprietors welcome visitors. They will show you round the *chais*, explain their production methods, which differ from those of Cognac, and in some cases they may allow tasting of their brandy, although it should be appreciated that drinkable brandy is a great deal more expensive than young wine, and that many of those offering a tasting expect to make a sale.

As there are at least a hundred such properties, varying from historic châteaux to plain old farmhouses, and as the Bureau National de l'Armagnac refuses point blank to recommend any particular one lest they be accused of favouritism, I offer the following suggestions as being worthwhile from my own experience, either from the point of view of interest, or the welcome offered, or both.

Tenarèze

Château de St Puy lies 6 km south of Condom by the D654 to St Puy. This was the birthplace and youthful home of Blaise de Massencôme, Sire de Monluc, usually known as Blaise de Monluc, who became a Marshal of France. He served the rulers of France in one reign and one foreign war after another, being captured at Pavia with Francis I when he was nineteen. A devout Catholic, at the age of sixty-three he was appointed Lieutenant General of Guyenne, by Catherine de Médici, with orders to suppress the Protestants in the region. As a professional soldier he answered atrocity with atrocity, but was disgusted by the St Bartholomew's massacre, which he did not regard as a military action, and retired in his old age to write his *Commentaires*, lamenting the cruelty which war forced upon him.

The château now produces *Pousse-Rapière*, a liqueur based on fruit macerated in Armagnac. The production is explained in the cellars, and together with the exhibition of old machines once used in the making of Armagnac, and another concerning the life of Monluc, it adds up to an interesting visit.

Haute Armagnac

Reached from Condom via the D931 and then left on to the D208, the **Château de Cassaigne** is a former residence of the Bishops of Condom. It has an interesting sixteenth-century kitchen, equipped and furnished as it was in the past, while in another room is an exhibition explaining the production of Armagnac.

From Cassaigne take the D229 towards Lagardère, but turn right at the second crossroads 4 km from Cassaigne to the **Château de Busca-Maniban**, which features an impressive interior with some fine period furniture. There are also two eighteenth-century kitchens with their utensils and furniture, and a fifteenth-century chapel with

235

seventeenth-century Italian paintings.

Bas Armagnac

Château de Ravignan is a fine historic château at Perquie, just outside Villeneuve-de-Marsan, which is reached from Éauze by the D30 and the D1. It is within easy reach of the two excellent restaurants already mentioned in that town – Francis Darroze and Hôtel De l'Europe (see p. 191). So after a good lunch, you could make the short trip to the Château de Ravignan, and perhaps take your digestif by tasting the excellent Armagnac made on this property.

Château Castex d'Armagnac is reached from Éauze by the D30 via Estang and Castex-d'Armagnac. By contrast with the other, older châteaux mentioned, this one was built in Napoleonic times and is still the home of the de St Pastou family, who offer a friendly welcome to visitors. Even by the standards of Gers, where the farms are larger than in most other parts of the south-west, this is a big property, covering nearly 600 hectares, about 1,400 acres. The *chais* include stocks of Armagnac up to fifty years old or more, the most recent bottlings being those of the harvests of 1968 and 1972.

The house, with some fine panelled rooms and period furniture, is interesting as an example of the lived-in home of an old Gascon family, rather than a château-museum. As the area headquarters of the Resistance during the Second World War it was singled out and bombed by the Germans. The damage has been repaired.

Where to stay

In addition to the hotels mentioned under Condom, Auch and Villeneuve-de-Marsan (Landes), there are others in the modern spa of **Barbotan-les-Thermes**, which is within easy reach of the Bas Armagnac area. On the northern limit of Gers, near Lot-et-Garonne, Barbotan-les-Thermes is pleasantly situated on the side of a pretty, wooded valley. As well as a number of hotels and restaurants, it has a modern thermal establishment treating rheumatism. There is also a leisure centre just outside the village on the edge of the Lac de l'Uby, where the facilities for sailing, windsurfing, swimming, tennis and a camp site, are popular with the young and healthy.

Hôtel Château de Bègue, 32150 Cazaubon, Gers, tel. (62) 69 50 08, lies between Barbotan-les-Thermes and Cazaubon. It is a country house in attractive grounds, with thirty-five rooms at a little above average prices, and a swimming pool. Open from 1 March to 1 November. The restaurant, whose prices are also a little above average, is open from 1 May to 1 October.

Hôtel Cante Grit, Barbotan-les-Thermes, 32150 Cazaubon, tel. (62) 69 52 12, has twenty-three rooms at average prices, and a restaurant which is also reasonably priced.

Hôtel Paix, Barbotan-les-Thermes, 32150 Cazaubon, tel. (62) 69 52 06, offers thirty-two rooms at average prices and a moderately priced restaurant.

Further information on Armagnac brandy is contained in the section on Eating and Drinking (see p. 78-9).

Useful Reading

General literature
For an understanding of the people and the life of the region:
Pierre Benoît, *Mademoiselle de la Ferté* and *L'Ile Verte*
E. Le Roy, *Jacquou le Croquant*
The novels of François Mauriac (particularly *Thérèse Deyqueroux*)
Blaise de Monluc, *Commentaires*

Aquitaine in general
S. Baring Gould, *Deserts of Southern France*
Michael and Sybil Brown, *Food and Wine of South-west France*
P. de Gorsse, *Splendeurs et Gloires des Pyrénées*
Larousse (publishers), *Pays et Gens d'Aquitaine*
Lyn Macdonald, *Bordeaux and Aquitaine*
Pierre Minvielle, *Les Pyrénées*
L. Papy (ed.), *Midi Atlantique*. This gives a very comprehensive survey of life, industry, agriculture and tourism in Aquitaine.
E. Penning Rowsell, *The Wines of Bordeaux*
Regine Pernoud, *Aliénor d'Aquitaine*

Dordogne
Marc Blancpain, *Le Périgord*
J. P. Bouchard, *Périgord – Terre de Memoire*
Philip Oyler, *The Generous Earth*. Although it was published nearly forty years ago, this book still gives a valid insight into the minds and attitudes of the peasant farmers of the region, as well as the land itself.
Jean Secret, *Le Périgord*
Freda White, *Three Rivers of France*. First published in 1952, but still good reading.

The Basque Country
J. Casenave, *La Côte Basque, Le Pays Basque*
P. S. Ormond, *The Basques and their Country*
Vivian Rowe, *The Basque Country*

Rulers and Governments of France

The Capet Dynasty

HUGUES CAPET, believed to have been born about 938, was elected king of the French in 987. The election was not unanimous. The rulers of Flanders, Aquitaine and Toulouse voted against him. The dynasty he founded lasted more than 300 years. He married Adelaide of Aquitaine (1), and Constance de Provence (2). Died 996.

ROBERT II (The Pious). It is not known when he was born, but he was the son of Hugues Capet and succeeded him in 996. He married Rozala of Flanders. Died in 1031.

HENRI I, probably born about 1008, came to the throne in 1031, married Anne of Kiev. He was the son of Robert II and died in 1060.

PHILIPPE I, born 1052, came to the throne in 1060, married Bertha of Holland. He died in 1108. Relationship to predecessor, son.

LOUIS VI (The Fat) born 1081 and came to the throne in 1108. Married Lucienne de Rochefort (1), Adelaide de Savoie (2). Died 1137. Relationship to predecessor, son.

LOUIS VII (The Young), born 1119. Came to the throne 1137. He married Eleanor of Aquitaine (1), Adele de Champagne (2). Died in 1180. Relationship to predecessor, son.

PHILIPPE II (Philippe-Auguste) born 1165. Came to the throne 1180. Married Ingeborg of Denmark, and then Agnes de Meranie. Died in 1223. Relationship to predecessor, son.

LOUIS VIII (The Lion), born 1187, came to the throne 1223, married Blanche de Castile. Died in 1226. Relationship to predecessor, son.

LOUIS IX (St Louis), born 1215, came to the throne 1226, married Marguerite de Provence. Blanche de Castile was Regent during his minority. He died in 1270. Relationship to predecessor, son.

PHILIPPE III (The Bold), born 1245, came to the throne in 1270. He married Isabela de Aragon. Died 1285. Relationship to predecessor, son.

PHILIPPE IV (The Handsome) born 1268, came to the throne 1285, married Jeanne de Navarre. He died in 1314. Relationship to predecessor, son.

LOUIS X (The Battler), born 1289, came to the throne in 1314, married Marguerite de Bourgogne. Died 1316. Relationship to predecessor, son.

JEAN I born in 1316, came to the throne in 1316, and died in 1316.

PHILIPPE V (The Tall) born in 1291, came to the throne in 1316, married Jeanne de Bourgogne. Died in 1322. He was the uncle of Jean I.

CHARLES IV (The Handsome) born 1294, came to the throne in 1322. Married Blanche de Bourgogne (1), and Marie de Luxembourg (2). Died in 1328. Relationship to predecessor, brother.

The Valois Dynasty

PHILIPPE VI (Philippe de Valois) born 1293, came to the throne in 1328. Married Jeanne de Bourgogne (The Lame). Died in 1350. He was the nephew of Philippe IV, and so was only distantly related to Charles IV, his predecessor.

JEAN II (The Courageous) born 1319, came to the throne in 1350. Married Bonne de Luxembourg. Died 1364. Son of Philippe VI.

CHARLES V (The Wise) born 1337, came to the throne in 1364. Married Jeanne de Bourbon. Died 1380. Relationship to predecessor, son.

CHARLES VI (The Mad), born 1368, came to the throne in 1380. Married Isabeau of Bavaria. Died 1422. Relationship to predecessor, son.

CHARLES VII born 1403, came to the throne 1422. Married Marie d'Anjou. Died 1461. Relationship to predecessor, son.

LOUIS XI born 1423, came to the throne in 1461. Married Charlotte de Savoie. Died 1483. Relationship to predecessor, son.

CHARLES VIII born 1470, came to the throne 1483. Married Anne of Brittany. Died 1498. Relationship to predecessor, son.

The Valois-Orléans Dynasty

LOUIS XII (The Father of the People) born 1462, came to the throne 1498. Married Jeanne de France (1), Anne of Brittany (2) and Mary of England (3). Died in 1515. He was descended from the first son of

Louis d'Orléans, the brother of Charles VI, so was only distantly related to his precedessor.

The Orléans-Angoulême Dynasty

FRANÇOIS I born 1494, came to the throne 1515. Married Claude de France. Died in 1547. His relationship to his predecessor was remote, as he was descended from the third son of Charles d'Orléans, another brother of Charles VI.

HENRI II born 1519, came to the throne 1547. Married Catherine de Médici. Died 1559. Relationship to predecessor, son.

FRANÇOIS II born 1544, came to throne 1559, married Mary Queen of Scots. Died 1560. Relationship to predecessor, son. Catherine de Médici ruled as Regent.

CHARLES IX born 1550, came to the throne 1560. Married Elizabeth of Austria. Died in 1574. Relationship to his predecessor, brother. During his minority Catherine de Médici was Regent.

HENRI III born 1551, came to the throne in 1574. Married Louise de Vaudemont. Assassinated 1589. Relationship to predecessor, brother.

The Bourbon Dynasty

HENRI IV (Henri III of Navarre) born 1553, came to throne 1589. Married Marguerite de Valois (1), and Marie de Médici (2). Assassinated in 1610. He was only remotely related to his predecessor, being descended from the sixth son of Louis IX.

LOUIS XIII born 1601, came to the throne in 1619. Married Anne of Austria. Died 1643. Relationship to predecessor, son.

LOUIS XIV (The Sun King) born 1638, came to the throne in 1643. Married the Infanta Marie-Thérèse. Died in 1715. Relationship to predecessor, son. During his minority France was, in effect, ruled by Cardinal Mazarin. When he died in 1660, Louis began his fifty-five years of personal rule.

LOUIS XV born 1710, came to the throne 1715. Married Marie Leczinska. Died 1774. Relationship to predecessor, great-grandson.

LOUIS XVI born 1754, came to the throne 1774. Married Marie-Antoinette of Austria. Died 1793, on the guillotine.

The First Republic

Set up in 1792 by the leaders of the French Revolution.

The First Empire

Napoleon Bonaparte became Emperor of the French in 1804. He had been born in Corsica in 1769. After his defeat by Wellington at Waterloo, he was exiled to St Helena where he died of cancer in 1821.

Restoration of the Monarchy – the Bourbon Dynasty

LOUIS XVIII born 1755, came to the throne 1815. Married Marie-Josephine de Savoie. Died 1824. He was the brother of Louis XVI.

CHARLES X born 1757, came to the throne 1824. Married Marie-Thérèse de Savoie. Deposed after the July Revolution 1830, when he fled to England. Died 1836. Relationship to predecessor, brother.

The Bourbon-Orléans Dynasty

LOUIS-PHILIPPE, born 1773. Came to the throne 1830. Proclaimed king in 1830. Married Maria Amelia of the Two Sicilies. Died 1850. His relationship to his predecessor was remote. He was descended from Philippe d'Orléans, brother of Louis XIV.

The Second Republic

1848–52. Elected President, Prince Louis Napoleon.

The Second Empire

NAPOLEON III (Louis Napoleon) born 1808, became Emperor in 1852. Married Eugenia de Montijo. Died 1873.

The Third Republic

September 1870 to July 1940.

The Fourth Republic

November 1945 to May 1958.

The Fifth Republic

September 1958–

Golf Clubs

Aquitaine

Golf d'Arcachon, 35 Boulevard d'Arcachon, 33260 La Teste-de-Buch, tel. (56) 54 44 00. Open all year. Eighteen holes. Par 71.

Bordeaux-Cameyrac, Sporting Club de Cameyrac, Cameyrac, 33450 St Loubes, tel. (56) 72 96 79. Open all year. Eighteen holes. Par 72.

Golf Bordelais, Domaine de Kater, Avenue d'Eysines, 33200 Bordeaux-Cauderan, tel. (56) 28 56 04. Closed on Mondays. Eighteen holes. Par 67.

Golf Municipal de Bordeaux, Avenue de Pernon, 33300 Bordeaux, tel. (56) 50 92 72. Closed on Tuesdays. Eighteen holes. Par 72.

Golf Club de Bellevue, Centre Sportif Jean Trillo, Avenue Marcel Dassault, 33700 Bordeaux-Merignac, tel. (56) 34 44 33. Open all year. Nine holes. Par 33.

Golf de L'Ardilouse-Lacanau, 33680 Lacanau-Océan, tel. (56) 03 25 60. Open all year. Eighteen holes. Par 72.

Golf de Mont de Marsan, Pessourdat, 40090, Saint-Avit, tel. (58) 75 63 05. Open all year. Nine holes. Par 34.

Golf de la Côte d'Argent, 40660, Moliets, tel. (58) 48 54 65. Open all year. Nine-hole beginners' course. Eighteen-hole competition course. New courses opened in 1988 and designed by Robert Trent Jones.

Golf d'Hossegor, Avenue de Golf, 40150 Hossegor, tel. (58) 43 56 99. Closed on Tuesdays in winter. Eighteen holes. Par 71.

Golf de Chiberta, 104 Boulevard des Plages, 64600 Anglet, tel. (59) 63 83 20. Closed on Thursdays in winter. Eighteen holes. Par 71.

Golf de Biarritz, Avenue Edith Cavell, 64200 Biarritz, tel. (59) 03 71 80. Closed on Tuesdays in winter. Eighteen holes. Par 69.

Golf de Chantaco, Route d'Ascain, 64500 St-Jean-de-Luz, tel. (59) 26 14 22 or (59) 26 19 22. Closed on Tuesdays in winter. Eighteen holes. Par 70.

Golf de la Nivelle, Place William Sharp, 64500 Ciboure, tel. (59) 47 18 99. Closed on Thursdays outside holiday season. Eighteen holes. Par 70.

Golf Club de Périgueux, Domaine de Saltgourde, 24430, Marsac, tel. (53) 53 02 35. Closed on Tuesdays. Eighteen holes. Par 36.

Royal Golf Club Artiguelouve, Domaine St Michel, Artiguelouve, 64230 Lescars Cedex 02, tel. (59) 83 09 29. Near Pau. Open all year. Eighteen holes. Par 71.

Golf Club de Pau, Rue du Golf, 64140, Billere, tel. (59) 32 02 33. Open all year. Eighteen holes. Par 69.

Golf de Salies-de-Béarn, Helios 64270, Salies-de-Béarn, tel. (59) 38 37 59. Open all year. Nine holes. Par 33.

Golf Club Agen-Bon-Encontre, Lieu dit 'Barre', Route de St Ferreol, 47240 Bon Encontre, tel. (53) 96 95 78. Open all year. Nine holes. Par 70 (5520 m).

Golf d'Albret, Pusocq, 47230 Barbaste, tel. (53) 65 53 69. Closed on Tuesdays from 1 October to 15 March. Eighteen holes.

Golf de Castelnaud de Gratecambe, Lieu dit La Menuisière, 47290 Castelnaud de Gratecambe (near Villeneuve-sur-Lot), tel. (53) 01 74 64. Open all year. Eighteen holes, Par 72. Nine holes, Par 28.

Midi-Pyrénées

Golf Club de Toulouse-Palmola, 31680 Buzet-sur-Tarn, tel. (61) 84 20 50. Closed on Tuesdays. Eighteen holes. Par 72.

Golf Club de Toulouse, Vieille Toulouse, 31320 Castanet-Tolosan, tel. (61) 73 45 48. Closed on Tuesdays. Eighteen holes. Par 69.

Golf International de Toulouse Seilh, 31700 Seilh, tel. (61) 42 90 31. Open all year. Eighteen holes, Par 72. Second eighteen holes (shorter), Par 63. New courses opened in October 1988.

Association Sportive du Golf Club de Guinlet, Guinlet, 32800 Eauze, tel. (62) 09 85 99 or (62) 09 80 84. Open all year. Nine holes. Par 36.

Special Interest Holidays and Excursions

Winter Sports – Cross-country and Alpine Skiing

Full details of amenities at **Arette-Pierre-St Martin**, altitude 1,650 m from *Office de Tourisme*, 64570 Arette-Pierre-St Martin.

Full details of **Gourette-Les Eaux Bonnes**, altitude 1,400 to 2,400 m from *Office de Tourisme*, 64400 Les Eaux Bonnes.

Full details of several ski centres in the **Laruns/Artouste** area from *Office Municipale de Tourisme*, Laruns 64440.

Agence Touristique du Béarn, BP816, 64008 Pau, tel. (59) 30 01 30, will supply information on any of the above resorts.

In the Basque country the **Domaine d'Iraty** has more than 200 km of cross-country skiing, from easy to difficult. Details from *Agence du Tourisme du Pays Basque*, 1 Rue de Donzac, BP247, 64108 Bayonne, tel. (59) 59 28 77.

Cookery and Gastronomy

Gourmet cookery courses and tours in Quercy and Périgord: Country Special Holidays, 153b Kidderminster Road, Bewdley DY12 1JE, tel. (0299) 403528.

Cookery courses and gastronomy in Dordogne: Francophiles Discover France, 66 Great Brockeridge, Bristol BS9 3UA, tel. (0272) 621975.

Horse Riding and Horse-drawn Caravans

Short pony-trekking holidays with escort, food and accommodation in south-west France: La France des Villages, Model Farm, Hightown Green, Rattlesden, Bury St Edmunds IP30 0SY, tel. (044 93) 7664.

Auberge Cavalière de la Vallée d'Aspe, RN134 Accous 64490 Bedous, tel. (59) 34 72 30. This is a centre for daily rides, pony trekking, and also for guided mountain walking. Equivalent of village inn accommodation and some camping.

Horse-drawn caravans in Dordogne, three to fourteen days: Slipaway Holidays, 90 Newland Road, Worthing BN11 1LB, tel. (0903) 821000.

Motoring Holidays

About fifty British tour operators offer motoring holidays in France with pre-arranged hotels, or selected self-catering. Some with motoring itineraries in south-west France include: Air France Holidays, Brittany Ferries, Cresta Holidays, Fairway Travel, France Voyages, Rendez-Vous France. Check with any reliable travel agent, or the French Government Tourist Office (see p. 96 for address).

Painting

Painting holidays in Dordogne: British Airways Holidays, PO Box 100, Hadford House, 17–27 High Street, Hounslow TW3 1TB, tel. 01-748 7559.

Painting in Dordogne: Nicholls Painting Holidays, Belfrey House, Pain Hills, Cobham, Surrey. No telephone.

Cycling Tours

By air, or self-drive, easy going cycling tours with accommodation in family-run country hotels: Madron's Holidays, Lloyds House, 22 Lloyds Street, Manchester M2 5WA, tel. (061) 834 6800.

Rafting, Canoeing

Two weeks' rafting on the Dordogne: Pleasure Holidays, 11 Woodlands Road, Northfield, Birmingham B31 2HU, tel. (021) 475 2560.

Some 160 km of downstream rafting on the Dordogne, camping en route: River Running Holidays, Wee Knockina'am, Portpatrick, Stranraer DG9 9AD Scotland, tel. (077 681) 473.

One-day excursions, weekends, five-day courses, in pneumatic rafts on the Gave D'Oloron: Rafting Eaux-Vives, 10 Rue des Cimes 64400 Bidos, Pyrénées-Atlantiques, tel. (59) 39 29 40.

Rafting or kayaks on 200 km of mountain rivers: Centre des Sports Nautiques, Soiex, 64400 Oloron-Ste Marie, tel. (59) 39 61 00.

Walking

Five to sixteen nights' walking from hotel to hotel in the Pyrenees (luggage transported): Inntravel, Hovingham, York YO6 4J2, tel. (065 382) 741.

Luxury walking tours in Dordogne: River Running Holidays, Wee Knockina'am, Portpatrick, Stranraer DG9 9AD Scotland, tel. (077 681) 473.

Walking holidays along the Pyrenees: Sherpa Expeditions, 131a Heston Road, Hounslow TW3 0RD, tel. 01-577 2717.

Mountain Walking: Bureau des Guides, 'La Goutte d'Eau', Cette-Eygun, 64 490 Bedous, tel. (59) 34 78 83.

Walking Holidays in the Pyrenees: Waymark Holidays, 295 Lillie Road, London SW6 7LL, tel. 01-385 5015.

Wine

Wine tours by car to the Bordeaux region: Just France, Eternit House, Felsham Road, London SW15 1SF, tel. 01-788 3878.

Wine and Gastronomy: David Walker Travel, 10b Littlegate Street, Oxford OX1 1QT, tel. (0865) 728136.

Escorted wine holidays by coach to Dordogne and Bordeaux vineyards: Wessex Continental Travel, 124 North Road East, Plymouth PL4 6AH, tel. (0752) 228333.

Quality wine tours escorted by experts to Bordeaux vineyards, by air or coach: World Wine Tours, 4 Dorchester Road, Drayton, St Leonard OX9 8BH, tel. (0865) 891919.

The above lists are indications of what is available and are not selected recommendations. Further information and addresses can be had from the *Office de Tourisme* in any region which interests you (see pp. 95-6).

Index